MAXIMUM
MORPHONIOS

MAXIMUM MORPHONIOS

The Life and Times of America's Toughest Judge

Ellen Morphonios
with Mike Wilson

WILLIAM MORROW AND COMPANY, INC.
NEW YORK

Recognizing the importance of preserving what has been written, it is the policy of William Morrow and Company, Inc., and its imprints and affiliates to have the books it publishes printed on acid-free paper, and we exert our best efforts to that end.

Library of Congress Cataloging-in-Publication Data

Morphonios, Ellen, 1929–
    Maximum Morphonios : the life and times of America's toughest judge / Ellen Morphonios with Mike Wilson.
      p.   cm.
    ISBN 0-688-09155-5
    1. Morphonios, Ellen, 1929– . 2. Women judges—Florida—Miami—Biography. 3. Criminal justice, Administration of—Florida—Miami—History. I. Wilson, Mike, 1961– . II. Title.
KF373.M573A3   1991
347.73'14'092—dc20

Printed in the United States of America

First Edition   90-38794

1 2 3 4 5 6 7 8 9 10   CIP

BOOK DESIGN BY M. C. DEMAIO

For Dale and Dean
And Carol

CONTENTS

INTRODUCTION
THROWING THUNDERBOLTS

JAMES CANNADY WAS a hard-working young man. His career was robbery.

In the first three months of 1987, Cannady, twenty-eight, robbed six Miami businesses. He held up a Circle K convenience store three times and a Shell gas station twice. He worked so hard that by the end of January he had robbed two men named Kenneth and two men named Riley. He stood five feet eight inches tall and weighed only 140 pounds, but somehow he still intimidated people. Maybe it had something to do with the revolver.

Johnny Riley and Kenneth Smith were the first victims. It was January 2, the night the University of Miami lost to Penn State in the Fiesta Bowl. The two friends were sitting outside the FINA gas station where Riley worked. They had the football game on the portable TV. Midway through the second half, Smith went around the corner to relieve himself. When he got back, he found a man standing in the shadows near the side of the building. Smith assumed he was a customer.

"What's up?" Smith said.

"This is a robbery," James Cannady said, displaying his gun. "Don't move and nobody gets hurt."

Riley gave the robber the few dollars he had in his pockets. Smith handed over a gold chain, a medallion, and a ring with his initials engraved in it. During the holdup, a bus stopped in front of the gas station. The driver stepped off, saw what was happening, climbed back onto the bus, and got the hell out of there.

Cannady was just getting started. He robbed another Kenneth and another Riley ten days later. Ernest Riley, a truck driver for a bakery, was delivering a rack of rolls to a Church's Fried Chicken store. He knocked on the back door and Kenneth McGee, the manager, opened it. When Riley passed through the door, James Cannady, who had been hiding nearby, followed, carrying his big silver gun. He waved the two men inside and told them to lie on the floor. Then he gave the same instruction to the rest of the store's employees.

"I have AIDS, so I have nothing to lose," Cannady said. He didn't have AIDS, but the people at Church's Fried Chicken didn't know that. And they thought it best not to question him. So they just lay there in terror, knowing that this man might, at any moment, place the barrel of his gun behind their ears and squeeze the trigger. Cannady made off with the money from the register and six hundred dollars in cash and checks that Ernest Riley had collected on his rounds that day.

To the bakery worker, that was a lot of bread.

"I was scared to death," he would say later.

Cannady went on and on. On February 5, he robbed a convenience-store clerk named Marcia Staples. He went back the next night and robbed her sister, Linda Munoz. It went so well that he returned on March 4 and robbed Linda again. Cannady committed all three crimes with a rusty knife. Then he returned to the gun: Joseph Alexis, a cashier at a Shell gas station, was held up on March 9 and 13. Alexis would later say, "Almost every fifteen days Cannady stopped by to get some money."

Cannady outdid himself on February 23. That afternoon, he walked uninvited into the Progressive Day Care Center and helped himself to the day's receipts. Before he left, he lined up the teachers against a wall so that he could keep track of them. Naturally, they thought he was going to shoot them to death one by one.

The thirty-five preschoolers watching from the doorway thought the same thing.

The police finally caught up with James Cannady on March 19. He probably figured it was the worst thing that could happen to him.

Then his case was assigned to me.

I am a judge in the criminal courts of Miami, Florida. Part of my job is to uphold the Constitution of the United States—to make sure that each defendant who comes before me receives a fair and speedy trial. It isn't easy. Crime is Miami's biggest industry. Each year I preside over more than two thousand cases, ranging from burglary to kidnapping to robbery to first-degree murder. It's hard to take the time to make eye contact with all those defendants, much less give them fair and speedy trials. But I do my best.

The other part of my job is to protect the people of Dade County—Johnny Riley, Ernest Riley, Kenneth Smith, Kenneth McGee, Marcia Staples, her sister, Linda Munoz, Joseph Alexis. You too, if you're ever in Miami. Call me old-fashioned, but I happen to think that decent, hard-working people have a right to stroll the sidewalks without being beaten, robbed, raped, stabbed, strangled, bludgeoned, or otherwise disturbed. I don't think law-abiding citizens should have to share breathing space with lawless creeps. So I give violent criminals the longest prison sentences I can under the law. A writer once said that I "inflict justice like a god throwing thunderbolts." I thought the god part was a vast overstatement. But I liked the part about throwing thunderbolts. That's what I do when a criminal really rubs me the wrong way. I throw thunderbolts.

James Cannady stood trial in my courtroom six months after his arrest. After three days of testimony, the jury found him guilty of eighteen felonies, including several counts each of robbery with a firearm and robbery with a deadly weapon. The state of Florida's sentencing guidelines recommended that I put him away for twenty-two to twenty-seven years.

I didn't think that was enough. As far as I was concerned, Cannady had proved he was a career criminal. He had been hauled in twice on robbery charges when he was still in his teens. In his early twenties, he had been sent to jail for committing two more robberies, but he had escaped before completing the sentence. He was still a fugitive when he began the crime spree that landed him in my courtroom. Here was a man with no regard for the law, or for law-abiding people. He was a dangerous individual, a complete menace who was only growing bolder and more ruthless. He had not killed anyone, but he had scared the living hell out of a lot of people, including thirty-five children. It was more than I could take. No way could I give this guy just twenty-seven years.

So I hit him with a thunderbolt. I sentenced James Cannady to 1,698 years in prison. It made me feel much better about things.

Not long ago, some TV reporters came to my courtroom to tape a story about me. They asked me about Cannady's sentence, and naturally I said I thought he richly deserved each and every day of it. Then they went to see Cannady in prison. They sat him down in front of the camera and asked him how he felt about me.

"Deep down inside," he said, "she's a bitch. A low-down, slimy bitch."

If you think he was upset, imagine how I felt when, early in 1990, an appeals court overturned the convictions on a technicality. The court said Cannady was entitled to a separate trial on each robbery charge instead of one trial encompassing all the charges. It seemed like a silly ruling to me, but I had to live with it.

Soon, Cannady will return to my courtroom for his first new trial. He will get a fair shake from me, as every defendant does. I'm going to put aside what I heard at the first trial and presume him innocent as I do everyone else. What will happen is anyone's guess. Maybe Cannady will walk out of my courtroom a free man.

Or maybe he'll get another chance to call me names.

ONE

TELLING STORIES

People tell a lot of outrageous stories about me. Most of them are true.

The one they tell most often is known as "The Gams Story," and it's a beaut. The story goes that I was sentencing a guy who had been convicted of a particularly nasty sex crime, and that I didn't like him one bit. That certainly is believable. I don't like violent criminals, and, unlike too many judges today, I'm not afraid to let them know it. Anyway, according to "The Gams Story," I sentenced this guy to a few hundred years in prison, then told the bailiff to get him out of my sight before I got angry and gave him an even longer sentence. So far, the story is credible. I have probably done all of those things dozens of times.

That was when it really got interesting, according to the story. The bailiff was leading this guy past the bench when I held up my hand and said, "Wait a minute." Then, the story goes, I reached down, lifted my black silk judge's robe, and exposed my honorable ankles to the prisoner. He stood there staring at my legs, astonished that a judge would do such a thing. The other people in the courtroom—the lawyers, the clerk, the court reporter, and the bewildered bailiff—supposedly froze in disbelief, almost afraid to know what I would do next.

"Get a good look at these gams, pal," I am supposed to have said, "because they're the last ones you'll be seeing for a long, long time."

This is my one and only life story, my singular opportunity to clear the record, so please believe me: It didn't happen. Really. It's not my style. I know that everyone at the courthouse in Miami believes "The Gams Story" is true. I know too that the people from the television program *60 Minutes* spread the story to several million more people when they aired a segment about me in December 1988. Those things are not my fault. Some people might think it sounds like something I would do. But I didn't do it. Yes, I might have said something to the guy. I might have told him it would be a damned long time before he laid eyes on a nice pair of legs. But I can state right now, as a woman sworn to uphold the law, that I never knowingly revealed my gams to any man in handcuffs.

If I had done it, I would own up to it in a skinny minute.

I have never understood why so many people like to spread that story. Not that I'm upset about it. Hell, I don't care. Let them say what they want to say. It's just that, well, the true stories are so much sexier.

Once, a defendant named Alfonso Ponton appeared in my courtroom. He was charged with armed robbery and aggravated battery, and now it was time for trial. We were about to begin when his lawyer approached the bench and asked permission for Ponton to use the bathroom. I was annoyed and I said so.

"Why didn't he go before he came in here?" I said, snarling the way I sometimes do.

The lawyer turned, looked at the defendant, and said, "Oh, my God. I think it's too late."

Ponton, about to stand trial on serious charges, was standing near the defense table, peeing and grinning. Now, I have seen a lot of things in my years in the courtroom. I have seen men stand and play with themselves right in front of me. But I must say I had never seen someone express his opinion of me and my court in such a liquid way.

Ponton was peeing in full view of the jurors, who were sitting no more than fifteen feet away. I quickly ordered the jurors to step into the jury room. I didn't want the defendant's bad manners to prejudice them against him, even if he was a fool and a jerk.

When the defendant finished his business, he stepped out of his jail-issue trousers and stood before me wearing nothing—and I mean nothing—but his shoes, socks, and shirt. I was pretty disgusted with Ponton by then, so I barked at the bailiff, "Get him out of here."

Ponton started to complain that he needed a dry pair of pants, but I cut him off in a hurry.

"You wanted to bare your ass in here," I said, "and now you can walk bare-assed out of here."

And that's just what he did. (Ponton was hung like a horse, incidentally.)

By the time I was done with him, Alfonso had been convicted of armed robbery in three different trials in my courtroom. In five days in 1981, he had robbed a used-car lot, pistol-whipped an old man in a junkyard, and held up a moving company and a business-forms company. His weapons of choice were a .45-caliber semi-automatic pistol and a shotgun. I sentenced him to 467 years in prison after the first two trials. When he was convicted in the third trial, I really got fed up. I added 730 years to the sentence, for a grand total of 1,197 years in prison.

May he live long enough to serve every day of it.

Nobody, except maybe the defendant, got too upset at that last sentencing. I was lucky. Usually, someone from the defendant's family is in court for the sentencing hearing. And sometimes they get bent out of shape when they hear what the sentence is going to be. Sending a man to prison for 1,197 years or so can ruin his family's whole day. Sometimes the relatives want to tear me apart, and they say so. That's why, when preparing for what I know will be a particularly difficult and emotional hearing, I have been known to carry a silver-plated .22-caliber pistol under my robes. I have never had to use it, but I would if I had to. If I had to choose between the life of some crazy defendant and the life of an innocent person in my courtroom, including me, well, that would be no choice at all.

I have found that the best way to maintain order in the court is to keep things moving. When things get out of hand, I don't scream and yell and get excited. I just go on with my business. Once, I was sentencing a guy for dealing in drugs, which is practically everybody's second occupation in Miami. (It's like having a real estate license in Los Angeles.) I gave this fellow a few years behind bars. It didn't seem to bother him, but his mother went off like a bottle rocket. She began to curse at me and scream and weep like crazy. Things were starting to get a little tense when, mercifully, she passed out from lack of oxygen, landing face-first in the aisle. Someone ran to call the paramedics. I pounded my gavel.

"Next defendant," I said. "Step forward. Step over the body."

Was it a cold, heartless thing to say? Some people thought so. But I had a good reason for saying it. If I had lost control of the courtroom, other members of the drug dealer's family might have started a riot, and a lot of innocent people might have been hurt. By proceeding to the next case, I kept firm control of the situation. If the woman's feelings were hurt, I'm sorry, but I had more important things to consider.

I have a habit of saying exactly what I am thinking. Whatever comes up comes out. People don't always appreciate it. Once, a guy who was charged with killing his wife in a gruesome way appeared in front of me. The guy, sadly, was as crazy as he could be. During the entire hearing, he kept insisting that he had to get back home as soon as possible. It was imperative, he said. "I have to take care of my wife," he said.

"Seems to me you've already taken care of her," I said.

Another time, a guy was on trial for the attempted rape of a young Miami woman. He had cornered her in her office one evening, beaten her, and tried to rape her. He would have succeeded, but she managed to push him away and get back to her desk, where, lucky for her, she happened to keep a revolver. She shot the guy and then called the police.

During the bad guy's trial, the prosecutor asked the young woman for details of what had happened.

"And where did you shoot the defendant?"

"In the groin," the young woman said.

That got my attention. "Nice shot," I said.

A lot of people don't like that story. "You can't do that," they say. "You're a judge. You just can't say things like that. It just isn't done." Give me a break. I can't always be utterly proper and dignified. I have to do whatever my personality dictates. And if it occurs to me that the groin is a pretty good place to shoot a rapist, I'm likely to say so reflexively, damn the critics. If people don't like my style, they can vote for someone else in the next election. This is a democracy. The voters can dump me anytime they want to.

People have been telling me all my life that I couldn't do this or couldn't say that. I have never listened to them. If I had, I wouldn't have gotten anywhere in life. When I decided to enter law school without having gone to college first, people said, "You can't do that." I could, and I did. When I wanted to become Florida's first woman felony prosecutor, people told me I shouldn't even try. "The courtroom is a rough place," they said. "A woman would never be able to handle herself." They were wrong about that too. I tried all kinds of cases, no matter how dirty the language or how vicious the crime.

When I decided to run for judge in the felony courts, people doubted me again. So far as I knew, no woman judge in Florida had ever made it beyond the juvenile and traffic courts. People told me I was brave to try, but they also told me I would lose. The discouraging words had no effect on me whatsoever. It's not that I was over-confident. I just thought that if I lost, it would not necessarily be because I was a woman.

I won. I was sworn in on January 5, 1971, and I have served as a judge in Miami ever since.

Some judges like to lecture the people they sentence to prison, or to probation. "Listen, son," these judges will say, "I hope this teaches you a lesson," and so on. Some of them go on for quite a long time that way.

I don't do that. Most of the people I sentence wouldn't listen to a thing I have to say. They don't care any more about my words of wisdom than they did about the people they shot or robbed or mutilated. They just stand there looking at their shoes and smirking while their lawyers check their watches and wish it were over. If a guy is going to go straight, he is going to do it because he wants to, not because I tell him he should. Why should I waste my breath?

Besides, I don't have time to give speeches. I can't devote that kind of attention to a single case. The criminal justice system in America is overcrowded beyond most people's wildest imagination. It is not so much a system of jurisprudence as it is a gigantic, spinning, whirring machine. Sometimes it churns out justice and sometimes it doesn't.

How crowded is it? In 1989, Miami prosecutors filed about forty thousand felony charges. The cases were then assigned to the twenty circuit court judges in the criminal division. That means that each judge saw about two thousand defendants, each of whom had a legal right to a trial before a jury of his peers. Most felony trials take at least two days; some take a couple of weeks. You don't need a calculator to figure out that, no matter how hard we may toil, we judges are constantly behind in our work.

Among the general public, I am known mostly for being tough.

Sentencing guys to 1,698 years in prison will do that for you. Among the people at the Metro-Dade Justice Building, though, I am probably even better known for being fast. I try to be the fastest and most efficient judge in Miami. In a typical week, as many as one hundred cases are set for trial in my division. That's a long calendar, but I almost always get to the end of it, either by trying the cases, taking guilty pleas, or, if the lawyers have a damned good reason, granting continuances.

How do I do it? I work extremely hard, and that means nights and Saturdays when necessary. And when I'm working, I don't waste much time on small talk and frivolity. I allow one continuance to the prosecution and one to the defense, and then it's time for trial. And if a defendant is having trouble deciding whether to plead guilty, I tell the bailiff to fetch me a jury. When the defendant hears the jurors' feet clomping down the hall, the state's plea offer usually starts to sound pretty good.

Early in 1988, I received a call at my office from Jim Jackson, a producer for the CBS news show *60 Minutes*. Harry Reasoner and the crew had heard about me and wanted to fly down to tape a story, he said. I didn't know if they really thought I was so interesting or if the crew just wanted a late-winter vacation in Florida, but anyway I told them I would be delighted to talk to them. I hadn't done anything they could skewer me for, at least not that I knew of.

The day Harry Reasoner came, I was as nervous as a whore in church. He is, after all, a legendary newsman. I needn't have been scared. He turned out to be unaffected and congenial, surprising characteristics in a man whose stories have exposed dozens of crooks and frauds. I was happy to be on his good side, I'll say that. He addressed me always as "Judge" or "Your Honor," and I always addressed him as "Mr. Reasoner." I wouldn't have dreamed of calling him Harry.

The crew spent several days with me. They were everywhere: in the courtroom, in my chambers, at home, at the gun range where I shoot. They even took pictures of me and my family fishing. When they finished, Jim Jackson told me he liked the story, and said he thought I would too.

He was right. It aired for the first time on December 11, 1988. The title was "Maximum Morphonios." This is how Mr. Reasoner started the piece:

"If you've ever thought that one of the answers for the law-and-order problems in this country is tougher judges, well, we've found just the one for you. She's Ellen Morphonios, and around the Dade County Circuit Courthouse, they call her Maximum Morphonios. During her four terms as an elected district judge, she has handed out the biggest sentences the law allows.

"The defendants know this going into her courtroom. She'll tell them right up front what will happen to them if they don't take the plea bargain and want to go to trial."

Then they cut to a picture of me telling a defendant that he could get fifteen years if he was convicted. "Ask and you shall receive," I said.

We were sitting in my chambers when Mr. Reasoner asked the question everybody asks me sooner or later. It has to do with conscience. He wanted to know if I ever woke up at night and wondered if some guy I had sentenced to 1,698 years in prison might actually have been salvageable.

I'll tell you the same thing I told him: No, I don't. You would be surprised how little I think about criminals when I go home for the day. To begin with, I don't sentence someone to a long prison term unless I have thought it through and decided he really deserves it. A person has to be truly evil to get that sort of sentence from me.

I don't pass those sentences to get featured on TV news shows, either. I do it because I want the prison system to know that this defendant is incorrigible, a menace to society. The wardens may not incarcerate these guys forever, but my thinking is that if I impose a truly startling sentence, maybe they will hold them a little longer than they might have. I get satisfaction from that.

Mr. Reasoner also wanted to know if I was always so hard on criminals. "When they call you Maximum," he asked me, "what are they talking about? Would you give ten years instead of six months for vagrancy, for instance?"

"No," I said, and that's the truth. When it comes to routine nonviolent cases, I don't always give the maximum. If a guy makes a mistake and seems remorseful about it, I don't hammer him. Look, everybody makes mistakes. I've made plenty, though not the kind that could have landed me in prison. I believe people deserve a second chance, as long as their first mistake wasn't killing or inflicting bodily harm on someone. The guys who get second and third and fourth chances—and still screw up—are the ones I get angry at. I think they're the ones the public is most sick of too.

After the 60 Minutes piece aired, I received a request for an interview from the producers of the Australian version of the same show. I said, "You want to talk? Come on over."

Things didn't go so well. Just as the Americans had done, the Aussies took me out to the gun range. One of the guys there gave me a machine gun to fire, and I happily began blasting away. I was wearing high heels and standing on soft ground. When I squeezed the trigger, that gun started to buck like a wild horse. Before I knew it, I was falling backward. I landed flat on my ass. If I hadn't let go of that trigger, I might have bagged a couple of TV people.

The Australians were awfully nice about it. They aired the footage of my fall, but they didn't make any nasty remarks, such as, "And here, the crime-busting judge falls on her can." I appreciated that.

The media feed on the media. It's amazing. If you're at all interesting, the local paper writes about you, which gets the local TV people interested, which might get you on the national TV news, which gets you a book contract and catches 60 Minutes' interest, which alerts People magazine, which tips off the late-night talk shows. When it's all over, you've accumulated a lot of frequent-flyer miles and a small amount of notoriety, for whatever that's worth. The 60 Minutes piece landed me on lots of TV and radio shows, the most fun of which probably was Pat Sajak's late-night talk show in Los Angeles.

When I got to Sajak's studio on the day of the taping, I was shown into my own private dressing room, then led to the greenroom, where the producers had left a spread of food and booze about the size of Delaware. I didn't touch the liquor. I can barely control my mouth when I'm sober.

I came on right after Lola Falana. I wasn't drunk, but I wouldn't have blamed anyone for thinking I was. I don't know if it was nerves or jet lag or what, but I started babbling on as if I were the host and Pat Sajak were a stagehand who had accidentally wandered onto the set. I was dressed very conservatively in a lovely pink suit, but I sounded like a very available female.

"My God, you're even cuter than I thought," I said. "How

come Santa Claus won't put you in my stocking? I ask him every year and he won't do it."

I was in some mood. I told Pat that I wasn't fooling around with anyone at the moment, but that I thought about it a lot. "Do you think that old ladies of sixty are sitting around crocheting and baking cookies? This one's not."

He made a joke out of the compliment, saying, "At forty-two years old, I discover that the whole world has the hots for me."

But I wasn't kidding. That man was handsome.

Ah, men.

I used to get married from time to time, with the changing of the tides and the coming of the full moon. I'm retired now. To hell with it.

I married Husband Number One in 1950. I was still just a kid then. I didn't know what I was doing. Alex Morphonios and I had been friends for several years, and when he asked me to marry him, I thought, Heck, why not? I probably should have thought it through a little better. I also should have learned something from the experience, but I didn't do that either.

Husband Number One and I quit communicating sometime in the second year of marriage. The next nineteen years were all downhill. Alex was a nitpicker. If I missed a spot while I was dusting, he pointed it out. If I didn't cook the string beans thoroughly—and I often didn't, for I am a lousy cook—he told me so. For a while, I tried to please him. Then I just quit listening.

Alex liked dog racing. Late in our marriage, he began to breed greyhounds. He also hired a dog trainer and moved him into the house. It was a mistake. The dog trainer was a pretty fetching guy. Before long, Alex became ex–Husband Number One and the dog trainer, John Rowe, became Husband Number Two.

John and I got married in a funeral home in East St. Louis, Illinois. Having been through it, I wouldn't recommend that anyone else get married in a funeral parlor. It tends to get couples off to a bad start. John and I got along well for the first, oh, two days or so, but then the relationship started to deteriorate.

It ended when I got beaten to within an inch of my life, which I also do not recommend.

My love life has been the subject of a lot of vicious, and unfortunately very true, gossip. I'm not going to lie about it: During both marriages I had a lot of boyfriends on the side. They were interesting guys. One was a journalist and political maneuverer. Another was a former governor of Florida. A third was a police detective. A fourth was a defense lawyer. Usually I broke it off with one before starting up with the next, but not always. There were times when I had a husband and a couple of boyfriends all wondering if I was being faithful.

Oh, it was never dull. Once, an angry wife literally chased me and her husband through the streets of Miami. We eluded her. Another time, one of my husbands chased one of my boyfriends on foot through a Miami neighborhood, but he didn't catch him. Gosh, I liked men.

I was utterly faithful to Husband Number Three, a handsome police detective. He was sixteen years my junior and we had a wonderful relationship. We were close friends and wonderful lovers. I didn't know if I was going to spend the rest of my life with him—I had grown understandably cynical about marriage—but I sure wanted to try.

It didn't work out. When I give interviews now, I am always candid about what happened between the detective and me. I tell the whole story—and then I politely ask the interviewer not to use it. Some agree, some don't. The breakup of my third marriage tore my family asunder, and I have always preferred that those tragic days not be recounted in the pages of my local newspaper. I will tell the story here not because I want to, but because this book is intended to be a complete history of my life as I have viewed it. The divorce was without a doubt the most significant event in my later life. To include it in this memoir will be painful, but to leave it out would almost be dishonest.

What happened? My third husband fell in love with my son Dale's wife, and there was nothing I or Dale could do about it. In 1983, we all got divorced and the detective married my daughter-in-law. My grandchildren suddenly had a new father. He was the man they used to call Grandpa.

Maybe now you're beginning to understand why people tell stories about me.

But there is still so much I haven't told. I have not told about the time I spent several hours locked up with a monkey. Or the time

I was named, wrongly, in a public corruption probe. Or the time I nearly quit the bench to go into show biz. Or the time I tried a man for first-degree murder twenty-four days after he was arrested. Or the time, as a young beauty contestant, I sued the people who ran a crooked beauty contest. Or the time I lost an election for judge— and applauded the voters for their good judgment.

Some, I'm sure, would prefer that I not tell my story. (The monkey is not among them. I know him personally, and he has no objection.) I respect their feelings, and I mean no ill will toward anyone, except possibly the many deserving people I have put in prison. But I am going to tell the story despite their objections.

I have spent a lifetime doing as I damned well pleased, and I'm too old to stop now.

TWO
A DAY AT THE ZOO

Behind the high-backed yellow vinyl chair in my fourth-floor courtroom hangs a sign that says, in big silver letters, WE WHO LA-BOR HERE SEEK ONLY TRUTH. I like the sentiment, but it is not entirely true. Some days we seek only truth. Other days, when the calendar is long and the defendants difficult, we who labor there seek only lunch.

Sometimes, we just wish we could all understand each other. One summer morning a man appeared before me on charges that he sold a small amount of marijuana to an undercover police officer. On the advice of his lawyer, he decided to plead guilty. The state asked me to give him twenty-seven days in jail—the time he had already served. I wasn't happy about it, but if that was what the state and the police officer wanted, I wouldn't interfere. There were far more important cases to hear.

The communication problems came up during the plea collo-quy. The plea colloquy is a list of questions judges ask to make sure that defendants know what they're doing when they plead guilty to a crime. They need to understand that they are giving up their consti-tutional right to a trial and so on. I think it's important that they know what they're doing. Some judges simply give the defendants a piece of paper to sign. I always ask them a series of questions. I sleep better that way.

Before I asked the first question, I noticed that the defendant was looking at me strangely. So I asked the question I always ask when someone does that.

"Do you speak English, pal?" In Miami, one never knows.

"Yes," he said, grinning.

"Are you sure?"

"Yes." As usual, the air conditioner in my courtroom was work-

24

ing hard, and the defendant, dressed only in prison slacks and a black tank top, was hugging himself to keep warm.

"All right," I said. "Do you understand that you are under oath?"

The clerk had already sworn him in. "Yes," he said.

"Do you understand what's happening here in court today?"

"Yes."

"Do you have any physical or mental defects that would prevent you from understanding what's happening here in court today?"

Answered the happy defendant: "Yes."

Just then, a man in the back of the courtroom stood. "Your Honor," he said, "I'm his brother."

"Well, thank God," I said. "Does he speak English or what?"

"No, Your Honor," the man said. "He speaks Creole."

The job of criminal court judge, at least in Miami, is one of much stress and craziness and precious little glamour. The legal system is often interesting, but it is just as often plain frustrating. To really understand me, you have to understand what I do each day and why I do it. I could tell you about virtually any day in my court, for every day is built of the same kind of madness. But I have decided to describe the morning the small-time Creole-speaking drug dealer appeared before me. Nothing newsworthy happened that day: No serial killers were tried and no famous robbers arraigned. It was a routine morning, which, in Miami, means it was just another day at the zoo.

It was a Monday, the beginning of another week of hearings and trials in Courtroom 4-6. I arrived at the Metro-Justice Building before seven-thirty A.M., as usual, and parked my van in a space under the building. Upon our election, we judges are assigned free spaces in the covered, guarded lot, which come in handy when it is raining or someone has threatened to kill us. (Fortunately, the rain is much more common.) Most of the other people who work in the courthouse—prosecutors, public defenders, bailiffs, and so on—have to park in lots a block or more from the building. Judges don't receive very many perks, but the parking space is a good one.

The Metro-Justice Building, a stark, blocklike structure, is an example of government architecture at its worst. The person who designed it must have had some sort of vendetta against the people of

Dade County; no lover of humanity would have bequeathed such a disaster to the public. Forget about proud marble columns and large windows with wood frames. The Metro-Justice Building, which opened in the early sixties (I was there), stands in the shadow of an expressway overpass. It is a gray concrete box with nine floors and, trust me, almost no character. No one approaching the building could possibly feel warmly toward it, which I suppose is fitting. Hardly anyone goes there voluntarily. The Metro-Justice Building is where people go when something awful has happened.

Inside, the place is not much prettier: The walls are tile, the ceilings are tile, and the floors are tile. The metal detector at the front entrance has uncovered over the years a trainload of guns, knives, and chains. Some of the weapon carriers come to the courthouse with an idea of hurting someone. Others are just every-day Miamians: They like to be prepared. A bank of elevators carries people upward from the lobby. Those who are in a hurry—that's just about everyone—take the escalator, which rises to the sixth floor and then, for no good reason, stops.

To get to my fourth-floor office, I took the elevator from the basement. For safety reasons, I try to stay off the escalators. I'm not afraid of guys who might have slipped a gun through the metal detector. Let them take their best shot, because the second shot is mine. It's the guys with knives I'm afraid of. They're braver, and usually more serious about hurting you. I have never had someone pull a knife on me, but if someone did, I wouldn't dare him to use it.

If I had taken the escalators to my office, I would have seen an amazing and memorable sight: the Monday morning courthouse crowd. Here you can find human beings of every stripe: prosecutors wearing dark suits and stern expressions; assistant public defenders bleary from a weekend of trial preparation; private defense lawyers, some with clients in tow, others scrounging for drunk-driving clients or court-appointed cases; jurors, some of them eager to serve, others already dreaming up reasons to be excused; crime victims stunned and angry about their losses and astonished at the teeming humanity; and those defendants fortunate enough to be out of jail pending trial. You'd think that maybe one day no one would commit any crimes and the courthouse would go on holiday. But it never happens. Other businesses may have slow seasons, but at the courthouse business just keeps getting better.

As always, my judicial assistant, Shirley Lewis, was in the office when I arrived, preparing the day's calendar and a pot of coffee. Shirley is not only my secretary but also my friend, protector, and sometimes drinking partner. We have been through everything together. In my first days as a judge, she was of more help than anyone ever knew. Every day, defendants came to me asking to be released from jail on bond. The decisions were always difficult, for I knew that anyone I released might go out and commit a crime, possibly a violent one. Thank God for Shirley. She had grown up and remained active in the black community, and still knew almost everyone there. Whenever a black defendant asked for a bond reduction, I looked out of the corner of my eye at Shirley. If she knew the guy and thought he wouldn't hurt anyone, she nodded her head very slightly so only I could see.

The sign on the bench said JUDGE MORPHONIOS, but it might as well have said JUDGE LEWIS.

After that, Shirley came to know me as well as I know myself, maybe better. She often accompanies me when I go out of town, whether I'm going to visit relatives in another state or to New York to do a radio show. Once, she accompanied me to the state prison at Starke, Florida, for a tour of Death Row. I was afraid that she might be upset when she saw the electric chair, for it is a disturbing sight, even to someone who supports the death penalty. After we saw Old Sparky, as it is called, I asked Shirley if she was all right. "Why wouldn't I be all right?" she said. "It's a fine chair, made of good, strong oak. They should use it more often." My kind of gal.

Shirley has always been there for me in bad times too. Near the end of my father's life, when he was too weak even to lift himself into bed, Shirley helped me to lift him onto a mattress so that he could sleep, and helped me to clean him when he could no longer control his bodily functions. She is family. She's also a heck of a good secretary.

A few minutes before 9:00 A.M., my bailiff, Tom Jordan, escorted me to a second-floor courtroom to begin work. Most days, I have to do only my own work, which is more than enough. But that day, one of the judges was out of town, so I had to cover for him before I went to work on my own trial calendar. When a building catches fire, you call the fire department. When a judge goes out of town and leaves behind his open cases, you call Morphonios. At

8:59 A.M., I burst through the door. Tom was right behind me, yelling, "All rise!"

Calling a trial calendar in Miami is insanity. The judge's job is to call each case and try to resolve it. In many cases, the defendants accept the plea bargains offered by the state. In others, one of the lawyers asks for more time to prepare for trial. Lawyers have to have a damned good reason to get a continuance from me, because any case I put aside this week will come back to jam my calendar next week. In a few cases each Monday, both sides say they are ready to go to trial. That's when I tell Tom Jordan to get me a jury. Everything happens so fast at calendar call that a person unfamiliar with the courts probably wouldn't know what was going on. Calendar call is a Chinese fire drill, a time of barely controlled lunacy. There is little time for small talk, no time for nonsense.

On this particular Monday, I called the first case before my rear end had even dented the chair. It was a bad start. The first defendant, who was being held in jail on a high bond, was not in court. I asked the court security officer where he was.

"He's up on the ninth floor," he said.

That was the officer's way of telling me that this person had psychological problems. The Dade County Jail, which is attached to the courthouse by a covered walkway, has a special floor for inmates in mental distress. It is almost always full. The police arrest a lot of crazy street people and folks who have blown their minds on drugs. I didn't know what this person's problem was.

I wasn't soon going to find out, either. Sometime earlier, I had ordered the psychiatrists at Jackson Memorial Hospital to evaluate the defendant. But when I asked for the report, the prosecutor said the doctor had never seen the guy. I was annoyed, but not surprised. Jackson is a gigantic institution, among the largest public hospitals in the nation, and its staff is always under intense pressure. I understand that. But without the report, I didn't know if the defendant was well enough to be arraigned and tried. The system is not supposed to prosecute people who don't know what is happening to them. I was faced with the prospect of continuing the case.

I hated to do it. Unnecessary delays are the justice system's worst enemy. Let me give an example. A woman coming home from the grocery store pulls into her driveway and gets out of the car with her purse hanging from her shoulder. She doesn't know it, but a guy

with evil intentions has followed her home from the store. As soon
as the woman gets out of the car, the guy grabs the purse and tries to
run. The woman, still connected to the purse by the strap, gets
dragged to the ground, and the guy, kind fellow that he is, kicks the
woman in the head a couple of times to get her to let go. Finally, he
wins the battle and makes off with the goods. The woman ends up in
the hospital. A couple of days later, she identifies the guy in a police
photo lineup and the cops go out and pick him up. He ends up in my
courtroom charged with robbery and assault. I see this kind of case
every day in Miami.

A few months pass while the defendant, unable to raise bail, sits
in the pokey. The state gathers its evidence and the defense lawyer
takes sworn statements from the victim, the arresting officer, and
everyone else he can find. But when the trial date finally comes,
something happens to delay the process. Maybe the lead detective is
off on some big case, or is testifying in someone else's courtroom.
Maybe a witness hasn't appeared in the defense lawyer's office for a
deposition. Whatever the reason, I practically have to continue the
case. No big deal, right?

Wrong. The delay hurts everyone. It hurts the victim, who
comes to each hearing seeking justice (and maybe repayment of the
money she lost and reimbursement for her medical bills). She is entitled to justice, but she isn't getting it. It hurts the defendant, who
hasn't been convicted of anything but is nonetheless rotting in jail
awaiting trial. Maybe, just maybe, the guy is innocent. Maybe the
woman picked the wrong guy out of the photo lineup. The longer he
smolders in jail, the worse the injustice to him. Even if he's guilty,
he has a right to a fair and speedy trial. The delay hurts the defendant's family members too. They come to court expecting to learn
what is going to become of their beloved Johnny or Billy or whatever
his name is. The delay also hurts the witnesses, who put aside their
other business to come to court, only to have their time wasted.

Finally, delays hurt the system. Every minute I waste is a minute
taken away from another defendant, another victim. As a judge, I
am the community's conscience, in some ways its last hope. I can't
tolerate a lot of needless, nonsensical delays in my court.

But in the case of that day's mentally disturbed defendant, I had
no choice. I had to continue the case. That was a loss, but then

there was a victory: I handled the rest of the calendar in thirty-two minutes and headed upstairs to begin work on my own cases.

My courtroom is a sober space, dark and colorless. The ceiling is high, the light dim, and the walls paneled in green. In the back of the room, an exit sign glows and a clock hums quietly. It is not always a serious place, but it is a place meant for serious business.

The back of the courtroom is reserved for the public. In Florida, the people are allowed to watch any part of any court proceeding, and that's the way it should be. They pay our salaries, and they have a right to know what they're getting for their money. My courtroom has about seventy-five seats—not nearly enough, especially when there is an interesting trial going on. It is not unusual for people to stand in the aisle and in the back doorway during a good case. The seats often hold an interesting mix of people. On this day, a police officer who arrested an armed robber sat a couple of seats away from the robber's family. They had nothing to say to each other.

The judge's bench sits at the head of the courtroom, on a platform about three feet high. I like sitting a few feet above the rest of the crowd. I think it's appropriate that the lawyers and defendants look up to the judge, because the judge is the ultimate authority, the one looking out for the people. I also think it is appropriate that I look down on some of the people I sentence. In most cases—the routine robbery, burglary, and drug-trafficking cases—I don't feel a thing when I pass sentence, except a burning desire to get it over with and call the next case. But in particularly bad cases, when the defendant is a ruthless rapist or killer, I get a certain pleasure in hovering over him like the Grim Reaper. Lowering my bench to floor level would be like removing Wonder Woman's wristbands. I would lose my sense of power.

From the bench I look down on a large and harried courtroom staff. On my right sits the calendar clerk, Susan Tepper, who keeps track of what is on my calendar for the day and for the coming week. She is a human computer, able to come up with the details of my schedule in the blink of an eye. In front of me is the court clerk, who places the lawyers' written motions in the files and makes notes on the docket about what happens in court. Her notes are the final word in each case: If the notes say something happened, well, it happened. To my left sits the court reporter, or stenographer, who, using a special typewriter, records every word spoken in my courtroom from the time Tom Jordan says "All rise" to the time I say "Court adjourned." Court clerks and calendar clerks have come and gone, but in all my years on the bench, the court reporter has stayed the same. Her name is Mona Gesse.

Mona grew up in my courtroom. She was eighteen years old and just out of high school when she began working for me. Usually, court reporters change courts after a couple of years, just for a change of pace, but Mona stayed. She became part of the family, and I would no sooner have her go to another court than I would ask my sons to get a new mother. When Mona started working for me, she was rather shy and innocent. She got a quick education. During one of my marriages I had a boyfriend who lived in the same apartment complex as she did. Mornings, I used to go to this fellow's apartment for breakfast . . . or whatever. Then I would emerge with him, arm in arm, and drive to work. The first time Mona saw us, her jaw hit the sidewalk. After a while, she got used to that sort of thing.

Now she is my conscience in the courtroom. Mona knows and likes most of the lawyers who work in front of me. When something ticks me off and I start to chew them out, Mona lets me know when I have gone too far. She looks up at me and frowns a terrible frown, as if to say, "Cool it, Judge." She does this without once taking her mind off her work. I happen to like the lawyers who work in my courtroom. Thanks largely to Mona, they can also tolerate me.

On this particular Monday, everybody in court was a little edgy. One of the court security officers had received word from an informant that a defendant, Micheal Connelly, was planning to try a jailbreak. He certainly had plenty of reason. Connelly was facing numerous charges, including aggravated assault, resisting arrest with violence (that is, slugging a cop), and robbery with a weapon. He was in jail awaiting trial, and he was going to be there a lot longer if convicted.

The jailers made sure he wouldn't get away. They brought him to court in enough chains to secure Fort Knox.

The security officers were happy to have him under control. A few days earlier, they had not done so well with another defendant who was appearing before me. The guy was a regular customer, the sort of guy who commits a minor crime, goes to jail for a couple of

months, then gets out and commits another one. This time he was
in jail for car theft. He apparently was getting tired of jail cuisine,
because when he got a chance, he leaped over a wooden railing and
headed for the door. He was halfway there before I knew what was
happening.

Fortunately, security officer George Trudeau was paying closer
attention. He caught the guy by the shirttail and tackled him, shoving him through the door and into the vestibule. The two men
crashed heavily to the floor, drawing blood from the defendant's
head and George's hand.

When it was over, George asked the guy, "What'd you go and
do a thing like that for?"

"I wanted to go home," the guy said.

I couldn't argue with that reasoning.

Putting people behind bars makes them cranky. Lisa Ott and
Horace Rucker were among the meanest I have ever seen.

Lisa Ott appeared in my court the same day the guy tried to
escape from George Trudeau. She was a habitual criminal, and a
nasty one too. For a while I thought she might be crazy, but the
doctors said no, she was just an unpleasant individual. Hell, you
didn't need a medical-school diploma to see that.

This time Lisa was in front of me on charges that she had violated her probation. A taxicab driver testified in court that she
flagged him down, tricked him into getting out of his car, and then
jumped into the front seat and drove away. As she left, she crashed
into three other cars and nearly mowed down a few dozen people
shopping in downtown Miami. Then, according to the cabbie, she
jumped out of the car, ran through the lobby of a hotel, and dived
into the Miami River.

The cabbie conceded, under oath, that he considered this unusual behavior.

"It was like a movie," he said.

Clearly, Lisa had violated the terms of her probation, which
obviously forbade her from turning downtown Miami into a demoli-
tion derby. I was going to have to send her to prison, and she seemed
to sense it.

"Don't you think I have better things to do besides sit my ass in
this goddamned fucking jail?" she yelled. "Bitch!"

I don't like to be called a bitch, even when I'm being one. But I learned early in my years on the bench that I should not get into shouting matches with angry defendants. Screaming at people takes a lot of time, and I don't have a lot of time. Besides, hollering back only raises tensions in the courtroom. The more I yell, the angrier the defendant and his loved ones are apt to get. Shouting back at someone could start a riot. So I sit there as still as the Venus de Milo and wait until the tirade is over.

Lisa Ott wasn't just a shouter. She was more dangerous than that. When she was done screaming at me, she reached over to George Trudeau's desk and grabbed his heavy police radio. Then, before we knew what was happening, she flung it at me. For a minute I thought the thing was going to conk me on the head, but George got his hand in the way and deflected it toward the trash can next to my seat. I was lucky. If that radio had hit me, it surely would have scrambled the frequencies in my brain.

Owen Chin, the defense lawyer, immediately asked me to have Lisa evaluated by a psychiatrist. He knew that would keep her out of state prison a while longer.

"No," I said. "Nothing is wrong with Ms. Ott except she's nasty. Not a thing in the world."

Lisa Ott was a Girl Scout compared to Horace Rucker.

Rucker appeared in my courtroom on February 22, 1973, at nine A.M. A short time earlier, a jury had found him guilty of robbery. He also was awaiting trial on another robbery charge. He was a bad man, and I fully intended to put him out of reach of other people's money for a long, long time. I had just begun the sentencing hearing when he began to wriggle like a hooked tuna. A half-dozen court security officers were watching his every move.

The transcript of that hearing is a well-known document in Miami. Many lawyers keep it pinned to their bulletin boards as a conversation piece. It is spicy stuff, but trust me, lots of defendants have said nearly the same thing in my courtroom.

THE COURT: Mr. Rucker, you have been found and adjudged guilty of the crime of robbery by a jury. . . . It's the judgment and sentence of this court that you be sentenced to the state prison for a term of ninety-nine years.

THE DEFENDANT: You should have gave me life.

THE COURT: Well, that's one thought, Mr. Rucker. You've been found and adjudged guilty.

THE DEFENDANT: I don't want to hear it.

THE COURT: You have a right to appeal.

THE DEFENDANT: Suck my ass, bitch.

THE COURT: In the event—

[Here, the court officers tried to restrain Mr. Rucker, who was growing rather animated.]

THE DEFENDANT: Don't touch me, honky.

THE COURT: Leave him here until I finish advising him. You have a right to appeal. You have thirty days within which to file your appeal. If you do not have funds with which to file an appeal or hire an attorney for that purpose, the court will provide counsel for you. In view of the fact that the public defender has represented you up to this time, the public defender is appointed for purposes of appeal.

The other case is number 72-5383, also robbery. And 72-326.

THE DEFENDANT: Fuck that shit, bitch. I don't want to hear that. I don't want to hear it. Motherfucker. You're a bigger crook than anyone. How the fuck are you going to give me anything? Motherfucker. You're a whore. And I pop you. You motherfucker, you're as guilty—slimy dog, bitch you.

THE COURT: We'll set him for trial for February twenty-third for the other case.

THE DEFENDANT: Stinking motherfucker.

THE COURT: Anything else?

THE DEFENDANT: Kiss my dick.

THE COURT: All right. Now, I want that record sent to the appellate court when it's appealed, completely in detail with all the four-letter words spelled out. Mr. Rucker, you have already been given ninety-nine years—

THE DEFENDANT: Fuck you, bitch. Do you want to give me some more?

THE COURT: I was thinking about it.

THE DEFENDANT: Go ahead, whore. Dog, motherfucker.

THE COURT [to the court reporter]: Do you want me to help you spell some of the words?

Recently, I received notice that Horace Rucker was out of prison. He had been released early—several decades early, in fact—and had successfully completed a drug-rehabilitation program. He was back on the streets. Of course, this came as an outrage. But not a surprise.

Julio Cabrera was charged with trafficking in drugs. The police had caught him red-handed, and now, as I called my Monday calendar, he wanted to plead guilty. He had no prior felony convictions, so the state offered what I considered a good deal—a year in jail and five years on probation. If the guy had gone to trial and been convicted, I could have sentenced him to thirty years in prison. Not that I would have. I usually don't give someone the maximum on the first offense. It isn't fair.

Owen Chin, the assistant public defender in my courtroom, wanted me to withhold adjudication in the case—to accept the plea deal without actually putting a felony conviction on Cabrera's record. To the defendant, this was a big deal. If I withheld adjudication, he could eventually ask to have the record sealed so that no one would ever know of his crime. If I didn't, he would no doubt have a hard time getting a job in the future and he would lose his civil rights—the right to vote, to travel outside the country, and so on. Felony convictions stay with you like garlic breath. So naturally Owen asked for a withhold.

"Judge, I don't think he has any prior felonies, Your Honor," he said.

"Well, what did y'all negotiate?" I said.

Phyllis Kilby, the prosecutor, spoke up. "Judge, this will be an adjudication," she said. The state attorney does not pay Phyllis to keep felons' records clean.

"I see no reason to override the state's recommendation," I said. "I mean, we have got a trafficking charge, for God's sake. No."

Owen tried another route. "Mr. Cabrera's daughter was holding the bag, Judge."

"No. No," I said. Then I did a double take. "Who?"

"The daughter," Owen said.

"Whose daughter?"

"His daughter."

"You think that gives him brownie points?" I said. "How old was the daughter?"

"She's an adult," Owen said.

"It's still a no," I said.

•   •   •

Owen lost another fight later that morning.

His client, a woman, was charged with battery on a police officer. According to the police, she was trying to steal some cheap clothing from a store when the store detective caught her. When the police came, the woman tried to get away by biting one of the officers. Cops don't like that, so the woman, who had an arson conviction on her record, wound up in jail. If convicted at trial, she could have been sentenced to five years in prison. This was not, I thought, the crime of the century.

Owen apparently knew I thought so. He asked me to place his client in pretrial intervention, a program for people in trouble for only the first or second time. The idea is to give people a chance to go straight if they want to. Those who stay out of trouble while in the program have their charges dismissed automatically. Owen thought it would be a good way to handle this case.

I didn't. Battery on a police officer is a serious charge, and this lady was in jail with her bond set at one thousand dollars. It's not my practice to spring people who bite cops. Hell, I probably wouldn't put a dog on pretrial intervention if it bit a police officer. If Owen's client could raise the one thousand dollars to get out, fine. But I wasn't going to release her.

The state offered the woman a year of community control, also called house arrest. Owen wasn't crazy about it, and I didn't blame him. House arrest means you can't go anywhere, period. If you leave home and you get caught, you go straight to prison. The state has to offer house arrest as an alternative to imprisonment because the jails are so crowded, but few people can complete their sentences successfully. Only the most desperate people agree to house arrest.

This woman apparently fit the description, because she took the deal. That jail food must be lousy.

Before I passed sentence, I explained the deal to her and her relatives.

"You all understand community control is house arrest? She has to stay home. She does not go to the store. She does not go out to get a bottle of milk. She doesn't go to the post office to mail a letter. She doesn't do diddly-squat.

"Make no mistake, folks," I told her relatives. "If she fails to do it, she's going to prison. I want you to know so you don't come back upset."

"We understand," they said.

"Swear the lady," I said, and the defendant raised her right hand.

Another deal done.

It had been another long, weird morning on the bench. But there was one big compromise yet to come.

The case of Devona Daniels, also known as Tony Anderson, typifies the way the justice system works. Daniels was charged as the wheel man in an armed robbery case. One fine Miami day, a guy walked into a pizza parlor, drew a gun, and demanded money from a couple of the female patrons. The women, sensibly, handed over their purses. But the robber apparently didn't think one rotten act was enough, so he pistol-whipped the young ladies for good measure. Then, according to the police, the robber ran outside and jumped into a car driven by our friend Mr. Daniels.

Someone called the police, and a car was dispatched. The cops quickly got behind Daniels's car and started to chase it through the streets. Daniels and the robber were cornered on a highway entrance ramp. The driver was arrested right there, but the robber himself got away, only to be picked up a short time later. Mr. Daniels, or Mr. Anderson, or whatever his name was, was on probation for attempted robbery when all this was happening. The state charged him with armed robbery, which, under Florida's sentencing guidelines, was punishable by up to seven years in prison. So naturally he was going to go away for a long, long time, right?

Well, no.

Daniels's lawyer was Owen Chin, the same guy who defended the woman on charges of cop-biting. Owen, a nice guy and a good lawyer, filed a motion to dismiss the armed-robbery charge, saying the state had no evidence that Daniels had participated in the robbery itself. Yes, he had picked up the robber outside the pizza parlor, but where was the proof that he knew the guy had just committed a robbery? There wasn't any. Maybe Daniels was just a dupe. Maybe the robber had tricked him into participating in the crime. Maybe he had just landed from Mars and didn't speak Earth languages. Yes, he had stomped on the gas when the cops showed up, but that was long after the robbery had taken place. At best, Owen argued, the state could charge him as an accessory after the fact, a much less serious charge.

The prosecutor, Phyllis Kilby, apparently saw the handwriting on the wall, because, in exchange for a guilty plea, she offered to reduce the charge to accessory after the fact. If it had been a first offense, Daniels could have gotten probation. But he was already on probation, so, under Florida's sentencing guidelines, I could sentence him to twelve to thirty months—not years—in prison. What looked like a seven-year sentence had suddenly become a thirty-month sentence at most.

But he wasn't going to get the most. Owen Chin wanted the state to offer the guy a year in prison. He was in a good position to make such a request. If the state brought Daniels to trial on an armed-robbery charge, it stood a good chance of seeing him acquitted. Apparently, Phyllis knew it, because she agreed to the deal. When the two lawyers came to me, I practically had to accept it. We simply must accept guilty pleas because, as I have said, we can't possibly try every case that comes into the system. As I said in court that day, I would go to the bottom of the guidelines on Jack the Ripper if everyone agreed to the deal.

So I sentenced Devona Daniels to a year and a day in state prison. I didn't like it. I'm sure the victims didn't like it. The arresting officers, who came to court that day, didn't like it either. I could tell by the disgusted looks on their faces. I couldn't do a damned thing about it. "Sorry, guys," I said. "Some days the bear bites us."

But that is not the worst of it. In Florida, as in every state, the state prisons are terribly overcrowded. To make room for new prisoners coming in, the prisons have to release people early. Most people know this as "time off for good behavior," but the fact is that most guys get time off whether they behave well or not. As I write this, inmates in Florida are serving about one quarter of the time they're sentenced to. That means someone sentenced to ten years in prison is likely to serve between two and three years. So when I sentenced Devona Daniels to a year and a day, I was, in all likelihood, sentencing him to three months in prison. He had already been in jail several weeks awaiting trial. Soon he would be out.

People demand justice in their community, and by God they deserve it. But they never know how difficult and how frustrating it is for us to provide it.

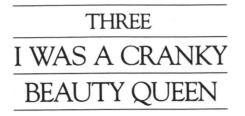

THREE

I WAS A CRANKY
BEAUTY QUEEN

My earliest memories are of justice.

As a little girl growing up on the rural east coast of North Carolina, I had a lot of pets, including dogs, chickens, and even a mule named Gin. But one of my favorite pets was a kitten that I adopted when I was only two or three years old. I played with her all day and took her to bed with me at night.

One day the kitten dragged herself into the house and collapsed. She was obviously in terrible pain. She had been in a fight with a tom cat, and she was bleeding all over. Her hind legs were paralyzed. I knew we would have to shoot her: She was going to die anyway, and the longer we waited, the worse her pain would be. I cried as my father took her outside and laid her away.

When he was done, he came back inside and said, "Now I'll take care of that tom." I knew what he meant. With Daddy, there was never any misunderstanding his meaning, never any guessing what he was going to do. Wesley James was a steely-eyed, no-nonsense sort of man, and he had an unerring sense of what was right. He was said to be related to the outlaw Jesse James, but there was no crook in him. He believed in hard work, family, fairness, and, maybe most of all, justice.

He got justice from that tom cat. He strode into the yard with his rifle at his side, cornered the cat, and killed him with a single blast. Then he buried the tom without so much as a prayer and walked back into the house.

"Not to worry," he said. "It's taken care of."

Later during the Depression, some son of a bitch gave Daddy a worthless check. I don't remember what Daddy had done for the man, but I imagine he sold him a cord of firewood or some animal hides. We were poor, and Daddy did anything he could to bring in some money. He cashed the check in a store and used it to buy food and other things for the family.

Then the check bounced, and the store held Daddy responsible. Whoever had written the check was long gone now, enjoying the fruit of Daddy's labor, so Daddy had to pay the money back. It was damned hard, but he paid it back, every dime. On Mama's birthday, he told the store manager he was going to hold a little back so that he could buy Mama a pair of stockings. Every other week he gave that store every penny he could set aside. That meant eating less and waiting longer for new shoes, and our meals weren't too big nor our shoes too new to begin with.

It was a bitter time for my father, who couldn't understand what kind of person would do such a thing. He never forgave the man who passed that bad check.

Those experiences, and my father's reactions to them, probably shaped my thinking as much as anything else that happened in my youth. As angry as I was at the tom cat for killing my kitten, I was sorry when my father killed him. No little girl wants to see an animal, even a cruel or dangerous one, put to death. But I understood why he did it. He was trying to teach me that no bad deed goes unpunished, and that awful things happen to those who do wrong. We never again saw the man who wrote the bad check, but I am inclined to think he paid, somehow, for what he did to us. My father, I knew, felt the same way. He believed that those who choose to commit crimes, even petty crimes, pay a price for making that choice. I came to believe it too.

I was born on September 30, 1929, in a little wooden house in Ponzer, North Carolina. It was grape-picking time. As my mother, Lydia, lay in bed struggling to give birth, the pickers kept sneaking up to the window for a peek. Mama spoke for years of how awful that was. My parents named me Lydia Ellen James. Daddy would always laugh and say, "Liddie Ellen came a-yellin'." I was their first and, as it happened, only child.

My father, the son of Montana farm people, went to Miami in the mid-1920s to spend a summer roughing it in a tourist camp. There, he met my mother, Lydia Winfield, the daughter of farmers from the Pungo River region of North Carolina. He married her in Miami in 1927 and then moved with her to North Carolina to work in farming and raise a family.

We lived mean lives in Ponzer. We were among the poorest of the rural poor, which means we didn't starve, but we didn't have any luxuries either. Daddy rented our home from a relative. It had no electricity and no running water. Our day began when the sun rose and ended when it set. When we needed drinking water, we lugged a pail out to the well, worked the pump, and then carried the water back inside.

I remember only the frightening and painful moments from those days. One was the death of my kitten. Another was when my maternal grandfather died. My parents laid his casket in the house until my aunt could come from Miami to bury him. I knew by my mother's tears that he was dead, not sleeping. I remember too the 1935 hurricane that roared through and blew down the big tree in our backyard. We were grateful for the firewood, mournful of the lost shade. That's rural life. God giveth and God taketh away.

When I was about to start grade school, we moved into a one-room shack next to the schoolhouse. It wasn't much of a place—we cooked and ate only a few feet from where we slept, and we still did not have plumbing—but it was all we could afford.

Daddy had bought the place partly because he wanted to make it easy for me to get to school. But then the state closed the schoolhouse and told us Ponzer kids that we would have to attend classes in a faraway swamp town. Daddy would have none of it. He traveled 150 miles to the state capitol in Raleigh to lobby against the plan. He won, and in 1936 I started school in Belhaven, North Carolina, twelve miles from my home. It was the first time I had ever seen a place with toilets and running water.

Getting to school was always an adventure. Each morning a bus picked us up and carried us over rocky dirt roads to the school. Sometimes the bumps were enough to shake my teeth loose. When it rained, which was often, the roads got so muddy that the bus couldn't pass over them. All the fathers in Ponzer knew what time the bus was supposed to bring us home. When it did not show up on time, they grabbed their shovels and planks and walked the road until they found us. Then they dug us out and rode home with us on the bus. To us, it was all very exciting. We loved getting stuck.

The schoolhouse in Ponzer stood empty now, so in 1936 Daddy bought it and converted it into a home for us. At last he and Mama had their own bedroom and I had mine. But we still had no electricity. And going to the bathroom often still meant braving a biting

North Carolina winter wind to get to the two-holer outhouse in the backyard.

Daddy worked hard to support us. He worked mostly as a farmer, raising potatoes, cotton, tobacco, corn, and soybeans. I often went with him when he picked or worked the plow, and I loved his company more than I can say. But farming was never enough to support us, so he also raised and sold hogs, dug ditches with Roosevelt's WPA, trapped furs, and worked in the tobacco barns. I'm sure there were times when he wondered where our next meal was coming from, but I never knew it. Nor do I remember ever going to bed hungry.

But being poor can hurt you even if you're not starving. One night, a terrible storm rolled into Ponzer. The night rumbled with the sound of thunder and the lightning turned the sky an angry blue. Out in the barn, our mule, Gin, was frightened. He stuck his snout out the window to see what was happening. It was a fatal mistake. A lightning bolt hit the barn, traveling into the window frame and killing the mule instantly. We found him dead in the morning.

Gin's death was a terrible blow. We had considered him a friend, even a member of the family. What's more, we had counted on him to better our lives. When we made the twenty-mile round trip to my Aunt Blanche's place, it was Gin who pulled the cart. And we didn't have a tractor, so we had relied on Gin to pull the plow in the fields. Everything worked out in the end—we borrowed another mule when we needed one—but for a time we did not know how we could get along. That's how much a mule can mean to a poor family.

In the Great Depression, my father could not find enough work in Ponzer to keep us fed and clothed. So he went to Newark, New Jersey; Washington, D.C.; and Baltimore, Maryland, to work as a roofer. The economies in those places were, as they were everywhere, dismal, but a man could still make a dollar laying down a hot-tar roof in the summer sun.

The days when Daddy went away were awful for me. I still don't like to think about them. It broke my heart when he had to leave. I would cry and cry and beg him not to go, but of course he always went. Finally, Mama decided it would be best if Daddy just slipped away before I got up, or while I was at school. I would awaken or arrive home in the afternoon to find him gone. And then I would spend the rest of the day, sometimes the rest of the week, sobbing uncontrollably.

Summers, we joined Daddy wherever he was working. He, Mama, and I would bounce around from rooming house to rooming house, always looking for a place we could afford. My mother had no trouble dealing with the landlords and slumlords. Once, Daddy got home from work to find Mama and me sitting in the car with all our things. Some landlord had mouthed off to her, so she had told him where to stick it. And then she had walked out.

Mama always said exactly what she thought. When, as a little girl, I told her I wanted a piece of candy or something, she always said, "You may want horns, but you'll die butt-headed." I say the same thing today when lawyers tell me they want something. I was closer to my father than I was to my mother. But my friends say I have my mother's personality traits. I never shut my mouth when I have a chance to open it, and I don't take any grief from anybody.

I almost didn't make it this far. In 1938, back in Ponzer for the school year, I contracted mastoiditis, which at that time was a life-threatening illness. I had internal bleeding, kidney problems, and any number of other complications. I spent several weeks in a hospital forty miles from home, but then the doctors ran out of ideas and sent me home to die. The neighbors all said it would be a blessing if I just passed away, because I was sure to end up a vegetable if I didn't.

Finally, we found a young doctor in Belhaven who had heard of a new drug that was supposed to lessen the effects of the illness. He began experimenting with the drug, giving me larger and larger doses and watching my reaction, and eventually I started to get better. The process of recovery was slow and painful; I missed an entire year of school. Daddy was away much of the time, but he took special care of me when he came home. Spring mornings, he would carry me from my bed to the front yard so that I could see the daffodils blooming.

At age twelve I discovered boys. I knew I would never be the same.

That year, 1941, Daddy moved us to Virginia so that he could work in the navy shipyard in Norfolk. The world was at war, and family men like Daddy could at last find steady work. We lived with my older cousin Mavis in Cradock. For the next five years, I saw shiny new ships steam proudly out of port, and sometime later saw them limp back, tattered but still afloat.

More exciting than the ships, though, were the boys. In Ponzer, I had not had much opportunity to spend time with other children, male or female. Of the few children in my school, most lived on farms miles away from me. My best friend by far had been Daddy. I was his little short-haired girl, more like a son than a daughter. He had taught me how to shoot and spit and swear, for all of which I'm still grateful.

Cradock, Virginia, though, was a big city, or at least it seemed so to me, and it was teeming with new friends. I made plenty of girlfriends, but I remember the boyfriends better. I started to go steady with a boy shortly after we arrived there. When he and I got sick of each other, I went steady with someone else. It was all very innocent, believe me. We traded fleeting kisses, but we didn't do anything heavy. I did not even know what heavy was. It was all a wonderful game, the most fun game I had ever played.

Then everything changed: I met Jimmy.

He was a student at a military school in Virginia. We met in summer, when he was home on vacation. I was fourteen and he was a couple of years older. Many nights we went to Ocean View Beach and rode the roller coaster and ferris wheel. Other times I met Jimmy at the movie theater where he worked as a projectionist. He used to sneak me into the projection room and we would smooch like crazy until it was time to change the reel. The amazing thing was that we never got caught.

It's hard to find words to describe the way I felt. In romance novels, girls say they can feel their boyfriends' embrace hours after the boys have gone home. That was how I felt about Jimmy. We were deeply, profoundly in love. I think grown-ups make a mistake when they say, "Aw, she's only a kid. She'll get over it." I don't think people ever experience emotions more intensely than they do when they're fourteen or fifteen years old. I, for one, have never felt so strongly about anything as I did about Jimmy that wonderful summer.

We wanted to get married, and we were completely serious about it. But we agreed that we should wait until I finished high school and Jimmy had started his career, whatever it might be. It was

1944. We decided that we would be married on June 24, 1947. The wedding was still a long way off, but I started making plans anyway. I got a piece of paper and made a list of things I would need in married life: house, silverware, pots, pans, dishes, dog, cat. I was very methodical, and romantic as hell.

But I was not sophisticated. My parents found the list. All hell broke loose when they found out what Jimmy and I had in mind. It wasn't that they didn't like Jimmy. They just didn't want me to run off and get married when other girls my age were still playing with dolls. Mama was afraid I would have sex with Jimmy and ruin my reputation. "The worst thing that can happen to a girl is to get petered," she'd say. "No man wants a girl like that for a wife."

Daddy and Mama kept an eye on us after they found the list. Often, Jimmy and I spent evenings rocking back and forth on the green glider on my front porch. The glider squeaked and squawked in a persistent rhythm as we rocked in it. If Jimmy leaned over to kiss me, the noise stopped and we got company in a hurry. Sometimes I would catch Daddy sneaking around the corner to check on us even when we weren't doing anything.

I still have that green glider, by the way. I plan to put it on the porch of my North Carolina farmhouse when I retire.

After two years of dating, Jimmy and I began to have arguments. We argued mostly about silly, unimportant things, but the fights grew intense because we both had strong personalities. Once, we had a particularly bad one. The fight itself was pretty bad, but I made it worse by being as sarcastic and as difficult as I could be. I pushed Jimmy as far as I could, and he responded by slapping me, hard, in the face.

When Daddy found out, he was damned furious. He went straight to Jimmy's house to talk it over with him. He was gone a long time, and soon I began to wonder what he had done to my boyfriend. But when he came home, he told Mama, "You know, Ellen caused a lot of it." And then he told me not to see Jimmy anymore.

Jimmy and I continued to see each other anyway, but things weren't the same. We were growing older, drifting apart. The relationship might have ended naturally if something unnatural had not happened first.

On New Year's Eve, 1945, my uncle Fountain Davenport died

in Miami. Aunt Maggie brought the body home to Ponzer for burial, and of course we were there. My aunt owned a taxicab, and after the funeral it was decided that we would move to Miami and Daddy would go to work driving it for her. With the war over, work at the shipyard was growing scarce. Daddy needed new work, and warm, sunny Miami seemed like a fine place to get it. Besides, Daddy and Mama had always talked about moving back to the city where they had met.

I was excited about the move. I did not want to leave the friends I had made in high school, especially Jimmy. But I was intrigued by the lights and the mystery of the city. I thought it would be a good place to spend my senior year in high school. We arrived in Miami on July 10, 1946, my parents' nineteenth wedding anniversary.

For a year I did not write to Jimmy, or even think much about him. Then, on June 24, 1947, the day we were supposed to have been married, I thought of him again. I remembered the great times we had had, and wondered if he thought of them too. So I sent him a telegram. It consisted of one word:

"Remember?"

Yes, he did. He called me right away and invited me to his military-school graduation ceremony. By the time I got to Virginia, we were both thinking once again about marriage, except now we were old enough to go through with it. He was going to be an engineer in Massachusetts, and I was going to be an engineer's wife. I even went so far as to pick out a silver pattern.

We probably should have been more realistic. By then, Jimmy had already met and begun dating someone else, someone he cared for very much. I also had found new boyfriends. What seemed like a wonderful idea at Jimmy's graduation ceremony soon began to seem less wonderful, and eventually we called off our plans. I had never before wept about the end of a romance, but I wept about that one.

Forty years later, Jimmy, I can still feel your arms around me.

Miami in 1947 was a magical place. There were no interstate highways or beachfront condominiums then, so the city still seemed very much like a small town. Downtown Miami bustled with shoppers, and the tourists enjoying their postwar vacations made Miami Beach as prosperous as it had ever been. But the city was still quaint enough for a North Carolina farm girl to appreciate.

I enrolled in Miami Edison Senior High School for my senior year, and promptly latched on to a boy named Teddy. He had been going steady with someone else for quite some time, but I didn't care about that, and when I arrived, he didn't seem to care either. We went everywhere together, but we were never alone. All the cab drivers in town used to follow us around and then report back to Daddy about where we had been and, worse, what we had done.

Once, Teddy got a chance to try out for a job as host of a teen radio show on WGBS, so I tagged along to watch him audition. I had never before been in a radio station and was eager to see how one worked. While Teddy auditioned, I horsed around outside the studio with some of the other kids. Afterward, the people at the station thanked Teddy and he and I started to leave.

Then the producer came running after us. "Young lady," she said. "Wouldn't you like to audition?"

Well, why not? I sure liked to gab. And I didn't see how gabbing into a microphone would be any different from gabbing to my friends. So I went into the studio and read a piece of paper the station had prepared.

I got the job. Teddy didn't. It didn't do much for the relationship.

I sure had fun doing radio. The live program—if audio tape even existed, we kids didn't know about it—aired for a couple of hours each Saturday afternoon. Three other kids and I put on skits, read the latest news from each of the high schools, and filled in the rest of the time fooling around. It might not have been the greatest radio show ever produced, but we had fun, and lots of kids listened. Also, I'm sure it made money for the department store that sponsored it.

It didn't take me long to figure out that there was money in radio. I was nothing if not an industrious, cocksure kid, so at age eighteen I went out and put together my own radio program. Called "Bridal Consultant of the Air," it offered the prospective bride everything she could want, save for a handsome husband. I gave advice on wedding etiquette (I learned it by going to the library and reading books by Emily Post), suggested places to buy invitations and party favors, and even reported on some of the society weddings taking place in the city.

Once I had put the show together, I went out and sold it to the radio stations. It wasn't hard. The people who ran the stations were

all men, and by now I had begun to take on womanly proportions—
35-22-37. It was, I must say, the sort of figure most men could not
say no to. Not too many of them made eye contact with me, that's
for sure. But they never tried to get me into the sack. I wouldn't
have known what it meant if they had: I was a virginal bridal consultant.

The radio show did not make me dream of getting married, incidentally. After Jimmy, my romantic notions of marriage faded away,
at least temporarily. I was interested in the radio program only so far
as it could make me money and, yes, make me famous. So I guess I
was also a mercenary bridal consultant.

The job as a radio wedding expert was not the last one I would
get because of my blond hair and big boobs. While I was still doing
the radio program for teens, a photographer noticed me and asked
me if I would like to model. What young woman would say no to
that?

I went to work for the Cornet Modeling Agency, a small firm
that provided models for fashion shoots. When I think of my modeling days, I think of animals, and I don't mean the photographers. I
posed with all kinds of beasts—monkeys, flamingos, mules, dogs,
cats. You name it, I posed with it.

It wasn't always as glamorous as it might have seemed to other
people. Often, I would go with a photographer to shoot one of those
sexy bathing-suit pictures. He would tell me to lean against a tree,
stick out my boobs, and smile. Smiling was the hard part, especially
when bugs were crawling off the tree and down my bathing suit.
When I posed with flamingos, they sometimes used my legs as
scratching posts. Instead of pictures of a young chick in a swimsuit,
the photographer would get shots of a very annoyed person with
bleeding legs screaming at a pink bird.

Most of the good pictures ended up in local department-store
advertisements, but a few appeared in national publications such as
Life magazine. I was just a kid, too young to fool with, so the photographers generally left me alone. The *Life* photographer was the only
exception. He was hell-bent on getting me in the sack, and he didn't
give a damn if I was an eighteen-year-old virgin. He did not succeed.
I sent him back to New York without any piece of me.

It was a short step from model to beauty contestant. Miami had

lots of beauty contests in those days. Some were big ones, like the
Miss Miami contest, but most were local events with little in the way
of prizes. From my senior year in high school to the time I was
twenty-three, I entered every one I could.

I disagree with people who say the contests are nothing but
meat markets that exploit women. In all my time in pageants, nobody ever tried to force me into doing something that nice young
girls didn't do. I really enjoyed myself. I also learned how to carry
myself in front of people, a skill I have used often in my life. Most of
the pageants required that the contestants show their talent. Well, I
had no talent. I couldn't sing, dance, play the guitar, whistle, juggle,
perform magic tricks, or even do bird imitations. I was born without
a talent gene.

So I talked. It was the one thing I could do really well. When it
was my turn to show my talent, I grabbed the microphone (if there
was one) and began to chat with the audience. I started by saying,
"Hello, ladies and gentlemen, my name is Ellen James, and I'm
mighty pleased to be here tonight." And then I shared my thoughts
on whatever subject popped into my mind—books, teen concerns,
whatever. I probably should have been nervous, but that didn't occur
to me then. I could sense that people were pulling for me. My North
Carolina accent, stronger then than it is now, didn't hurt me any.

I did well. In 1947, I was runner-up for Tequesta Queen. In
1949, I became Coconut Harvest Maid, which I thought was a funny
title even then, and came in third in the Miss Miami contest. I
probably won or placed in a few more, but forty years after being
Coconut Harvest Maid, who remembers?

The most important event was the contest to become Orange
Bowl Queen. For the winner, it meant a ride on the float on New
Year's Day, some prize money, and probably a pretty good modeling
contract. I thought being Orange Bowl Queen would be quite an
honor, and a lot of fun.

But when I entered the contest in 1949, I found that the orange
was rotten.

Sometime before the competition, the Orange Bowl Committee
summoned us all to a local department store to be fitted for the
queen's gown. The committee members said they wanted to have the
dress ready for whomever was chosen queen.

The competition was held at the Coral Gables Country Club.

Right in the middle of the event, an early edition of the next day's paper hit the stands. The front page carried bad news. One of the finalists, it said, had been chosen Orange Bowl Queen and would ride at the head of the float in the parade. The paper even carried a picture of her being crowned, which was pretty suspicious, considering the contest wasn't over yet.

In fact, it was over. The committee members had long since selected the winner. They only wanted us to think that we still had a chance. The trip to the department store and the contest itself had been shams. The committee members had no need for my measurements, except possibly for their own amusement. We went on with the competition anyway, but we were none too happy about it, especially when it started to pour.

Well, I was one cranky beauty queen. But I wasn't one to cry, or to complain about how badly I had been cheated. People in my family didn't do those things. It wasn't dignified.

So I sued them.

Yes, this was the future judge's initiation into the legal system— a small-claims suit over a matter of principle. Do I think it was the most important case ever to hit the American judiciary? No. Do I regret bringing it? No, indeed. If the courts aren't there to help us resolve disputes and settle grievances, what are they there for?

For several days I tried to serve the papers on Dan Mahoney, the chairman of the Orange Bowl Committee and, incidentally, the publisher of the *Miami News*. Somehow, I kept missing him. I don't know if my timing was bad or he was trying to avoid me. But nothing was going to keep me from suing. So I parked myself in the lobby of the newspaper building and waited for him. Finally, he stepped out of the elevator and I slapped him with the suit.

The committee, I'm sure, did not know what to make of me. But it certainly didn't want any publicity about its shabby and unfair treatment of the city's fine young ladies. So, a few weeks after I brought suit, the committee settled out of court. It agreed to pay us for the gowns that had been ruined in the rain if we would drop the suit.

It seemed like a good deal to me. I got $50, which was $15 more than I made in a week in my job as a legal secretary. The other girls, Cathy Blakely and Karen Von Unge, received $158.50 and $52.95, respectively. The *Miami Herald* even took a picture of us receiving the checks, but they didn't print the real story of what had happened.

The picture caption said, "Feeling happier about the 1950 Orange Bowl Queen contest are these unsuccessful candidates, shown as they received checks from the Orange Bowl Committee paying for damages to their clothes when it rained during the coronation ball and parade."

I would have been happier if they had printed the real story, but I was satisfied. I had gotten my dress money back, and I had made the committee reconsider the way it did things.

It never double-crossed a beauty queen that way again.

My first lover ended up in politics. I'm sure he was more faithful to the voters than he was to me.

His name was George Dubreuil, and I was not madly in love with him. After dating Jimmy, other relationships seemed insignificant in comparison. But I liked George very much. He was fun, imaginative, a little unpredictable. Also, he was several years older than I was, which added to the mystique.

We dated for a long time, but we never did anything beyond necking and groping. Even at age nineteen or twenty, I was mindful of my mother's warning about sleeping with men before marriage. I didn't want to be the scourge of the neighborhood, nor did I want to forever soil the James family name. Which were things I really thought would happen if I got horizontal with this man.

One night, George came to me looking forlorn. He sat me down, gazed into my eyes, and began to talk in very solemn tones.

"Ellen," he said, "we've been dating for quite some time now. You know I'm very fond of you, and I would never want to be with anyone else. We have been great friends. But after a while, just being friends isn't enough. I want us to be more than friends, see? I know you're a nice girl, but this nonsense just has to stop, and it is going to stop. Understand?"

Poor George. He must have been so frustrated.

I didn't want to quit seeing him, so I gave in. To use my mother's phrase, I let him peter me. It was not a memorable occasion. Skyrockets did not go off. Alarms did not sound. Bells did not ring. Lydia Ellen James did not know what the big deal was. She would find out later—oh, would she ever—but that night she just thought it was a bother.

Because I had let him have his way with me, I felt the only honorable thing for George to do was to marry me. I mean, he couldn't very well use me up and then throw me away like a dirty dish towel, which is how lots of men would have viewed me after what I had done. So I told him to start shopping for a ring, and, to my surprise, he said he would.

But he was not sincere about getting married, at least not to me. George owned a restaurant near the airport. He worked there day and night, night and day, trying to get a good start in life so he could eventually become someone. I respected that, and wanted to help. So, many nights I went to the restaurant and worked in his place so he could get some rest.

Our engagement ended when I learned that he was getting it with a girl named Jo in Fort Lauderdale.

FOUR

SETTING TRAPS
FOR GRANDPA

When I broke off the engagement, my friend Alex Morphonios was there to help me get through it. It is still not entirely clear to me how I wound up married to him.

I had met Alex a few months after my high school graduation. When the new school year began, Miami Edison Senior High School's alumni association held a meeting for its new alumni, and as a loyal Red Raider, I naturally decided to go. Alex, who had graduated nine years earlier, was the head of the association. He and I immediately found something to talk about—he was in engineering school, and so was my cousin St. Clair. I thought Alex was a nice fellow, but I didn't think anything more than that.

At that time I lived with my folks in an apartment owned by my aunt. To say it was an uncomfortable place would be an understatement. In the bathroom we had only a large sink to wash in, so we had to fill the basin with warm water and scrub ourselves standing up. My bedroom was divided from my parents' only by a dark curtain, which didn't provide much privacy, to say the least. The kitchen had nothing more than a little stove. I don't know what Daddy paid my aunt to live there, but it couldn't have been much. We didn't have much to give.

The night after the alumni-club meeting, there was a knock at the door. I opened it and there stood Alex. I was stunned. What the hell was he doing there? Naturally, I invited him in, because a decent person didn't leave someone standing in the doorway. But I immediately had a problem. I knew Daddy and Mama would want to size up this young man who had come unannounced and uninvited. But I couldn't remember his name. We had met only once, and now my mind was a blank. I was going to be in big trouble if my folks found out I didn't even know this guy. So, thinking fast, I said, "I'd introduce you, but I can't pronounce your name."

53

I would have been screwed if his name had turned out to be Smith.

We became good friends, and I learned a lot about him. Alex had had a tough upbringing. His father was a mysterious and unpredictable fellow who had disappeared one day and left his wife and children alone. His mother was domineering, and sometimes downright unpleasant. Alex had two sisters, one of whom hated him so much that when he went off to serve in World War II, she said, "I hope you get killed." His kid brother, also a soldier, did. It was a loveless, fractured family, and Alex grew up with the heavy responsibility of keeping it together. He worked a lot of jobs so that his family could eat. Not that anyone ever thanked him. The Morphonioses never hugged, kissed, or even touched. But when I met him, Alex seemed to have done a good job of overcoming all that. It would take me a long time to learn that he really hadn't.

He was like an older brother to me. I often consulted him on whom to date. Once, I made a date with one boy for Saturday and a date with another for the sixteenth, only to find out that Saturday and the sixteenth were the same day. I asked Alex what to do, and he told me the only wise thing to do would be to break both dates. Apparently he was always interested in being more than my friend, but I didn't realize it. I should have. He always saw something wrong with the boys I was dating.

After I broke up with George, Alex and I started to become more serious about each other. I was lonely and hurt, and Alex finally admitted that he had been waiting for an opportunity to be close to me. We dated for a short time and then Alex asked me to marry him. I said yes. I had known him for a long time and was very fond of him. Also, he was very steady, very serious. He was good husband material.

My parents were not crazy about him. My father, roughneck that he was, didn't think Alex was a real man, whatever that meant. But in a way they liked him. In high school, I had dated an Arab, an Italian, and a Jew. My parents never forbade me to go out with them, but I knew they would have felt better if I had dated, as my father said, "a regular American." By the time Alex came along, they were happy to settle for a Greek.

We were married on February 5, 1950.

*   *   *

The early days of our marriage were among the happiest days of my life. We didn't have any money, but I was used to that. Alex, who was still in school, got seventy-five dollars a month from the G.I. Bill and worked part-time at the Barfield Instrument Company as a technician. I earned about fifty dollars a week as a secretary for Roscoe Brunstetter. We ate scrambled eggs and cheese for two years, and not only because I was a lousy cook.

When we got married, we pooled our money and came up with about $500. (I had been keeping my part, about $300, in a piggy bank.) We used part of it to make a down payment on the house in Miami where we would live for the next twenty-one years. The house cost $10,300. With the rest, I went to a department store and bought a bedroom set, a living-room set, and a few other things. You could get that much furniture for a few hundred dollars in those days, and it was damned sturdy furniture. It was a nice home, a home I'd be proud to have even today.

I was no good in the kitchen—not if I was cooking, anyway. I'm still no galloping gourmet. I once burned some hot dogs so badly that even my dog, Jeff, wouldn't eat them. He took them out in the yard and buried them like bones. Another time, I decided to cook a can of pork and beans—by putting the can directly on the burner. Why dirty a pot? I just grabbed the can, fired up the burner, and laid the thing on top. About two minutes went by before the can exploded and the pork and beans were blown all over the ceiling. I could make blueberry pancakes and scrambled eggs, but even then I was no great hostess. I used to give each person a fork, lay the skillet on the table, and let everyone dig in.

We always seemed to have relatives and friends living with us. We began taking people in during the early days of the marriage and just kept taking them in for years and years. The door literally was never locked. At first, Cathy Blakely, my maid of honor, moved in with us after she had had some trouble at home. Then Betty, one of Alex's many nieces, moved in, and later brought her boyfriend with her. All I remember about him is that his feet smelled like a closet someone had died in.

Alex's niece Carole lived with us the longest. She was a sweet little thing, with blond hair (it's now red) and a nice figure. She didn't get along with her mother worth a damn, so she moved in with her uncle Alex and aunt Ellen. We were a lot more fun. Or at least I was. In coming years, Carole worked with me on political campaigns (mine and others'), and eventually became an assistant to Florida Congressman Claude Pepper. She also assisted me in another way: In later years, she covered for me when I wanted to be with a boyfriend and didn't want Alex to know.

I had one boyfriend who drank a bit. One night when I was in law school, he called me from a bar and told me to come and get him. Carole came along with me. She was only fourteen years old then. When we got to the bar, I found that there were too many people inside who knew me. I could hardly go in and drag out my boyfriend with all those people there. So I sent Carole in.

"You're kidding!" she said. "I can't go in there. I'm underage."

"I'm not kidding. Get your ass in there and get him out here on the double."

She did as she was told. Sweet kid.

I was a good wife for about a year. It didn't pay.

I did everything for Alex. Our house had wood floors, so on weekends I swept them, cleaned them with mineral spirits, and then waxed them so shiny you could almost go ice-skating on them. Alex would walk into the house, take one look, and say, "You missed a spot." So I would run to the spot and sweep and oil and wax it until it was perfect, and he would say, "I don't see why you can't get things right the first time."

I put up with it for about a year before my bullshit alarm went off. When it did, I quit housekeeping altogether. He'd say, "Aren't you going to wax the floors?" And I'd say, "If you want the floors waxed, wax them yourself, pal." Alex was older than I was, and he wanted to push me around. That wasn't the sort of answer he was expecting. Two decades later, during our divorce, the judge admonished Alex for losing control of his household. Alex sounded so sad when he answered. "But Judge," he said, "you don't understand. Ellen Morphonios is an unusual person."

Alex was not a thoughtful fellow. On my first birthday after the wedding, he didn't get me anything. The people in my office had made me a cake and given me presents, but my husband didn't say a word. I thought he had forgotten it was my birthday, but he hadn't. He had ignored it on purpose. He told this weird story about how he once put all his faith and trust in a girlfriend, but when he got back from the war, she was pregnant with someone else's baby. Apparently, he felt he couldn't risk giving another woman that sort of love and attention. But I was his wife, and I thought I deserved better.

Not only did Alex not give me things, he didn't want other people to give me things, either. On our first Christmas, Daddy and Mama gave me a fur cape. It wasn't a mink or anything, just an inexpensive fur. I appreciated it, especially knowing what a sacrifice it had been for my parents to buy it for me. Alex was furious. When my parents left our house that day, he said, "If anybody's going to buy you furs, it's going to be me." He felt Daddy and Mama had upstaged him, and he wanted me to return the gift. He might as well have asked me to drill a hole in my forehead.

But Alex's worst trait was his failure to understand people from different backgrounds. He was terrible. I may have been a Southerner, but I was raised to respect people of all colors. Once, when I was a little girl, I was walking with my father when a black lady passed us by walking in the other direction. I thought she was a prostitute. For some reason, maybe because I had seen someone else do it, I stuck my nose in the air as if I thought she were beneath me. Daddy had his prejudices, but he would not put up with prejudice in me. He grabbed me by the arm right there and said, "Don't you ever do a thing like that again. You're no better than anybody else, and don't think that you are."

Alex never learned that lesson. In later years, we had a black housekeeper named Sarah Lewis. I loved her. She was a close friend and confidante, and I trusted her with my life. Alex was not so warm. When he drove her home after a day's work, he made her sit in the backseat so that no one would see him sharing his seat with a Negro. It was appalling, and I found myself apologizing to Sarah all the time.

Once, Alex, Carole, my sons, and I were driving somewhere on vacation when we stopped at a restaurant for lunch. The waitress, who was black, came to take our order. Alex wouldn't even look at her. "May we have another waitress, please," he said. I'll never forget the look of humiliation and hurt on that poor woman's face as she went to get a white waitress. I was deeply embarrassed, and Alex's niece was so ashamed she wanted to cry.

Why would a woman go on living with such a man? Women stay in bad marriages for all sorts of reasons. In court, I often meet men who are charged with beating the hell out of their wives. And just as often I see the wives, their bruises just beginning to fade, come to court to have the charges dismissed. These women seem to be under their husbands' control—not so much physical as emotional control. They believe, despite all the evidence to the contrary, that their husbands aren't so bad, that maybe these men will change. Worse, they start to think that, if they're getting beaten regularly, they must have done something to deserve it.

I was a prisoner of my own thinking, not Alex's. I stayed with Alex for the simple reason that I did not believe in divorce. I thought that divorce would shame me, would make me a pariah in the community. Worse, I thought it would kill my parents. Alex's niece often asked why I didn't just leave him, but I would always say, "Not while Daddy and Mama are alive." At the same time, I knew it was not, and never would be, a good marriage. So I just tuned Alex out. I ignored him the way I would have ignored a knock in the pipes or a minor leak in the roof over the garage.

We stayed married for twenty-one years, but the marriage really was over before our third anniversary.

Our relationship might have seemed stranger if not for the truly odd relationship between Alex's parents. It was the weirdest relationship in Miami, and naturally it was conducted under my roof.

Mrs. M Grandma—that's what I called Alex's mother—had lived in her own home in Miami for years. But in her late fifties, she began to get very sick with high blood pressure and other ailments, and soon it became clear that she could no longer care for herself. We learned this in a rather disturbing way. One day she called and told us that her dog wouldn't wake up. It was no wonder. Poochie had been dead for a week.

So we packed up her things and moved her into an apartment in our garage. I soon found out where Alex had gotten all his charms. Mrs. M Grandma used to come into the dining room, lean her back against the wall, reach around the corner into the kitchen, and say, "Give me a drink of water, please. I can't stand to come into your messy kitchen." If she had not been so pathetic I would have decked her.

For all she and Alex had in common, they didn't get along too well. Alex treated her like dirt. He would walk into the garage, push her, and say, "Come on, you old bitch, why don't you clean up?" Mrs. M Grandma wasn't my best friend by a long shot, but I couldn't stand to see her treated that way, as sick and crazy as she was. Alex and I had some of our worst fights over the way he treated her.

Soon our domestic life became even stranger and more complicated. Alex had been looking for his father, on and off, for many years. As any son would have, he missed his father and wanted him back in his life. Once, when Alex and I were on vacation in Georgia, we got a call from a friend who said he had heard that Alex's father was in Columbia, South Carolina. At the end of the week, I went back to Miami, and Alex went to South Carolina.

When he came home, he had his father with him. Mr. M Grandpa, as I always knew him, was a tiny, happy-go-lucky man with a bald head and a silly smile. He had lived in the United States for many years, but he spoke no English, only Greek. When he got excited about something, which was often, he rubbed his hands together and giggled like crazy. For reasons I have never completely understood, he called me Miss Lady. I adored him.

Mr. M Grandpa moved into the back bedroom, which was empty then. This created an odd situation: He was now living under the same roof with the woman he had walked out on some twenty-five years earlier. They were not happy to be together again. Living with Mrs. M Grandma apparently reminded Mr. M Grandpa of all the reasons why he had left her. And it convinced Mrs. M Grandma that she had been right to forget about the guy and put the whole thing behind her. The two did not even speak. They would pass each other in the living room on the way to breakfast every morning and not say a word, not even make eye contact. It could have been worse, I guess. At least they didn't fight.

Mrs. M Grandma was not the only one who was losing her mind. Mr. M Grandpa had a few screws loose too. In his wallet he carried an old, tattered newspaper clipping from the days of the Depression. It was an advertisement for a chiropractor, and Mrs. M Grandma's picture appeared in it. Apparently the chiropractor had asked her to pose for the ad, and she had accepted. Well, Mr. M Grandpa had assumed that his wife was diddling the chiropractor. He used it as one of his excuses for leaving her.

By the time he came to Miami, Mr. M Grandpa was too old to take care of himself anymore. But you couldn't tell him that. He used to run away all the time—not so much because he didn't like living with us but because he had been on the road for years and wanted to stay there. At night, he would slip out of the house and roam the streets, eventually stopping to sleep at a three-dollars-a-night flophouse. We never knew, when we woke up in the morning, if Mr. M Grandpa would be in the house or somewhere in downtown Miami, roaming the streets and looking for a handout.

To keep better track of him, I made him an identification bracelet with our address and phone number printed on the inside. I also wrote, "This is Mr. Morphonios. He's harmless. If you should find him, please send him home." It worked well. In the next few months, I met police officers from all over Dade County and beyond. One of them told me he had tried to speak to Mr. M Grandpa in English, but had gotten nowhere. "He speaks Greek," I said. "Lady," the cop said, "he doesn't make any sense in Greek, either." I even set traps for him to keep him at home. I filled coffee cans with screws and nails and left them by the door, so that when Mr. M Grandpa tried to sneak out at night, the cans spilled everywhere and I could run out and catch him.

When he got old and sick, we had to put him in a nursing home. I hated to do it, but I could no longer care for him the way I wanted to. When he got very sick, he went to a hospital, where he died. We were with him there, but that is not what I remember most about him. What I remember most is something that had happened a few months earlier, when he was still in the nursing home. The director had called us to say that Mr. M Grandpa had completely lost his faculties, that he no longer remembered anyone or anything. My two small sons and I hurried to the nursing home, afraid that we would never again see Alex's father with his senses intact. It would not, we were sure, be a happy visit.

When we walked into his room, Mr. M Grandpa's eyes brightened with glee. "Miss Lady, Dale, Dean!" he said, and there was no doubt he knew exactly who we were.

He was a con artist of the first order.

FIVE

HOW I WENT THROUGH LAW SCHOOL PERPETUALLY PREGNANT

One day in the winter of 1953, I made a major career move, a decision that would change the very course of my life. As usual, I gave it about as much thought as I give to brushing my teeth in the morning.

That day, my boss, an attorney named Roscoe Brunstetter, dictated a letter to the dean of the University of Miami law school. It was a recommendation for a client who, it turned out, wanted to become a lawyer. This client ran a grocery store in the Florida Keys, but was now giving it up for a life at the bar. My boss described the man in glowing terms and urged the dean to accept him into the law school. I knew the letter would carry a lot of weight: Mr. Brunstetter was a trustee of the university. It always helps to have connections.

As I sat taking dictation, I got an idea. It was as if the notion had been buzzing around the room like a fly and had landed in my ear. It happened that suddenly, that unexpectedly. Anyway, once the idea was in my head I couldn't get rid of it.

I was going to become a lawyer and that's all there was to it.

When my boss finished dictating the letter, I went back to my desk and typed it up. Then I brought it into Mr. Brunstetter's office for his signature. He was about to sign it when I said, "As long as we're at it, would you mind writing one of those letters for me?"

He looked at me as if he thought I had been talking to somebody else. "I beg your pardon?"

"I got to thinking about it while you were dictating that letter, and I think I'd like to go to law school too," I said.

I could tell he thought it was a harebrained idea. Actually, he was right. Even I knew that there were a couple of serious obstacles to my becoming a lawyer. First, I hadn't even been to college. Jumping straight from high school to law school would be like running for governor after one term as dog catcher. It was possible: In those days, the University of Miami law school admitted high school graduates who could show, through tests and recommendations, that they had the equivalent knowledge of a college graduate. But it would be tough, and I knew it.

Second, as most people couldn't help noticing, I was a woman. There were some female lawyers in those days, but not many. It was 1953, and women were expected to get married and have babies and keep house. I knew that by asking for a recommendation to law school, I was wandering into territory that traditionally belonged to men. It wasn't the first time, and God knows it wouldn't be the last.

It was my gender that Mr. Brunstetter seemed to be thinking of when we discussed my request. He said I was too young for law school, but I could tell he really meant that I was too female. And I said no, I'm not so young, I'm twenty-three years old, but what I meant was that it didn't matter if I was a woman or a golden retriever.

"I think I'm ready," I said. Actually, I hadn't thought about it at all. It wasn't as if becoming a lawyer had been my life's ambition. There were no lawyers in my family, so the inspiration didn't come from some successful relative. I never paid much attention to the old Perry Mason radio dramas, so that wasn't it either.

So why did I decide to go to law school? Mr. Brunstetter himself was a small part of the inspiration: He was a decent, gentle man and I thought his work was rewarding and worthwhile. He seemed to have a good life.

The best explanation, though, is that I saw an opportunity and decided to grab it. All my life, no matter what I wanted to do, people have told me, "You can't do that. It just isn't done." I have never listened to them. I have always done pretty much what I wanted to do, damn the consequences. Hell, I made the decision to go to law school without even consulting my husband. "It would be nice if you told me about these things before you did them," he said at home that night.

Mr. Brunstetter apparently sensed how determined I was, because he finally gave in and dictated a second letter. The law school took me even before I had passed the entrance exams.

*   *   *

One of these days, when some criminal does something that really ticks me off, I'm going to sentence him to three years in law school. Now, that's punishment.

I entered the University of Miami Law School in late February 1953, three weeks into the semester. It was interesting at first. The course I took in criminal law that semester fascinated me. Before taking that course, I hadn't even known criminal lawyers existed. I thought all lawyers practiced civil law—tort actions, divorces, and so on.

Subsequent courses cured me of my enthusiasm for law school. They were tedious, mind-numbing ordeals, and some days I could hardly stand the thought of going to class. Learning about wills and trusts is about as interesting as plucking your eyebrows. I couldn't see the point of it, but, then, I couldn't see the point of most of the things I was learning.

I might have liked it better if my days had not been so hectic. In my second year, eager for a change in atmosphere, I left Mr. Brunstetter and went to work as a secretary for a banker named Hoke Maroon. It was a demanding job, and my class schedule only increased the pressure. Once, I made the mistake of taking a course in corporations on my lunch hour. Each day at noon I rushed to school, sat through the class, and then drove like hell back to Mr. Maroon's office, which was clear on the other end of town. To complicate things, the man who taught the course always rambled on way past the allotted time, making it that much harder for me to get back to work promptly. I worried so much that semester that my stomach began to eat itself. I never took a midday course again.

My schedule wasn't always that heavy, but it was never light. Throughout law school I got up early, picked up my housekeeper, brought her back to the house, headed to the office, worked hard all day, and then went to school. I always seemed to have a ten P.M. class, so I usually didn't get home until eleven-thirty. Sometimes I would nod off at the wheel on the way home, only to awaken to the sound of my tires on gravel. It was tough. Years later, when I was holding court until ten or eleven P.M., the lawyers would complain about their long days and I would say, "Shit, these are bankers' hours."

At times I wanted to quit school, but I never would have allowed myself to do it. I wouldn't give anyone the satisfaction of saying, "See, I told you it couldn't be done." My attitude didn't have a thing to do with my gender, by the way. It had to do with my ego. I have never been out to prove that a woman could do something—only that I could do it.

A couple of things happened that made law school more tolerable. First, I ran for the school senate on a write-in ticket and won. It didn't give me any great power, but it made me feel accepted. Second, I met a man who would be my best friend—and more—for many years.

Don Petit, a slender, dark-haired, dark-eyed man, was seven years my senior. A native of Vermont, he served as a combat correspondent in the Marine Corps and then went on to a career in newspapers. He joined the *Miami News* in 1946 and quickly became one of the paper's best political and investigative reporters. In the late forties, he wrote an exposé on Miami's many illegal gambling joints, naming names and giving addresses and phone numbers. It took a lot of guts. In those days, the hoodlums owned Miami, and few people dared to cross them. Don's series closed a lot of those gambling parlors for good.

Another time, long before such stories were popular among crusading journalists, he wrote shocking articles about the lack of attention given to the mentally ill. His stories about the Ku Klux Klan got people's attention—and got him and his photographer roughed up by some angry bigots. That didn't bother him. He was a rugged, old-fashioned, hard-nosed newspaperman, a tough guy who would do anything for a story.

He was also scrupulously fair, which earned him a lot of respect among politicians. By the time I met him, he was already acquainted with any number of senators, governors, mayors, and judges. In later years, he supervised several gubernatorial campaigns and even worked briefly for President Lyndon Johnson. He liked shaping the news as much as covering it, and he did both almost all his life.

Now he was going to law school, not because he wanted to practice law but because he thought knowledge of the law would be useful to him. One of my classmates, a police officer, introduced us, and the three of us began to study together at my house.

Don and I took to each other right away. One night, Don took me aside and asked me if I would like to have lunch with him. I was not naïve; I knew what he really wanted. I also knew he was married. His wife, Jean, and I were becoming fast friends. I accepted the invitation anyway. We had lunch the next day, and the day after that, and soon we were together every day of the week. At first we just ate lunch, then we just held hands, and then—well, then there was nothing just about it.

It was not a passing fancy. We were lovers, on and off, for almost twenty years. When Don was home, it was on, and when he was away on business, as he frequently was, it was off. We did not make excuses for ourselves then, and I won't make them now. Don and I were deeply, foolishly, in love, and instead of fighting it we accepted it. We talked sometimes about getting married, but we were just being romantic, just indulging our fantasies. I wasn't happy with Alex, but I was used to him, and I couldn't imagine being without him. Besides, marrying Don would have meant getting a divorce, and I didn't believe in divorce.

How could I do such a thing to my husband? It was easy. I had gone to the altar with a gentleman, a friend. But I had found myself married to an angry and troubled man, a relentless nitpicker who was unable to forgive anyone anything. I listened to his griping for a year or two. I did what I could to please him. When I found out there was no pleasing him, I gave up. I didn't leave him physically, but I certainly left him emotionally. He was still the man I lived with, still the guy next to me in bed at night. When the roof had a leak or the car had a flat tire, I went to him. But when I wanted affection and romance and real love, I went to other people. Don was the first one I went to, and the greatest.

I don't think our relationship was any great secret around town. Certainly Don's newspaper friends knew about it. They saw us together all the time, and knowing Don, who was rather a ladies' man, they assumed we were an item. Naturally, we tried to keep it a secret from Jean and Alex, but I don't guess we did a very good job. Once, the four of us went to the Firemen's Ball, and Don and I danced together most of the night. Later, a friend told me that her husband had seen us dancing and said, "If I were her husband or his wife, I'd kill them both."

Don and I had some close calls. In my kitchen one evening, Jean started talking about Don's philandering. She said she hoped that anyone who was having an affair with him would understand that she had children and that she wasn't getting any younger. If someone was going to take Don away from her, she didn't want it to happen when she was too old to start over. She never mentioned me directly, but I think that, in her dignified way, she was trying to tell me how she felt about it. She was coming at me with a butter knife, not a pitchfork. Another time, when he was very small, my son Dean told Alex, "In the afternoons I have to be quiet because that's when Don and Mommy go into the bedroom to rest." Alex blew his stack over that, but it wasn't true. Don and I did a lot of things, but we never screwed around in either of our homes. That could have gotten us killed, and we knew it. We always went to neutral sites, some of which had neon signs. I think Dean made the remark about our afternoon rests only because Alex harassed him into it. Alex was, justifiably, a suspicious fellow. He spent a lot of time cross-examining people.

Alex seemed to know what was going on. Sometimes, when he got angry, he made sarcastic remarks about Don and me, but he never directly accused me of screwing around. One night Don and Jean had a disagreement, and Don went out and got drunk with some newspaper buddies. He called me from the bar and asked me to come and pick him up. That wasn't unusual. Don and Jean had many disagreements, and Don spent many nights on our couch. Alex never complained. This time, though, was different. "Don't you go get him," Alex said. "You're not to leave." He said it in a very threatening way, as if to assert himself as the head of the family. I listened carefully, considering every authoritative word. And then I left. Alex was already in bed, fuming, when Don and I got back.

Alex and I had our pleasant moments. One of them made me pregnant.

It was halfway through my first year of law school and I was not pleased. I had always assumed that Alex and I would have a child or two, Don Petit or no Don Petit, but I certainly didn't want one now. I had too many other things to do. I was working days and going to law school nights. I had no time for a kid. I didn't want a kid.

I was so upset about it that for a while I even considered getting an abortion. They were illegal then, but, like a lot of people, I knew of phone numbers I could call to make an appointment for a back-room operation. It would cost a few hundred dollars and nobody would be the wiser. (I know now that a person could get killed by one of those hacks, but I didn't know it then.) I thought long and hard about making an appointment, but in the end I decided against it. I just couldn't do it. I thought it was wrong—not for someone else, maybe, but certainly for me.

I went into labor on August 9, 1954, during a summer recess from law school. The doctor gave me something to put me under, and when I woke up the next morning, voilà!—Alex and I had a son, Dale. I didn't feel a thing, which was exactly how I wanted it.

I thought I would be overcome with emotion when my first child was born, but I wasn't. Maybe it was because Dale looked so bad. It turned out that while I was sleeping, Dale was having a hell of a time being born. The doctor had had to use forceps to draw him out, and by the time he emerged he looked like he had gone ten rounds with Joe Louis. His eyes were black and his head was swollen. I had given birth to a living bruise. When the nurse brought him to me, I thought, Gee, I thought there was supposed to be a magical aura around me when I gave birth. But there wasn't.

I was exhausted, and I wanted Dale's bruises to fade.

I got pregnant for the second time a year later. I still didn't think I had time for children, but what could I do? I had to live with it.

Dean was not as polite as Dale. He had the bad manners to arrive in April, right in the middle of the spring term. I couldn't take time off, so I kept working and going to school right until the day of delivery. I have never liked taking days off. If I had a baby today— which is unlikely as I am past sixty—the doctor would have to come to the courtroom and deliver the baby between witnesses.

Having the second child was not going to be as easy as having the first. Shortly after I went into labor, I went out and got a roast beef sandwich. The doctors had told me not to eat anything, but hell, I was hungry. When I got back to my room, the labor pains intensified and my doctor told me I was going to have the baby immediately. So the orderlies came and rolled me down to the delivery room.

The anesthesiologist put the mask on my face to put me under and, naturally, I immediately threw up the roast beef sandwich. Then I passed out. When I came to, I could hear the doctor telling someone, "What do you mean you can't find her husband? You have to find him." Alex was off someplace with Don. The doctor was shouting now. "Don't you understand that this is an emergency?" Nice words to wake up to.

When I got my senses, I became aware of two unpleasant facts. One, I was going to have a baby. Two, I was going to have a baby while I was wide awake. I was not happy about it. Natural childbirth was not my idea of a good time. If I could have had the baby delivered by room service, I would have. At the very least, I wanted to be in la-la land. Clearly that wasn't going to happen.

I had Dean without taking drugs. I had to stay in the hospital for three weeks after his birth. It took that long to clear my lungs of roast beef.

I graduated from law school in June 1957—pregnant again.

For the first time, I was really excited about it. I had been working so hard when Dale and Dean were born that I hadn't been able to spend much time with them. Now, with law school behind me, I would finally have time to be with my infant child.

Alex and I already had two boys, but I wanted another one. I don't think I would have known what to do with a girl. Boys are easy, predictable. Give them an expensive new toy and they'll do what comes naturally: They'll destroy it. I like that kind of dependability.

Girls are much more complicated. If I was lucky enough to have a daughter who liked to fish and shoot and swear, I figured I'd be fine. If I had one who liked expensive clothes and sweet perfumes, I knew I would be useless. I can spend about thirty minutes shopping before I need a straitjacket. I don't think God makes too many mistakes, but I have always thought he goofed when he made me female. So I was praying for a son.

A month after graduation, I came home from work one day and noticed that I was spotting, the way I sometimes did at the beginning of a period. I wasn't overly concerned. I had heard about women who had experienced this, so I tried to put it out of my mind. Before long, though, the trickle turned into a flow, and I knew I was in serious trouble. I was five months pregnant. Pregnant women aren't supposed to bleed, not that much.

About four A.M., Alex drove me to the hospital. I was ushered into a room and left there, presumably until a doctor could come and examine me. By now I had cramps, and the bleeding was heavier. I was thinking, When are they going to come and stop this?

All at once I knew I was going to lose the baby, and no doctor could do anything to stop it.

I delivered my stillborn child alone. It was over in seconds. Moments later, a nurse came into the room and took the child from the bed. She placed the tiny baby in a pan and left it on the dresser while she went to call a doctor. When she left, I got out of bed and went to the dresser. The child, my third son, seemed to be sleeping.

Later, I would come to understand what had happened. For some reason, the baby hadn't been able to get nourishment in my womb, and had therefore stopped developing. I think my doctor knew what was going to happen: The day before the tragedy, he had unexpectedly done an internal examination on me. He must have known then that the baby would not be born alive.

In the coming weeks I would blame law school for the child's death. If I had not been so preoccupied with getting my degree, I thought, I would have taken better care of myself and the baby would have lived. It was crazy thinking, but I needed a scapegoat, and law school was it. Shortly after the baby's death, I threw my diploma into the top of a closet and left it there for a long time.

I spent two days in the hospital after the stillbirth. One morning I threw on some clothes and made my way to the pediatric ward. From the hallway I could look through a window and see the newborn babies, some of them too tiny or sickly to survive despite the hospital's best efforts. I looked at those babies and knew that God, in His wisdom, had decided that the world didn't need another sick or handicapped child, and therefore had taken mine from me. It was all for the best.

I wasn't supposed to be out of bed. So I stood still by the window, looking at the babies and crying softly so no one would hear.

I took the bar examination a couple of weeks later. It was a bad idea. I could barely remember my own name, much less the fine points of civil and criminal law. I had no business taking that test, and it showed in the results: I failed with flying colors.

I shouldn't have been disappointed, but I was. I had never failed at anything before, at least not anything important, and I was inconsolable. I was still mourning the lost child, still blaming law school for my troubles. Alex and Don tried to make me smile, but they couldn't. I just lay in bed, crying and feeling sorry for myself.

Then somebody called my dad.

"What the hell are you doing?" Daddy said. He had a way of saying things that could wake up a bronze statue. "You're quitting? You're giving up? I've never heard of such a thing. You get up and you go out there and do better next time."

I got up in a hurry.

Failing the bar exam didn't mean I couldn't work as a law clerk. Under the law, I could not speak in court or sign my name to pleadings, but I could do legal research and draft motions. So I went to work.

I had a hell of a first job. My first law partner was Fuller Warren, the former governor of Florida.

Fuller Warren, who grew up in Blountstown, Florida, never wanted to be anything but governor. He ventured into politics at thirteen, running for page in the state House of Representatives. He was defeated, but that didn't dissuade him. He was elected to the Florida legislature when he was a junior in college.

He became governor in 1948. His campaign promise was to get the cows off the highways. It was a big issue then: Under state law, drivers had to pay for the cows they hit, and they whacked a lot of them. Fuller Warren ushered Florida, until then a rustic, untamed place, into the twentieth century. He built the modern system of schools, encouraged tourism, and battled the Knights of the Ku Klux Klan, whom he called "covered cowards, hooded hoodlums, and sheeted jerks."

People called him the silver-haired, silver-tongued governor. He could talk about anything, even something he didn't know anything about, and sound as if he were delivering his doctoral dissertation. Once, in a speech at a football game, he said, "I want to thank you for this tumultuous reception, this incredible ovation, this thunderous welcome. It is more than I expected and almost as much as I deserve." He could also be as cutting as a meat cleaver. In an angry moment he referred to a political enemy as "a foul blot upon the escutcheon of human propriety and decency." Being criticized by Fuller Warren was like being beaten with a dictionary.

I would like to be able to say he had a blissful term as governor, but I can't. In the middle of his term, he got into a mess that soiled his reputation and flat-out ruined his political career. In the early fifties, Estes Kefauver's Senate Crime Investigating Committee began uncovering racketeering operations across the country. Kefauver, scrambling to build his name for a presidential bid, started his work in Florida. He had good reason: In those days, an outfit called the S & G rackets syndicate controlled Miami. The syndicate operated gambling parlors and bookmaking joints around the clock. Instead of hiding from the cops, the S & G simply paid them off and worked openly. You couldn't walk past a hotel in Miami Beach without hearing the clang of pinball machines and the whir of slot machines. Every salesman from Topeka knew Miami was the place to buy a broad and place a bet.

Kefauver didn't take long to tie Fuller Warren to the racketeers. He discovered that several known gamblers had contributed anonymously to the governor's 1948 campaign, funneling the money through political connections. When the governor refused to testify, Kefauver blackened his name with a vicious television and magazine campaign. It was not fair. Throughout his term, Fuller Warren had made life miserable for racketeers. He had suspended six sheriffs and a dozen other law-enforcement officers for failing to enforce gambling laws. He had also backed a tough antibookmaking law. None of that mattered to Kefauver and his gang. The governor finished his first term a scorned man.

He ran for the post again in 1956, but the voters just shook their heads. People loved him as a man, but they no longer wanted him as governor. Later, he would joke that the voters had given him "a mandate to remain in private life."

Don Petit probably was Fuller's closest friend in private life. They were strange bedfellows. During the Kefauver brouhaha, Don had written some damned critical stories about Fuller. But the governor never held it against him, because he knew Don was doing a fair, honest job. If there's anything a good politician appreciates, it's a decent, professional reporter, even one who writes unflattering things.

Don had introduced me to Fuller when I was still in law school. He had been trying to impress me, and it worked. Fuller had high cheekbones, an impish smile, and a big personality, and I liked him immediately. Shortly after I met him, I invited him to have Thanksgiving dinner with Alex, the kids, and me. I was really just being polite: Surely such an important man would have other plans. I almost fainted when he accepted. Things didn't go too well—the toilet backed up and nobody could use the bathroom all night—but Fuller still put me at ease.

Now, in 1957, Fuller was preparing to open his own law firm in downtown Miami, and I was going to be his partner. Don had arranged everything. Fuller would get 60 percent of the profits and I would get the rest. Fuller wasn't thrilled with the deal—as a beginning lawyer, I had little to contribute to the partnership—but he went along with it because he trusted Don with his life.

We opened an office on the sixth floor of the Ainsley Building, which was a landmark in downtown Miami in the days before skyscrapers. Neither of us had any money, so we went to a lumber store and bought wood to build our own bookcases. We rented our desks. Then we bought an American flag and a Florida flag and put them behind Fuller's desk, just because we thought they should be there.

We handled appeals, mostly. We took cases that clients had lost at the trial level and argued them before the Florida Supreme Court, which was the only appellate court the state had then. Fuller's job was to bring in the cases and do the courtroom work. Mine was to ensure that everything he needed was at his fingertips when we entered the courtroom. I never knew when we would have to fly off to argue a case, so I always kept a fresh skirt, blouse, and pair of underwear in the office, just in case. Fuller would not have cared to wait while I hurried home for a bra.

I argued my first case before Florida's Supreme Court. The client was neither a convicted criminal nor an aggrieved citizen.

It was me.

It all began about the time I went to work with Fuller. Shortly after we opened the law office, I got another opportunity to take the bar exam. To prepare, I left the kids with Alex each night and went to my parents' house to study. I worked as if my life depended on it, because it seemed to me that it did. When I sat down to take the test, I was utterly confident that I would pass.

I was wrong. When the results came back a couple of months later, I found I had failed. Again. I couldn't believe it. I was sure someone had made a mistake. Before long, I would learn I was wrong about that too.

Someone had not made a mistake.

Someone had screwed me.

Fuller and I were in the Tampa airport, waiting for a flight home after arguing a case in court, when we got our first clue about what had happened. As we walked through the airport, we bumped into a man who had been in my high school class. The man—a nice guy—now worked for the state. When he saw us, he came over and clapped me on the back.

"Hey, congratulations on passing the bar," he said. "You made it."

"The hell I did," I said. "I got word that I failed."

He looked shocked. "You couldn't have failed," he said. "I saw the list and it said you passed."

"Well, that's not what I heard," I said.

"Gee, I'm sorry," the fellow said. "I must have been mistaken." Then he walked away.

Something was fishy. What did he mean he had seen the list? Fuller and I didn't know what was going on, but we aimed to find out. To do so, we needed to get our hands on the list of people who had passed the exam. It wasn't going to be easy. To protect the privacy of those who took the test, all scores were kept out of the public view. It was going to take a magician or a thief to get them.

Fuller got them. I still don't know how he did it, but he did it.

We were shocked at what we found. There were several lists. The first one said that I had narrowly missed passing the exam. My score was just below the passing grade. The second list showed that the bar examiners had lowered the passing grade to let more lawyers into the bar. They often did that if they decided, in hindsight, that they had made the passing grade too high. With the change, my grade should have been good enough.

But my grade wasn't my grade anymore. Someone had lowered it to ensure that I wouldn't pass.

We didn't know who was responsible, but we had a pretty good idea. Governor Fuller Warren had made many friends in his days in politics, but he had made some enemies too. The animosity those people felt toward him lingered long after he left office. Fuller couldn't prove it, but he believed that those enemies were trying to spite him by hurting me. If I didn't pass the bar, I would not be able to help Fuller, and Fuller's practice would suffer.

Fuller understood that politics could be dirty, but this, we knew, was beyond dirty. Fuller's enemies didn't even know me, but they were jeopardizing my livelihood to carry out an old political vendetta. It was downright unfair, and we were hell-bent on doing something about it. So, calmly and rationally, in the most adult manner possible, we did what any two mature lawyers would have done.

We sued.

We dreamed up a damned good lawsuit, if I do say so myself. For some reason, the bar examiners had flunked an unusually large number of people. Would-be lawyers everywhere were cursing their luck. So we rounded up a few of them and asked them to join us in suing the bar examiners. They loved the idea. We argued that, by failing us, the examiners had placed themselves above the deans of the various law schools. The deans had believed in us enough to give us diplomas. How could the bar examiners presume to say they were wrong?

Fuller, working completely in the background, got Paul Raymond, the former dean of Stetson Law School, to represent us. He wrote the pleadings and argued the case. When we brought the case in front of the state Supreme Court, Raymond let me make part of the argument. Later, a lot of people joked about how I had started my career at the top and then worked my way down. Apparently the justices liked me: When I finished, one of them said, "It would be a shame to deprive this young lady of the right to practice law."

"She's already practicing law," another justice said. "She's just signing the name of Fuller Warren." Which was very perceptive of him.

Now we could only sit and wait for a decision. After a couple of weeks, we learned through Fuller's political sources that the justices were close to deciding in our favor. One justice, it seemed, was holding things up. Fuller had appointed this particular justice several years earlier, but now the holdout was aligned with Fuller's political enemies. I couldn't imagine how we would prevail with this guy standing in the way.

Fuller's imagination was more vivid. With the case still pending, he wrote to Tallahassee and announced his intention to run for a Supreme Court seat—the holdout's seat. I considered it a stroke of genius. The people didn't want Fuller in the governor's mansion, but they would have elected him to the Supreme Court in a skinny minute. The holdout justice was looking down the barrel of a very big gun. Too bad for him. Politics is a bloody business, and anybody who doesn't understand that shouldn't be in office.

The justice understood it. He changed his vote.

In the end, the justices threw out the results of the exam and allowed us all to take it again. I passed easily.

When I met him, Fuller Warren was a lonely man. He never belonged to any woman as much as he did to politics, and to his work. He had been married three times, most recently to a young Hollywood movie actress named Barbara Manning. Walter Pidgeon, Hedy Lamarr, and the whole Hollywood press corps had attended the wedding. But then, just as the others had, she dumped him. Now, in the late fifties, he was alone.

Which, I suppose, is why he couldn't help noticing me. We started by flirting and playing footsie, but it didn't end there. It never does. One day he made it clear that he wanted to be more than law partners. I certainly was available. My marriage was the same old thing, and Don was often out of town doing one thing or another. And I happened to find Fuller attractive, both for his looks and for his intellect, which was great. He was an enchanting man, a true romantic. So, very discreetly, we began to date.

He was wonderful. He wrote me beautiful love letters and left them on my desk at work. You could read a whole volume of poetry and never find anything so lovely as his letters to me. In later years, I took them all and burned them for fear that Alex would find them. I still regret it. Fuller wrote in a stylish, flourishing script, using a thick ink pen. My heart used to leap when I saw his handwriting.

Fuller proposed marriage a few times. He said he wanted me to divorce Alex and move into his house in Miami Beach, kids and all. I always said no. I was raised to believe that I should stay with my husband no matter how miserable I was, and that's what I intended to do. Besides, I wasn't head-over-heels in love with Fuller. I liked him very much, and admired him even more. But did I want to spend my life with him? Not really. He was a delightful man, and, incidentally, a great lover, but somehow he didn't capture my heart.

I had a way of stopping the marriage talk in a hurry. Every time the subject of marriage arose, I brought the boys to his house for an afternoon. He didn't have children of his own, so he didn't know what it was like to be with them all the time. Dale and Dean showed him. They would run around the place like little demons, knocking books off the shelves and breaking vases, and by the time evening came he wouldn't be so interested in fatherhood anymore. Weeks would pass before he would propose again.

In the end, the problem took care of itself: Don found one of the love letters Fuller had written me. Fuller and I were on-air guests at a radio station that day. While we were there, Don popped into the law office to see us. He didn't find us, but he found the letter, which left no doubt about what Fuller and I were doing. After he had read it, Don called the station and had me summoned out of the studio. Then he read me the letter and demanded an explanation.

"I don't know anything about that," I said. Oh, I was a poor liar.

"The hell you don't," he said. "I know exactly what's going on, and I want you to put a stop to it."

Which I did. Fuller and I remained law partners, but he never again examined my briefs.

SIX

THE DOCTOR WAS
THE BETTER LAWYER

A week into my first political campaign, I approached a man and handed him one of my brochures.

"Hello," I said. "I'm Ellen Morphonios and I'd appreciate your vote."

"Hello," he said back. "I'm Tom Duff, and I'm one of the people running against you."

"Oh," I said. "I don't guess I'll get your vote, then."

Don Petit was my Svengali. He created me as a politician.

Don, a bit of a dreamer, formulated the master plan for my career: I was to run for a series of political offices, win them, and then become the first woman Supreme Court justice in the state. Just like that. He fully believed that I could learn to do just about anything.

I wasn't so sure, but I was willing to try. In the first few years after high school, I was content to go wherever events took me, a grain of sand drifting with the currents. I suppose I was too young or unsure of myself to make any firm plans. But going to law school made me more conscious of my power to direct my future, to achieve goals, family or no family. Now, at thirty years old, I was ready to see what I could accomplish.

To become a judge was my secret ambition. Years earlier, during law school, Don had taken me to Tallahassee to visit with Supreme Court Justice B. K. Roberts, whom he had known for years. It was a Sunday, and Justice Roberts was showing us around the building.

We were in the courtroom when, all of a sudden, Justice Roberts pulled a black robe off a coat hanger and hung it around my shoulders. Then he went down to the dais and argued a case before me. I had goose bumps on my goose bumps.

When I left that day I knew I wanted to be a judge. And Don knew he wanted me on the Supreme Court.

Now it was 1960, and Don and I had decided it was time for me to seek office. We went over the list of possibilities and decided that I would run for judge of the juvenile court. Judge Walter H. Beckham was retiring after twenty-seven years on the bench, leaving his seat open. It's difficult, if not impossible, to defeat a sitting judge, so his seat was the natural one to go after.

My candidacy was in trouble from the start. First, I was a woman, and few women had ever been elected to the juvenile court bench. Second, I was only thirty years old. Third, I didn't know anything about the juvenile courts. Fourth, I had been out of law school for only eighteen months. I was only slightly better qualified than the neighborhood grocer.

Those things didn't faze me. What bothered me was that Fuller Warren was dead set against my running for office.

Fuller had been hurt badly in politics. Estes Kefauver had not only destroyed his political career but also dirtied his reputation. Fuller knew how nasty politics could be, and he feared that I would get hurt. Once, when I was away from work, he wrote a list of reasons why I shouldn't seek office and left it on my desk. I found it when I got in.

I appreciated his advice, but I didn't take it. I felt I had to learn about politics for myself. One day when Fuller was out of town, I went to the county clerk's office and formally entered the campaign. When Fuller got back to Miami, there was nothing left to discuss.

Nothing concerns people as much as crime. It has always been that way. If you check the newspapers from any year, you'll always find stories about inflation, poverty, and war, but never as many as you'll find about murder, robbery, and burglary. Crime affects not only its victims but also the victims' neighbors and friends and acquaintances. It pervades the consciousness of a community, inspiring anger and outrage and, most of all, a sense that the world is going to hell.

We certainly thought we had a crime problem in Miami in

1960, particularly a juvenile crime problem. Kids got drunk, stole cars, shoplifted, and broke into houses. Those crimes are minor compared to today's atrocities—drive-by shootings, drug wars, gang rapes committed by children—but people took them very seriously at the time.

My campaign platform that year was the same as it would be if I were running for juvenile court judge today: I believed that the criminal justice system was too lenient. By 1960, many so-called experts were beginning to theorize that it didn't matter what a kid did. The important thing, they said, was why he did it. Did he have a hard childhood? Did his parents neglect him? Did he grow up poor? Instead of punishing kids who broke the law, the system was beginning to pity them.

I disagreed strongly with that, and still do. I don't give a damn why Johnny stole the car. He stole it, and that's what matters. Interviewing him about his poor upbringing isn't going to do him any good. Kids accused of crimes should go to the lockup, at least briefly, and then have a trial, the same as adults do. And if convicted, they should be punished. I'm not saying we should send twelve-year-old car thieves to Alcatraz. But I don't think we should congratulate them, either.

Before the campaign began, I learned everything I could about the juvenile justice system. A cop who lived next door to me took me to every police station in the county so I could learn about the way law enforcement dealt with juvenile offenders. I also spent a lot of time watching the other juvenile court judges.

I found a lot wrong with the system, but I quickly came up with solutions. The cops in one city didn't have access to the criminal records of the kids in the next city over, so I suggested creating a central records system to track juvenile offenders. I found that many kids got in trouble because they didn't have anything to do, so I suggested creating a youth employment bureau and a better youth recreation program. I also suggested creating a child guidance clinic to treat kids with behavior disorders.

I was determined, above all, to conduct court in a friendly but dignified manner. Many kids' first contact with the American judicial system is with the juvenile court. I wanted them to feel that the system was fair, but also just.

Early in the campaign, Don printed a brochure detailing my

views. He wrote it in the form of a news story, and gave it the headline THE MORPHONIOS STORY. Anyone interested in the campaign found out in the first few paragraphs exactly where I stood.

"It's high time that we started letting youthful offenders know that they are not going to be coddled in our juvenile courts any longer," I said in the brochure.

"I have as much interest in the sociological and psychological needs of the problem child as any person in Dade County, but I believe a juvenile court judge has a responsibility to the property owner and the citizen as well as the offender.

"These difficult youngsters must be made to realize that they are going to be held to account for their actions. Unless we start to develop a respect for the court by the youthful offender, we are in for trouble.

"We are not decreasing juvenile delinquency with the old textbook ideas. Juvenile offenders know that an artificial shield has been placed around them in the guise of 'welfare.'

"Let's stop making excuses and face up to the fact that the increase in delinquency here is caused largely by the protective shield adults have built up for the young offender.

"This is reflected in the mistaken belief that these youngsters should be pampered and not made to realize that they are young adults."

I announced my candidacy in late January 1960. The headline in the *Miami Herald* said, MOM OF TWO IN RACE FOR JUDGESHIP.

When I entered the race, I had three opponents—Dixie Chastain, the investigating lawyer for the juvenile courts, and private lawyers Tom Duff and Victor Levine. All three were much older and more experienced, and any of them would have made a fine judge. But I firmly believed that, with hard work and a little luck, I could be elected.

When Dr. Ben Sheppard filed his campaign papers, I no longer thought so.

Ben Sheppard was a meek, bespectacled, slightly overweight pediatrician whose only wish in life was to help people. Everyone loved him, including me. When he entered the race, I knew I couldn't wage a negative campaign against him. What could I say? That he was unqualified? No. He was superbly qualified. Could I say I cared more for children than he did? No. He cared as much as anyone in Miami. Some people told me they weren't going to vote for him because they were afraid he would leave the bench every time a child got sick. That was as close as anybody came to criticizing him.

Some people might have quit when Ben Sheppard announced his candidacy, but I never considered it. I'm not a quitter. Once I've bitten into an apple, I eat it, core and all. I had promised myself that I would do my best in that campaign, and that was what I intended to do.

I had made the same promise to my supporters. When I worked on other campaigns, I learned that a lot of people depend on political candidates—family members, friends, contributors, and many others. Candidates can't disappoint all those people just because they think they might lose. Or, as in my case, because they know damned well they're going to lose. My job was not to win at all costs, but to campaign well and follow the wishes of the people—even if the people wished me to go away.

Early in the campaign, Don drove me to the building in downtown Miami where the county kept the rolls of registered voters. That year, as it did from time to time, the county was purging the rolls to eliminate the names of people who had died or moved away. Everyone who wanted to vote in local, state, and national elections would have to reregister.

"There's only one place in the county where you'll get registered voters and only registered voters, and that's here," Don said, pointing to the front entrance of the building. "The people line up to register here every day. I want you to come here every morning and work that line."

Which I did. Each morning that March and April, I dressed in a business suit, grabbed a handful of palm cards, and headed downtown. I usually got there by eight A.M. and stayed until the office closed at four P.M. "Hello," I said to everyone I met. "My name is Ellen Morphonios. I'm running for judge and I'd appreciate your vote." I said it so many times that it used to ring in my ears at the end of the day.

I met some mighty nice people in that line. People were always pleasant, even the ones who told me they weren't going to vote for me. Some old-timers still approach me today and say, "I met you in the voter-registration line a couple of years back." I don't have the heart to tell them it was thirty years ago.

As nice as the people were, it was tiring to stand out there. Sometimes I got downright sick of it. Once, after working hard all morning, I decided to spend the rest of the day in the office with Fuller.

The phone was ringing when I walked in the door. It was Don. He was working as a public-relations man for the county manager at the time, and his office overlooked the voter-registration line. He had glanced out the window and noticed that I wasn't there.

"What the hell are you doing in the office?" he hollered. "You've got Fuller Warren's vote. Get your ass back out there. Now!" Back out I went.

I seldom took the kids with me when I worked the voter-registration line; they were still very small and couldn't stay in one place for long stretches. But they often tagged along when I worked the streets downtown. They both wore signs saying VOTE FOR MY MOM, which, if it wasn't the most effective campaign tactic, was certainly the cutest. Dale was old enough to make sense when he said things, so he was a good little campaigner. Most of what Dean said was just babble, but who cared? Most political speeches are.

They were good kids. Sometimes they got silly and rowdy, but I had a way of calming them down. All I had to say was, "It's important," and they would immediately straighten up. Once, I went to a meeting in Hialeah and the kids were behaving like little madmen, making noise and disrupting everyone. Finally, I grabbed Dale by the arm and said, "Why on earth are you acting like that?" And he said, "Mom, you didn't say it was important." And he was right. I hadn't.

Alex worked every bit as hard as the boys. He passed out palm cards, shook hands, mailed brochures, and helped to spread my name. He couldn't have avoided it if he had wanted to. We spent all our time with the Petits, which meant that even when we were socializing, we were working. Most of our conversations were about the campaign, and virtually everything we did together had something to do with it.

My running for office seemed to please Alex, seemed to make him feel special in a way that nothing else did. Campaigning gave him a chance to make speeches to civic groups and meet the people in Miami, his native city. It also allowed him to spread the Morphonios name, which I knew made him happy. I wasn't always glad he was around—we didn't always get along famously—but most of the time I was glad he was on my side.

I used Alex and the kids in every way I could. Their pictures were all over my campaign brochures. One snapshot showed Dale with Cowboy Gil Faver, the TV star. Another showed him campaigning with me downtown; he was wearing a cowboy outfit and a VOTE FOR MY MOM button. Still another photograph depicted the kids, the dog, and the cat with me and Alex. Was I trying to appeal to people's emotions? Absolutely.

The best campaign picture was the one with me, a couple of local politicians—and former president Harry S Truman. Don had used his connections to the local bigwigs to get me introduced to the president. It was a great day, believe me. Harry Truman was, in my opinion, the greatest political figure in modern times, followed closely by Barry Goldwater and Ronald Reagan. Truman had brains and guts, and I admire those qualities.

I was terrified to meet him. All Don wanted me to do was get close to Truman so that he could snap a picture, but I was afraid. So I just hung back. Don's friend Chuck Hall, a popular local politician, had to take me by the arm and pull me close to Truman so Don could take the picture. What we saw when we got the picture developed was a nervous woman being dragged toward the former president. It wouldn't have made a very impressive picture for the brochure. The caption might have said, "Candidate Ellen Morphonios makes ass of self with Truman."

The picture we ended up using wasn't much better. It showed me standing ten feet away from Truman, looking glumly at my shoes as if he had just told me to go stand in the corner.

Did all these famous people actually come out and pledge me their support? Of course not. That's why, on the bottom of the campaign brochures, we printed these words: "The candidate does not imply that dignitaries on this page necessarily endorse her candidacy." It was the only honest thing to do, even if we did use very, very small print.

Most of the campaign was not so glamorous. It was just hard work. I must have traveled the length of Dade County—seventy-five miles, and we didn't have expressways then—one hundred times in two or three months. I would give a speech in the south end at seven

P.M., then zip up to the north end and give another one a couple of hours later. I hated the travel, but I liked to give the impression that I was everywhere.

Once, on a terribly rainy day, I went to a rally where all the candidates were supposed to speak. When I got there, I found Ben Sheppard standing alone in the driving rain, waiting to say his piece. I couldn't believe it. I strongly believed he was going to win the election, so I went to him and said, "What are you doing here? You don't need to be here. Go home before you catch a cold." He mumbled his thanks—he was a mumbler—and left. Hell, I would have made his speech for him if he had wanted me to.

I didn't have such great experiences with other candidates. One night a friend took me to a meeting where I was supposed to debate Dixie Chastain. I didn't know what group I would be speaking to, but I found out quickly that it was a group of Dixie Chastain backers. Someone would ask her, "What do you think of the county's youth recreation programs?" She'd answer, and then someone would ask me, "Don't you think the leading cause of juvenile delinquency is working mothers like you who leave their kids at home?" I was fuming, but I had to stand and take it.

It wouldn't be the last time I would walk into dangerous territory without knowing it. A few years earlier, when he was working for the *Miami News,* Don had written a story about Communists in Dade County. It was the early fifties, and people were interested in that sort of thing. Don joined the group, pretended to be a Communist, and eventually worked his way up in the hierarchy. Then, on the night of the big meeting, the *News* photographers burst into the room with cameras flashing. It was a sensational story, but it didn't make Don too popular with the Communists.

One night during the campaign I was giving a speech somewhere, going through the usual routine, when I noticed that Don looked a little edgy. He kept shuffling back and forth during my speech, holding his hand over his face as if to hide himself. When at last I finished and we walked out, Don said, "That was a goddamned cell meeting." Communist groups are called cells. He had recognized some of the people and, not normally a religious man, was praying they wouldn't recognize him.

I woke up early on the day of the election, May 3, 1960. At six that morning, I went to the workers' gate at Miami International

Airport for one last bit of stumping. Hundreds of guys worked there, most of them registered voters, and I wanted to catch the ones coming off work and the ones coming on. I had been there many times during the campaign, but that morning I particularly enjoyed it. People seemed especially friendly and encouraging, as if they thought they might be looking at a winner, the next juvenile court judge. Of course, a baseball coach acts the same way toward the scrawniest kid on the team just before he sends him in to strike out.

I cast my ballot that afternoon, so I was assured of at least one vote. (I stifled the impulse to vote for Ben Sheppard.) That evening, twenty friends and relatives joined me in Fuller's office to wait for the returns. Don and Alex went down the street to the courthouse to watch the counting of the ballots. It was a hard night. I never expected to win, but, as Don had told me, the impossible could happen. I tried to look cool and detached, but I was secretly wishing it would.

It didn't.

A couple of hours after the polls closed, it was clear that Ben Sheppard and Dixie Chastain were headed for a runoff, and that Tom Duff, Victor Levine, and I were also-rans. For the record, I finished fourth. I was disappointed, sure, but somehow I knew the world would keep turning without Ellen Morphonios on the juvenile court bench.

I'm sure Dixie Chastain expected me to endorse her—for whatever that was worth—in the runoff election. She was a woman, and I had said in my campaign brochures that a woman should be elected because more than half the cases in the juvenile courts involved dependent children, not juvenile delinquents. But the fact was that I hadn't been hell-bent on getting a woman elected. I had only said it because it sounded good in the brochure. I liked Dixie very much—in later years, she got elected to the juvenile bench and became one of the giants in the field—but I couldn't support her.

On May 4, the day after the debacle, I returned to the airport at sunrise—wearing a Ben Sheppard sign. He won the seat in a landslide.

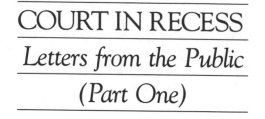

COURT IN RECESS
Letters from the Public
(Part One)

EVERY SIX YEARS, the voters of Dade County tell me what they think of my work. They go to the polls and vote to let me stay in office or to replace me with somebody they like better. So far, they have stuck with me. But I have learned that running for office is a sure way to find out what people think of you.

Between elections, it's sometimes hard for me to know what people think of my work. Save for the few who end up on juries in my courtroom, most people never see me on the bench, never get a chance to see whether justice is being done in my courtroom. Unless the newspapers or TV stations happen to pick up on one of my rulings, I generally work in semiprivate, far from the public eye.

But there have always been some people who, whether or not they have seen me in court, feel the urge to let me know what they think of me. They do this by writing letters. Sometimes they write nasty notes and sometimes they write nice ones. Either way, I appreciate that they take the time. And I always take the time to dictate a gracious letter back—even if I'd really like to send a nasty one.

Over the years, hundreds of letters have accumulated in my files. Here, in no special order (for that's the way I keep them in my files), is a sampling of what I consider the best of them.

Miami Police Officer Rolland J. Lane II was a fine young man and an excellent public servant. For no fame and little money he put on a gun and a badge each day and worked to keep Miami safe. One day, a low-life criminal named Willie Garrett thanked him for all his fine work by shooting him dead.

Garrett was waiting in the doorway of a downtown Miami hotel when the young officer walked by. It was three-thirty A.M. He shot him twice in the back. Then he walked out the doorway and shot him again. Lane wore badge number 131, the same number his father, Rolland Senior, had worn in his days as a New York State motorcycle patrolman.

Two Orlando police officers overpowered and arrested Garrett aboard an Eastern Airlines jet five hours after the shooting. For several years, Garrett bounced between mental hospitals and the county jail, unable to stand trial because he was incompetent. He appeared in my courtroom several times in that period for hearings on his competency. Shortly before one of those hearings, I received this letter.

Your Honor:

In the next few weeks you will be faced with a decision that you are not going to be envied for as I am sure not many people wish to be in your position at this time.

I'm certain I can assume you are aware of the fact that I am speaking about one Willie Allen Marcellus Garrett, for you see Officer Rolland J. Lane II was my daughter's fiance, and he also was like our very own son.

It wasn't easy for us to receive a telephone call from a police sergeant at 6 A.M. asking if we were Rolland's fiance's parents—only to be told that he had been gunned down. Nor was it easy to go to our daughter's room watching her peacefully sleeping with rollers in her hair possibly dreaming about her Senior Prom that night with her sweetheart. Plans had been in order for months. It was a very sad event for us to have to go to the Lane home where we could all be together searching for some sort of comfort from each other. It isn't easy to go to visit a square piece of earth covered by a marker inscribed Officer Rolland J. Lane II, Beloved Son and Brother. Where you sit for a few minutes and meditate about the might have beens and what ifs. He was more than just a run-of-the-mill kid. He was a good Christian, an excellent son, a super policeman and a real sweetheart. Everyone who knew him loved him. Our daughter was robbed of her wedding plans and who knows what else. We will never know. We do know, however, that Willie Garrett may possibly be set free unless you rule otherwise.

Is the time a criminal serves for murder only five years now? He has been fed, clothed, sheltered and medicated for five years. We along with his family and friends have struggled through the bad days trying to forget, but the pain never goes away. The scar remains tender and each time you touch it it hurts. You must know from your own experience that there is no medication perfected for a heartache. Yes, Your Honor, you are faced with the very tough decision and if you decide to let this creep go then I hope you can serve your conscience when you must face your own two sons.

He doesn't deserve the fresh air he is breathing. If you don't find him competent to stand trial for the cold-blooded brutal murder of Officer Rolland Lane then please in the name of justice will you find him mentally deranged to the point where he must be returned and confined to the South Florida State Hospital until such time as you feel he can competently stand trial for the crime he has committed. I beg of you—don't let us believe Rolland died in vain.

He protected you and I while we were sleeping. Let's you and I now let him at long last sleep in peace knowing his killer won't be turned loose to do this horrible thing again.

He must be kept out of society.

Respectfully yours,
Betty Ann Barnes

That is the sort of letter that reminds me that, as a judge, I am not just a civil servant but the conscience of the community. Every decision I make affects not just the life of the defendant but the lives of his victims and their families and friends. It is an immense responsibility, as Mrs. Barnes so eloquently reminded me.

As it happened, a couple of years passed before the case finally was resolved. Seven years after the killing, I adjudged Garrett competent to stand trial—as long as he took his medication. Instead of going to trial, he pleaded no contest. I sentenced Garrett to life in prison plus ten years.

After the sentencing, I received a second letter, this time from Rolland J. Lane II's heartbroken fiancée.

Dear Judge Morphonios:

I would like to take a few minutes of your busy day to thank you for a job well done.

I was the fiance of Miami Police Officer Rolland J. Lane II, who was brutally murdered on May 23, 1970. I must say I am relieved and very pleased that Willie Garrett has been sentenced to life plus 10 years.

I was kind of wary of our judicial system in this day and time but my faith has been restored. So many people who are guilty of a crime are set free because sometimes the system seems to be leaning their way. I know the system is not perfect but it is all we have, so we have to make do. A tricky lawyer gets hold of a certain case and then literally the person gets away with murder.

I feel that in this particular case justice has been served.

I knew that Willie Garrett would not have been electrocuted for Rolland's murder as our society just won't let it happen. Even if he was sentenced to die it would not bring Rolland back to us and I feel that the sentence that Garrett received was in good judgement. At least with life plus 10 years he will hopefully never walk a free man again. He will not be able to make someone else go through the pain and sorrow I had to.

Maybe now a lot of the hurt will go away knowing that the man who took Rolland's life is not free and able to sit back and laugh at us all.

Every time a police officer is killed I go through the same nightmare. Maybe now with Garrett away in prison I can pick up my life again and go on with all or at least most of it behind me. I will never forget, but now at least Garrett is paying for the wrong he has done.

I thank you from the bottom of my heart for the wise choice you made in this case.

Very sincerely yours,
Loma N. Barnes

I wish that had been the end of the Willie Garrett story, but it wasn't. After I imposed the sentence and Garrett was sent off to prison, the Third District Court of Appeal in Miami threw out the conviction and the sentence. The court ruled that the long delay between the killing and the sentence constituted a violation of Garrett's right to a speedy trial. I couldn't believe it, and neither could the prosecutors.

The state appealed the case to the Florida Supreme Court, which wouldn't grant a hearing, and then to the U.S. Supreme Court. The high court also would not hear the case. But two justices, Chief Justice Warren Burger and Associate Justice William Rehnquist, issued a blistering memo criticizing the appeals court in Miami for its decision.

"Only the most careless reading" of the Supreme Court's earlier decisions in such cases could have resulted in such a misguided ruling, Rehnquist wrote.

It was nice of those justices to take my side, but it didn't do me—or the family of Rolland Lane—much good. I don't know what became of Willie Garrett. For all I know, he could be in my neighborhood now, or in yours, with the blood of a police officer still on his hands. I only know that he was never brought to justice for his terrible crime.

In 1978, the Associated Press wrote an article about my efforts to speed up justice. Because of the tremendous backlog of cases in my court, I had decided to bring all cases to trial within 60 days of arrest—120 days faster than the law required me to try them. A lot of defense lawyers didn't like it. They complained that my new rule kept them from preparing a complete defense. The article quoted them to that effect. I didn't agree. I thought, and still think, that a good lawyer can be ready for most trials in a matter of a couple of weeks if he puts his mind to it. The article also quoted my point of view. That article prompted this letter from a lawyer in San Francisco.

Dear Judge Morphonios:

Let me commend your attitude and tempo. In earlier days, it was the view that defendants should be tried, speedily, in their own interest. As you were quoted to have said, "Defense attorneys seek delays with hope the witnesses will move, die or forget details as time ticks away." What a transposition of tactics from earlier days when it was thought just and proper to give the defendant a speedy trial, so that in the event of innocence, no cloud would unduly hang over his or her head.

Hope your pattern of procedure will be emulated and followed in the name of justice.

Respectfully,
S.

One of the defendants I tried in a hurry was Manuel Valle, who shot and killed a police officer in Coral Gables. I got a lot of criticism for the speed with which I began the trial (I'll go into that in another chapter). But the juror who wrote this letter didn't seem concerned about that. Rather, he was in awe of the system. He especially admired defense lawyer David Goodhart, who asked him not to recommend the death sentence for Valle, and prosecutor Hank Adorno, whose plea for the death penalty he ultimately heeded.

Dear Judge Morphonios:

I am so proud of you! I am proud of our judicial system, its dignity and fairness.

I served as a juror on the Valle trial this week. I've always wanted to serve on the jury, but was never called and I've always been curious about the procedure. I was impressed on how the jury was selected. I learned—and how. I never expected to be caught up in something so traumatic as a murder trial. Having worked in hospitals for many years, I was always concerned in saving life. Being religious, I felt that saving life was the most noble and important thing a human being could do—and here I was, torn to pieces by my strong feelings and my duty as a juror and as an American.

When Mr. Goodhart reminded me "Thou shalt not kill," that devastated me completely, but I felt, doesn't that apply to Valle? But I searched my heart and mind and felt I must do what is right—as much as it pained me.

I am so proud of men like Mr. Goodhart and Mr. Adorno—they were so intelligent, sincere, honest and eloquent. I'm glad I live in Miami. God bless you all.

Sincerely yours,
L.

Not everyone feels so rapturous about me and what I do. In 1972, *Time* magazine included me in an article about radio talk-show hosts around the country. The magazine photographed me sitting by a microphone. On the table next to me was my family's pet monkey, Toto. Not long after the article appeared, I received this letter from a man in a federal prison in Springfield, Missouri.

Dearest & Most Beautiful (racial & spiritual) Sister & Sweetheart Ellen:

I pray above all things that you and our beautiful white race may prosper and be in health. God is with us.

Have just seen the photo of you and a monkey (the monkey is symbolic of a nigger male, and your pose seems to reveal that you may practice fellatio on the aforesaid monkey) in the May 22, 1972 Time magazine. I read the accompanying article, in which you are called an "arch-conservative," which is a joke on you, me and every member of our beautiful white race! I feel that I (an Anglo-Saxon man who could satiate your every desire and make you much happier than a world full of monkeys or the entire nigger "monkey" race) could make you the most happy lady that lives if you could but visit me in this federal prison . . .

E.

E. went on that way for quite some time. He obviously had put a lot of thought and effort into his letter, but still I did not accept the invitation to visit him in prison. Instead, I sent a copy of the letter to the United States Secret Service. I thought the employees of that fine agency might be interested in E.'s prose style. They must have stopped by his cell for a chat, because I soon received a second letter from E.

Dearest & Most Beautiful (racial & spiritual) Sister & Sweetheart Ellen:

I pray above all things that you and our beautiful white race may prosper and be in health. God is with us.

Must have come on too strong about your practicing bestiality with your pet monkey . . . Please forgive me if you believe that I went too far, as I probably did. At any rate, your mouth is just the right size to receive the head of my hard penis, if you would have all your teeth extracted. Please don't take offense at what I say as I am very religious and would never let you do fellatio on me. So cheer up!

E.

I get lots of letters from defendants who have appeared in my court. For years, I regularly received letters from a prison inmate who wanted me to get his old job back for him, buy him a Cadillac, and find him a girl to "suck [his] dick"—in that order. He was a nice guy, but he didn't have the greatest manners.

One of my favorite letters came from a guy who had filed a motion for a reduction of his sentence. I don't remember what his crime was, but I know that I denied his motion and told him he would have to serve whatever time I had given him. He was upset with me. After I denied the motion, I got this letter from him.

Dear Judge Morphonios:

Denied. Denied. Denied. Denied. Denied. Denied. Denied. Denied. Denied. Denied. Denied. Denied. De-

nied. Denied. Denied. Denied. Denied. Denied. Denied.
Denied. Denied. Denied. Denied. Denied. Denied. De-
nied. Denied. Denied. Denied. Denied. Denied. Denied.
Denied. Denied. Denied. Denied. Denied. Denied. De-
nied. Denied. Denied. Denied. Denied. Denied. Denied.
Denied. Denied. Denied. Denied. Denied. Denied. De-
nied. Denied. Denied. Denied. Denied. Denied. Denied.
Denied. Denied. Denied. Denied. Denied. Denied. De-
nied. Denied. Denied. Denied. Denied. Denied. Denied.
Denied. Denied. Denied. Denied. Denied. Denied. De-
nied. Denied. Denied. Denied. Denied. Denied.
Have you ever heard of the word GRANTED?

R.

At least he wasn't profane.

You'd be surprised at how many former criminals write me letters to thank me for sentencing them to prison and helping them
straighten out their lives. I'll admit that the guys who do this are not
ruthless killers. Usually, they're average folk who get mixed up with
the wrong crowd or the wrong chemical and wind up making a big
mistake. Joe Smith (I have changed the fellow's name here because I
don't want to embarrass him), whom I sentenced to prison in my first
year on the bench, was that kind of guy. His lawyer sent me this
letter in 1975.

Dear Judge Morphonios:

In July 1971, Joseph Smith was arrested and charged
with breaking and entering a dwelling. All of his problems
came from his involvement with drugs and the unfortunate
subculture into which that drew him. I represented him at
that time and we pled him guilty as charged.

I worked at length with the probation officer, Terry
Olsen, and established a program for Joe's rehabilitation at
the Synanon Foundation in Santa Monica, California. You
might recall that I had a rather lengthy brochure which
contained everything from information on the foundation
to letters, etc. I do not believe our request [for a drug treatment program] was opposed by the probation department.

When we appeared before you for sentencing on January 20, 1972, you placed Joe on probation for three and a half years while withholding an adjudication of guilt. You allowed him to go to California to enter the Synanon Foundation.

I have recently been in contact with Joe's father. Joe has been back in the Miami area for a couple of months. During his stay at the Synanon Foundation, he prospered in every way and actually stayed there longer than he was compelled to. He then stayed in California for an additional period of time and worked with a construction firm renovating homes. He is now back in Miami and actively looking for a job. He apparently is a new person, according to his father, who was once most unhappy and depressed about his son's situation.

I know it was a difficult decision for you to make in 1972 to allow this boy to attend a program in California where supervision could possibly be so difficult. I did want to take the opportunity to share the good news about what appears to be the successful rebuilding of this young boy's life. I also want you to know that those of us who must appear before you, together with the families we represent, deeply appreciate the dedication and concern which you bring to your office.

Cordially,
C.

Among the letters I have received from prisoners themselves, I particularly liked this one for its sincerity and especially its brevity. I got it when I was still married to my second husband, John Rowe.

Dear Mrs. Rowe:

Thank you for giving me a chance and putting me on probation instead of sending me to jail again. Thank you very much.

J.

I liked the following letter not only for what it said but because it was written on a card with a picture of a furry white kitty on the front. I love kitties.

Dear Judge:

You have given me a chance for a new life. An adult life, which at 36 years old is something to be thankful for.

Your compassion and understanding will be rewarded by my efforts to finally become a human being and not a drug addict living in a different dimension.

I pray daily and you will be in my prayers for the rest of my life.

Thank you forever,
R.

Prison inmates make the strangest requests. I suppose they figure they don't have anything to lose. They're already in prison. What more can I do to them? Send them to hell?

One of my favorite letters came from an inmate in solitary confinement in the Florida prison system. The fellow started by saying that he was looking for a woman he had seen in court in 1975. She had sandy-red hair and "her physical body was beautiful and desirable." He said he wanted very much to meet her.

Ellen Morphonios:

. . . One day I was asking questions pertaining to you. The convict who was answering my questions said, "She sounds like Morphonios from the way the woman was described." Send me a picture of you so I can see whether or not you is this woman. I will send the picture back.

How about getting me a good book on prostitution and pimps? How old is you? I would like for you to be a lawyer owning your own firm. Have you ever thought about that? Start giving it some thought. If you be a lawyer, I might consider being your personal bodyguard. What do you think about a pimp?

E.

P.S. How about sending me $25?

H. didn't want money. He wanted a new trial. In 1977, he wrote and asked me to see if I could get him one. I will reprint the letter here exactly as he wrote it.

> Hello my lovely Lade and Most Beautiful one Mrs. Judge Ellenor Maphonies Row:
>
> You know sweetheart I allways like you and your fat leg self. Well baby I am up on cloud nine and i need some help you know my love.
>
> So you know sweeheart my mind said to drop you a line or two. And look here baby don't let me down because I wanted to come back to Miami town. And if you can get me down, well me and you might can drink a bottle of wine, and then grind.
>
> You know baby I always like you with the big blue eyes. And your yellow hair. You know baby, I am in prison from shooting at my girlfriend for attempted murder baby. And you know it was with a shotgun. And you know sweetheart I did not try to hurt her. And she wanted to drop the charge on me but I have not got back to court so far . . .
>
> Signed,
> H.

The people of Dade County have never let me forget that, though they may not ever come to my courtroom, they are watching me. When people feel that their homes and lives are threatened, they don't hesitate to take action, and I don't blame them. All we have are our homes and our lives, and we have a right to protect them.

In 1979, some residents of northeast Miami got sick of being victimized. So they got together and wrote this letter, copies of which were sent to every jurist in the county.

> Gentlemen:
>
> Within the last five days five homes in our neighborhood have been broken into. We are sick and tired of it to say nothing of the fact that we are scared.

Day after day, week after week, we read and hear that you judges—the last bastion of relief—have released and continue to release literally hundreds of proven criminal animals to perpetrate further crimes on the streets, in our homes, and against our person.

We do not believe that the American system of criminal jurisprudence ever was intended to work to the advantage of criminal scum who have no fear of the courts and look only with contempt upon the judge, and we suppose, one can hardly be surprised at this attitude when the record reflects such a constant abuse of judicial discretion that allows these criminal thugs to roam freely after scores of arrests secure in the knowledge that the odds are so great in their favor that jail becomes a big joke.

It is apparent to us, and we think probably to the rest of the community, that you are not doing your jobs and we see no evidence that you intend to change.

Hope springs eternal, however.

Very truly yours,
[32 residents of northeast Miami]

I didn't know what the other judges were doing with the letter, but I sat right down and wrote a letter back. In it, I suggested that all the authors pay a visit to my courtroom at their earliest convenience. So often, I said, people judge others without having all the facts. A day in my courtroom, I believed, would disabuse them of the notion that I was going easy on criminals.

A few days later, I received this reply from a couple who had signed the letter.

Dear Judge Morphonios:

We are pleased to learn that you are listening and that you cared enough to acknowledge receipt of the petitioned letter.

It is ironic that the one judge we feel is doing a worthwhile job would be the first one to respond. When we drafted the petition, we considered excluding your name, but in all good conscience we found no way to do so without arousing the ire of the other judges . . .

Very truly yours,
Mr. and Mrs. T.

SEVEN

BLONDE JAILS HOODLUMS

Losing the election wasn't enough to make me give up politics. How could I? Richard Nixon needed me.

I went to work for the "Nixon for President" campaign a week after my defeat. When I was asked to join, I gladly accepted. As a conservative, I wasn't overly enthusiastic about John F. Kennedy. He was handsome and charming and all that, but I didn't care for his politics. Nixon was no Harry Truman, but I thought he would make a much better president than Kennedy. Naturally, I didn't know at the time that he was dumb enough to bug his own office and then keep the tapes. But I still think he's great.

The Nixon headquarters were in downtown Miami, next to a shoe store. I went there whenever Fuller and I weren't too busy. The other volunteers and I wrote and mailed letters, made phone calls, handed out palm cards, and did whatever else we could think of to get support for the candidate. The kids came with me lots of times. Dale, who was a conservative even in kindergarten, was a great help. He used to stand on the corner, wearing a Nixon sign and handing out bumper stickers. He was six then, so of course everyone loved him.

Dean was, and still is, the family liberal. How he became one remains a mystery. Alex was a conservative, I was a conservative, both sets of grandparents were conservatives, most of our friends were conservatives, and still Alex and I brought forth a liberal. I discovered his leftist tendencies during the '60 campaign. He was four years old. When I wasn't looking, he would wander out to the sidewalk outside campaign headquarters and say, "Vote for Kennedy! Vote for Kennedy!" I would have to haul him back into the building before too many people took his advice.

Dean denies that he is responsible for Nixon's narrow defeat.

* * *

I enjoyed working with Fuller Warren. I learned a lot about politics, the law, public speaking, everything. And I made really good money, considering I had been a twenty-five-dollars-a-week secretary. But after my loss in the judicial race, I decided to leave Fuller. I wanted to go into public service.

I encountered a lot of people in 1960 who didn't give a damn about government, as long as their taxes didn't go up. I didn't have much to say to them. I met many more who really cared about the community, who wanted a clean, safe place to live. I liked those people. I also began to think that I wanted to work for them, to see if I could give them the kind of community they wanted. It might sound corny, but I thought that being a public servant would be a great and honorable way to make a living. At the very least, I knew it would be a good career move. Clearly, I wasn't going to become a Supreme Court justice by drafting wills in Fuller Warren's office.

So I applied for a job as a prosecutor in the Dade County State Attorney's office.

Why become a prosecutor? Because I thought I had all the personality traits a prosecutor needed. I liked to confront people. I could detect a lie instantly. And I thought I would take immense pleasure in giving criminals what they deserved. I could have applied for a job as a defense lawyer in the public defender's office, but I never seriously considered it. Generally speaking, defense lawyers work for people who have done something wrong. The defendants might not have done exactly what the state says they've done, but usually they've done something damned close to it. The lawyers justify their work by saying that they defend not just individuals but also the Constitution of the United States. I could appreciate that. I just didn't think I could do it. Years later, when I was briefly in private practice, I represented a guy on a criminal charge. I was talking to the judge when my client leaned over to tell me something. It distracted me, so I turned to my client and shouted, "Shut up!" Not a good way to build a clientele.

Even in 1960, I thought I was a born prosecutor. I was just hoping that Richard E. Gerstein thought so too.

Gerstein, one of the toughest prosecutors I have ever known, had been elected state attorney in a highly emotional campaign in 1956. Two years earlier, in 1954, a seven-year-old girl, Judith Ann

Roberts, had been abducted from her grandparents' apartment, raped, beaten, and savagely murdered. The crime had terrified and outraged the community. (This was in the days when murder was still front-page news in Miami.) The people had demanded that incumbent State Attorney George Brautigam bring the killer to justice, but he had not been able to. Gerstein, who had made his reputation prosecuting gamblers in the early fifties, took advantage of that. He blasted Brautigam, saying he would crack the case himself if elected. Don Petit, working behind the scenes as usual, dreamed up a devastating campaign slogan for Gerstein: "Make Murder a Crime in Dade County." It worked. The voters threw Brautigam out on his ear.

No one was ever convicted in the Roberts case, but that didn't detract from Gerstein's brilliant career. He prosecuted corrupt politicians, killers, rapists, bad cops, and every other kind of creep you can name. Once, a right-wing fanatic named Donald Branch took it upon himself to rid Dade County of people he considered liberals. He bombed the home of a newspaper editor, then decided to kill Gerstein himself. Branch was going to shoot Gerstein with a long-range rifle as the state attorney walked down the steps of the courthouse. Gerstein, brave as always, agreed to be a target while the cops tried for an arrest. For sixty-seven days this went on. The state attorney never got shot. But the lunatic did get arrested. Gerstein sent him away for twenty years.

Perhaps his greatest case was Watergate. In June 1972, Washington, D.C., police arrested five men, including some from Miami, for breaking into Democratic party offices at the Watergate hotel and office complex. Gerstein and his chief investigator, Martin Dardis, provided the first major break in the case. They discovered that President Richard Nixon's cronies had ordered the break-in and had paid the burglars to keep quiet after the arrest. Nixon resigned two years later after his own tape recordings proved he had tried to cover it all up. Gerstein and Dardis became key characters in the book *All the President's Men*.

But all that was still years away. Now it was 1960, and I was asking Gerstein to hire me as a prosecutor. It was a lot to ask. In those days the courtroom was still a masculine enclave. Female spectators weren't even allowed to hear the testimony in some cases. The judge would tell the ladies that the case involved indelicate language and activities of a sexual nature, and then he would invite them to wait in the hallway. A few women in Florida worked as grand jury prosecutors, but none worked in what lawyers call the pits, trying the cases and hearing the rough testimony. But that was exactly what I wanted to do. I had no interest in becoming a paper shuffler. I didn't want to sit in the law library and research cases. I still don't like to do that, though I do it when I have to. No, if I was going to go to work for Dick Gerstein, he was going to have to put me in the pits.

Fortunately for me, he was inclined to do so. Gerstein knew what it was to be a trailblazer. He was elected at thirty-two, making him the youngest person ever to serve as a state attorney in Florida. He was also the first Jewish person elected to that high an office. Whatever the political pressures on him, and there were many, he was not the type to deny me a job because I happened to be female. Besides, Don Petit wanted him to hire me. Like almost every other politician in South Florida, Gerstein trusted Petit implicitly. So I figured my application had a pretty good chance.

Late that year, Gerstein called me to his office for an interview. When the secretary showed me in, I encountered a tall, imposing man in a dark suit. His serious and thoughtful demeanor made it clear I was dealing with a substantial man. He had always been such a man. Serving in the Eighth Air Force in World War II, Gerstein had been a tremendous hero, flying more than twenty-seven bombing missions over Germany as the navigator of a B-17. In his last flight, in September 1944, his plane was hit by antiaircraft fire from below. The flak penetrated the nose of the plane, entered his head through his right temple, and exited through his left cheek. Severely wounded, Gerstein, only twenty-one years old, somehow remained conscious and guided the plane on its six-hour flight back to safety. He lost vision in his right eye, but his bravery won him the Distinguished Flying Cross and a host of other decorations. This was the legendary man whom I was now daring to ask for employment. He showed me into his office and immediately got down to business.

"Ellen," he said, "people give some very disturbing testimony in the courtroom. The things they describe are shocking, and their language is coarse, to say the least. Do you think you could put all that aside and concentrate on the job?"

It was a straightforward question, and I gave him a straightforward answer.

"I don't see why the hell not," I said.

He hired me.

Before I left, Gerstein told me what he told every assistant he hired.

"Ellen, in every case you handle for this office, I want you to regard the victim of the crime as you would a member of your own family. A burglary or robbery case may become routine to you, but it will never be routine to the victims.

"To them, that crime will be the most upsetting, the most terrifying thing that has ever happened. Remember that in your dealings with them. If you treat every victim as if he were a member of your family, you will never go wrong, because you will be serving people the way they expect to be served."

I became an assistant state attorney on February 16, 1961. I never forgot what Richard Gerstein said. I try to think about it every day of my life on the bench.

One of my first cases involved my father. He was not the victim. He was the accused.

It was in my first month on the job. I was working in traffic court, prosecuting drunk drivers and speeders. All new assistants started that way. Traffic court was a good place to learn because little was at stake. No killers would go free if I screwed up. No innocent men would go to the electric chair, either. If I blew a case by neglecting to ask a fundamental question, the world would not come to an end.

I was sitting at the table with another prosecutor when my father walked into the courtroom and approached the bench. Daddy, it turned out, had gotten a speeding ticket while driving his cab. It was news to me. He had not said a word about it, even though he knew I worked in traffic court. My colleague got up and read the charge. And then Daddy pleaded guilty. The judge levied the appropriate fine and Daddy nodded to me and started to leave.

"You know who that was?" I asked the other prosecutor. "That was my father."

He was flabbergasted. Daddy's last name was James, not Morphonios, so the guy had no way of knowing who he was.

"Are you kidding?" he said. "Why didn't you say something?"

I hadn't said anything because I didn't think my father should be treated any differently from anyone else. I had only mentioned it because I thought it was an interesting coincidence that he should come into my court. My colleague apparently didn't take the same view. As I sat at the counsel table, he walked over and whispered into the judge's ear. The judge looked at me and smiled.

And then he called Daddy back into the courtroom and suspended the fine.

Traffic court convened every night in several different cities: Miami Shores, Opa-locka, Coral Gables, Homestead, Hialeah, and downtown Miami. My job was to go to a different courthouse every week and prosecute cases. Traffic court, I thought, was aptly named: When I wasn't in court, I was in traffic.

My German shepherd, Jeff, always went with me. I had adopted Jeff after a police officer found him tied to the bumper of a stolen car. Whoever owned him must have trained him to be a guard dog, because Jeff protected a car as if it were Fort Knox. If someone approached my car when he was in it, he'd snarl like a chainsaw. Once, a friend needed to borrow the car for the day. I gave it to him—with Jeff in it. The guy drove to wherever he was going and parked the car. When he came back, the shepherd wouldn't let him open the door. Old Jeff was a good dog. I remember standing in a sixth-floor courtroom in downtown Miami and hearing him barking in the parking lot.

The people I prosecuted in that job were regular folk, not hardened criminals. But I learned quickly that even regular folk will do almost anything to get out of trouble. Once, a young woman showed up in court in high heels, a low-cut dress, and enough makeup to fill in the Grand Canyon. Apparently, she was planning to sweet-talk the judge, whom she obviously expected to be male. She was sorely disappointed when Mattie Bell Davis—very much a woman, and, incidentally, no fool—took the bench. Another time, in the Hialeah courtroom, some kids were talking loudly in Spanish about how they were going to lie to the judge. What they didn't know was that Judge C. P. Rubiera spoke Spanish fluently—and had heard everything they had said. When he took the bench and introduced himself in Spanish, they knew they had been had.

It was in traffic court that I first learned how important it is for judges to be efficient. People charged with traffic infractions expected swift justice. They wanted to come to court, stand before the judge, answer the charge against them, and get the hell out of there. I didn't blame them. They might have broken the law, but that didn't mean they should be sentenced to three hours on a hard wooden bench while the judge slogged through his cases. As the prosecutor, I called the calendar as quickly as I could. People loved the judges who could keep pace, and they loathed the ones who didn't. I promised myself then that if I ever became a judge, I would keep things moving in my courtroom.

In traffic court, I worked almost exclusively with men—judges, police officers, bailiffs, other prosecutors, defense lawyers. They all treated me beautifully, and we all got to be great pals. But it was hard for some people to believe that a woman could handle herself in that situation. Once in a while, some joker would come up to me and say, "Do you find it to be a disadvantage being the only woman with all these men around you?"

Some disadvantage. I was in heaven.

After a year in traffic court, my superiors called me into the office and gave me my first felony case.

A woman named Jean McCarthy had been charged with passing a worthless check in North Dade. Normally, a bad-check case is no big deal. But McCarthy happened to be a political mover and shaker: She knew every important politician in town. That meant the press would be covering the case, which meant Gerstein wanted badly to win it. No politician ever likes to look like a fool in the press. Since the defendant was a woman, somebody in the office decided it would be a good idea to have a woman as prosecutor.

I was assigned to work with a prosecutor named Eddie Klein, who also is now a judge. A lot of men looked twice when they saw me in those days, but Eddie was not among them. Eddie is a straight arrow. Not only has he had the same wife all these years, he also has had the same car. It's a 1956 Chevy. People no longer ask him, "How's the wife?" They say, "How's the car?" Anyway, Eddie and I investigated that case as if it were the Lindbergh baby kidnapping. Prosecutors almost always visit murder scenes, but they never go to the scene of a worthless check. But Eddie and I visited that one. We even interviewed the store owner, who must have thought his tax dollars were going a long way.

Before the trial, Aram Goshgarian, one of Gerstein's top assistants, called me to his office. Gosh—that's what everybody called him—weighed three hundred pounds if he weighed an ounce, and he had a voice like a foghorn.

He said he wanted to help me with my opening statement. He told me exactly how to begin.

"Ladies and gentlemen," I was to say, "my name is Ellen Morphonios. I am an assistant state attorney on the staff of your state attorney, Richard E. Gerstein, and I have been assigned to prosecute this case for the people of the state of Florida."

He made me repeat that phrase several times, to make sure I had it memorized. He seemed pleased when I got it.

"If you do what I'm saying," he told me, "nobody will remember that you're a female by the time you sit down. Get them to concentrate on what you're saying, and not what you look like or what you're wearing, and you'll never have a problem." I left his office feeling confident that I could handle the case.

The feeling had left me by the time I reached the courtroom. I was scared when we picked the jury, and I was downright terrified when it was time to begin the trial. My hands were trembling. Some prosecutors carry a big stack of books into the courtroom to keep their hands busy, but I hadn't done that. Soon, the judge asked me if I would like to make an opening statement. Remembering what Gosh had told me, I stood and told the jury, "My name is Ellen Morphonios . . ." And then I began to describe the evidence against the defendant. All of a sudden it was no longer scary. It was fun. I found I could look each juror in the eye and feel comfortable as I spoke. When I finished, I knew I had begun an important new phase of my life. Many people go through life without feeling they have a purpose, but that wasn't going to happen to me. In prosecuting felony cases, I had discovered the thing I was born to do.

When the trial was over, the jury found Jean McCarthy guilty as charged.

After that, I tried felony cases more and more often. I would work in traffic court for a while, then go downtown to try another felony case, then head back to traffic. I think Gerstein set it up that way. He was easing me into the job, making me feel comfortable with my skills before he gave me my own caseload. When he felt I was ready, he assigned me to a felony division and let me do the job.

My first division chief was Alfonso Sepe, a tough, handsome man who later became a judge. Al was a ladies' man and I was a man's lady, so we couldn't help noticing each other. But mostly we kept our minds on business. He liked to test me. As chief, it was Al's responsibility to decide which prosecutor would handle which case. When I first came into his division, he gave me a bunch of obscene-language cases, just to see how I would handle them. I showed him. I went into court and told the jury, in a clear, firm voice, "Ladies and gentlemen, the evidence will show that the defendant referred to the police officer as a nasty bastard and a motherfucker." I would draw out the colorful words for effect. Al appreciated that.

Later, the boss made me chief of my own division. That was fine with me. No problem. Now I could give the rinky-dink obscenity cases to somebody else. But it wasn't fine with some of the men in the office. Men simply did not work for women in those days. Some considered the very thought degrading, an affront to their masculinity. Some of the guys resented me, and said so.

One day, a prosecutor came into my office to complain. "I can't imagine why the boss made a woman division chief when so many of us have families to support," he said. "It just doesn't seem right."

I didn't say anything, but I was thinking, What does he think my sons are? Land crabs? Not that I really blamed him. No one had ever seen a woman felony prosecutor before, much less a woman division chief. I knew I would take some getting used to.

Soon, even the newspapers became aware of me. In November 1962, a *Miami News* reporter named Miller Davis spent a day with me and wrote a piece about it. His article was headlined BLONDE JAILS HOODLUMS. If you don't think things were different in 1962, get a load of this.

"A little blonde with a tough mind is helping State Attorney Richard Gerstein send bad people to jail.

"Assistant Prosecutor Ellen Morphonios, who grew up on a farm but learned big city ways fast, is 105 pounds of bad news to those who get in trouble and wind up in Criminal Court.

"'Men jurors melt under her tender gaze,' says one of Miami's top criminal lawyers who has several clients behind bars, courtesy of perky Ellen.

"Adds the same attorney ruefully, 'and in a good old-fashioned cat fight between Ellen and a lady defendant, the defendant usually leaves the witness stand with tears and mascara dripping down her face.'

"Almost every weekday Mrs. Morphonios stands in front of Judge Jack Falk's bench, hands on hips, tapping a high-heeled pump, and her voice is as warm and gentle as a Minnesota frost.

"'Well, sonny, make up your mind,' she barked at a 6-foot-2 robbery suspect recently, 'were you in the alley or in front of the store? And speak up nice and loud so the judge can hear about it too.'

"Born on the outer banks of North Carolina, Ellen grew up to a pleasant-looking 35-22-37 and came to Miami with a high school education, a legal pad and pencil, and a fierce interest in law.

"She served as a legal secretary for seven years for veteran Miami attorney Roscoe Brunstetter and used her natural endowments profitably as a part-time photographers' model.

"She attended the University of Miami Law School without ever having an undergraduate degree, was former Gov. Fuller Warren's very junior law partner for a while, and then ran for juvenile court judge.

"'I lost,' Ellen says cheerfully. 'Boy, how I lost.'

"But pride gleams in her blue eyes as she recalls that she was admitted to the bar on a Thursday in 1957 and tried her first law case before the Florida Supreme Court. Ellen later learned she had won.

"Gerstein named her an assistant in 1961, and her batting average for successful prosecutions is 94.1 percent.

"Sweaters and tight skirts help in some cases, claims Prosecutor Morphonios, and then there are times when a girl lawyer comes to court in something demure.

"'It's a simple matter of when and how you want to distract somebody,' she noted, with the matter-of-factness of an infantry officer sizing up a battlefield.

"Married and the mother of two, Ellen has a special sympathy for the work of juvenile courts.

"Maybe, someday, she will make the race again.

"'Right now I'm happy . . . I think I'm doing a man's job.'"

Happy did not adequately describe how I felt about my job. Ecstatic was more like it. Thrilled. Delighted. The job was my life. I felt like an Old West crime fighter, riding into town wearing silver pistols and a white hat and rounding up the lawbreakers. The Lone Ellen. I was doing the people's work, and they appreciated it. Every time I won a case, the victims of the crime would shake my hand, sometimes with tears in their eyes, and thank me for my work. I thought I had the most important job in the world. Everyone else's seemed dull in comparison.

But that sense of satisfaction came at a price. When I entered the state attorney's office, I was planning to use the job as a stepping-stone to a judgeship. It was all part of Don Petit's master plan. I would spend some time as a prosecutor, then, having gained the support of some lawyers and judges, I would resign and run for juvenile court judge. After that, it would be a short step to criminal court judge, and then a hop to the Florida Supreme Court. I was going to be Justice Ellen Morphonios, the first woman on the high court.

But now I knew those things weren't going to happen, at least not that way. Being a prosecutor had turned out to be more than just a rung on a ladder. It had turned into a career, a calling. I no longer wanted to walk out after two or three years. Don couldn't understand that. He often tried to persuade me to leave. Once, a judicial post came open and Don suggested, in his forceful way, that I run for it. I refused. He said, "Nobody is going to know who the hell you are if you don't get out there and run for something." I said I didn't particularly give a damn. We had a terrible fight, much worse than our usual spats. By refusing to leave the state attorney's office, I was rejecting Don as my Svengali. For the first time ever, I was not going to take his advice. He had wanted me to be his perfect creation, his masterpiece. But I couldn't do it. I had to be what I wanted to be.

It was the beginning of the end for us. My relationship with Don had been founded on our mutual interest in politics, and now I was knocking down that foundation. It wasn't that Don placed his happiness above mine; he wasn't a small man. Things simply had changed. And they kept changing. In 1962, my second year under Richard Gerstein, Don accepted a job as an aide to Florida Congressman Claude Pepper, the champion of the elderly, who died in 1989. He told me over dinner one night that he was moving to Washington, and I wept into my napkin. I loved him then, and I would never stop loving him. But our relationship would never be the same.

My parting with Don left me alone for the first time in years, if you don't count Alex, and I didn't. I wasn't alone for long.

Jack Headley was a detective in the Miami Police Department's worthless-checks squad. He also happened to be the son of Walter Headley, the chief of police. I had met Jack while working on cases, and had found him irresistible. He was over six feet tall and well built, and one of his front teeth slightly overlapped the other. I thought that was pretty cute. Once, when he was in my office helping me to prepare a case, I told him so.

"Goddamn," I said, "if I were ten years younger and I weren't married, I'd be after you."

I was coming on to him, of course. But Jack, who also was married, didn't accept the invitation right away. He was somewhat old-fashioned. Screwing around was not his hobby, as it was Don's. And he certainly didn't believe a woman should ever say "fuck," even if that was what she was doing.

Soon, though, he gave in, and we began dating. It was never dull. Once, we were driving to lunch in his police car when another driver suddenly turned into our lane. "Hold on," Jack said, "we're going to get hit!" Then came the pop of glass and the twisting of steel. The force of the collision nearly knocked me onto the floorboard. When the car stopped rocking, my knees ached and my head hurt.

As an assistant state attorney, I had every reason to be in a car with a police officer. We could have been going to a crime scene or driving to interview a witness. We could have been, but we weren't. And I didn't want to be part of any police accident report, just in case the press picked it up and made a story out of it. Nor did I want to be seen hanging around the accident scene.

So I opened the door and told Jack, "See ya." And then I hauled ass. I limped to a phone, called a fellow prosecutor who knew about the relationship, and told him to come and pick me up. When he arrived, we drove back to Jack's car to see if he was all right. He was. Jack told me later that one witness kept insisting a woman had jumped out of the police car and run away right after the accident. Jack assured him that he had been alone in the car.

That was not our closest call, not by a long shot. Jack's father, the chief, had an apartment near the waterfront. Jack and I used to sneak off to the apartment on our lunch hour, spend a few pleasant moments together, then go back to work. It sure beat Chinese food.

On one occasion, we were pulling out of the parking lot on our way back to work when I heard Jack say under his breath, "Oh, damn."

"What?" I said.

"My wife," he said. "She just pulled in."

Her car was right next to ours, and she was glaring at Jack through the window. I was mortified, so I did what any logical, intelligent person would have done: I hit the deck. Jack floored it out of there, thinking his wife would never follow. He was wrong. His wife gave chase. She followed us, the white-faced police officer and the kneeling, praying prosecutor, through the streets of Miami, screeching her tires after us and cursing us through her teeth. Fortunately, Jack was a much better driver than Mrs. Headley, and he finally shook her. When his wife called him at work that afternoon, he denied he had ever left the office. It was a ridiculous defense, but it was the best he could do.

I always used to predict that I wouldn't live past forty. I still don't understand how I made it this far.

EIGHT

SPEAK UP, PAL,
I CAN'T HEAR
YOUR HEAD RATTLE

The defendant was on trial for armed robbery. He had left only two things at the scene of the crime: a terrified store clerk and an old straw hat.

When I cross-examined the guy, he denied again and again that he had pulled the job. "You got the wrong guy," he said. "I wasn't there. I didn't do nothing." He was lying; I was sure of it. But how could I prove it?

I turned toward the prosecution table when the straw hat caught my eye. Then I got an idea. Suddenly, I stepped over to the clerk's desk, grabbed it, and handed it to the uncomfortable fellow on the witness stand.

"Here," I said, "put this on." Before the defense lawyer had a chance to object, he did.

The hat sat on his head like a thimble on a beach ball. It was at least three sizes too small.

Oops.

One of the nastiest cases I ever prosecuted involved neither an armed robber nor a mugger nor a cold-blooded killer. It involved a police officer.

Vivian Walsh Barron had been a Miami cop for thirteen years. For much of that time, she had worked the shoplifting detail in downtown Miami, and had done a fine job of it, arresting many habitual thieves and receiving a stack of commendations. The newspapers had written several articles about her, and not only because she was a good cop. She was a handsome woman with horn-rimmed glasses and a beautiful smile. Once, *True Detective* magazine wrote an article about her, calling her "Glamour Girl of the Law."

Nights, Barron moonlighted as the $2.50-an-hour store detective in Burdines, one of Miami's largest and most popular department stores. That's when her troubles began. In the time she worked at the store, Burdines began receiving an unusually large number of refund vouchers—slips of paper that customers presented when they wanted or needed their money back for an item. Each voucher the store honored meant money out of the cash register.

The store's managers suspected that the detective was involved, so they called the cops. Miami police, working with Sheriff Tal Buchanan's deputies, secretly watched their fellow officer for several days. Eventually, they figured out that she was signing customers' names to refund vouchers and then cashing them in. In all, she and an accomplice had taken four thousand dollars. The police arrested her, and I got the case.

I thought it would be a hard case to try. I was, and still am, a great supporter of the police. Cops do a dangerous, thankless job for mediocre pay, and I, for one, appreciate it. So I might have been inclined to give Vivian Walsh Barron a break—to tone down the rhetoric so the trial wouldn't be any more harrowing for her than it had to be.

But then bad things started happening.

My housekeeper then was Cheli Izquierdo, a delightful and tremendously loyal woman. One night during the trial, the phone rang and Cheli picked it up.

"It's too bad," the caller said in Spanish. "We know you're just a housekeeper, but you're going to have to die. We're going to kill that bitch, and we're going to kill you, too. We're going to kill the children. We're going to blow up the house."

I was the bitch they were referring to, and I was terrified. If somebody wanted to kill me, fine. I wasn't crazy about the idea of being turned into hamburger, but I understood that people in my job often made people angry. I could live with that. But I was shocked to think that someone would want to kill my children and my housekeeper too. My family and friends were not to blame for my career. They didn't choose to become prosecutors. Only I did. And I was damned upset that someone wanted to kill them out of anger toward me.

We all walked on eggshells for several days. Each morning, I would wake up, fix breakfast for the kids, grab a cup of coffee and a cigarette, then go out and start the car to see if it would blow up. In the afternoon, Cheli met the boys at the bus stop and walked them home. She was the only woman on the block who carried a butcher knife while strolling in the neighborhood.

In the next few days, Cheli received several more threatening calls. She was reluctant to tell me about them for fear she would worry me, but eventually she detailed every call the person had made, and related everything he had said. It was never very neighborly.

My boyfriend Jack Headley, who had a lot of good sources inside and outside the police department, began doing some detective work for me. It wasn't long before someone told him who was calling.

I knew the guy. On one hand, I didn't think he had the guts to make good on his threats. On the other hand, I thought he might do anything if he had a couple of drinks in him.

Of this I was sure: The guy was not making the threatening calls on his own initiative. He had no quarrel with me. Someone obviously had put him up to it. I knew through Jack that some cops were mighty angry with me for prosecuting Barron, the demure glamour cop. Perhaps some of those officers were behind the threats. The thought infuriated me. It also strengthened my determination to win the case, even though I'm sure Barron knew nothing of the calls.

It was a nasty trial. Once, in a heated moment, defense lawyer Norman Haft lost his temper and shoved me clear across the courtroom, right in front of the jury. Lawyers often get angry, but they rarely push each other around. I could have regained my balance quickly if I had wanted to, but I didn't want to. If the opposing lawyer was going to start attacking poor little me, I sure as hell was going to make it a good show for the jury. The next day Norman arrived in court to find several of Sheriff Tal Buchanan's rugged deputies sitting in the front row. They made it clear that they planned to intervene if he got rough again. He didn't. Tal Buchanan had a special incentive to want to help me out: He and I had been, briefly, more than friends.

Later, Norman got into a scuffle with Woodrow Melvin, Jr., the lawyer for the department store. Norman accused Melvin of coaching a witness, and Melvin took objection. Norman pushed the department-store lawyer into a sand-filled trash stand, and Melvin responded by socking Norman in the eye. The newspaper reported the whole thing, making both men look like children. Norman really wasn't a bad guy. He was simply caught in an emotional situation.

Two experienced prosecutors, Mike Hacker and Richard Essen, helped me during the trial. Their job was to prepare the opening and closing statements; mine was to deliver them. "This is an important case, and I know you want to win it," they told me before we picked the jury. Then they gave me a copy of the opening remarks. "Read this statement exactly as it is written. Don't deviate from it even once."

I did as I was told during the opening statement. But by the end of the week, I was no longer in a charitable mood. When it was time for me to make my closing argument, I tossed aside my colleagues' carefully typed statement and became Ellen the Merciless. I gave it to the accused cop with both barrels, using every bit of invective, vicious slang, and negative innuendo I could think of. The people in the courtroom must have thought I was prosecuting Jack the Ripper, not some department-store crook.

The jury deliberated for four hours before convicting Barron of ten felony counts. Judge Jack Falk immediately sentenced her to five years in prison. Justice may be blind, but it could read Vivian Walsh Barron's handwriting on a refund voucher.

The Barron case was brief—the trial took only three days—but it was significant in terms of my career and the development of my ideas. As I've said, my attitudes about justice, about crime and punishment, began to form when I was a girl growing up on the Pungo in North Carolina. They were reinforced by my parents'—especially my mother's—Old World ideals, and by my experiences as a mother and a young lawyer. The Barron case only hardened my feelings of contempt for the lawless. I saw Virginia Walsh Barron as a corrupt person, a woman who had been given a position of trust in the store and had willfully abused it. Here was a clear example of a person who committed crimes out of plain greed and avarice. There was no excuse for what she did. Trying that difficult case convinced me that my hard line against criminals—especially the greedy and avaricious ones—was indeed justified.

Not that I had doubted it.

As a prosecutor, I believed my job was not just to get convictions. It was to get justice.

Getting justice means getting a conviction in most cases, but not all. The police, in their zeal, occasionally make an arrest on evidence so weak that it would be an injustice to prosecute. The job title is prosecutor, not persecutor. I always tried to dismiss weak cases, but it wasn't easy. Cops generally are sensitive, prideful people. When they make an arrest, even a lousy one, they want it to stick. And they take it personally when it doesn't.

Crime victims can be even more demanding. People who get robbed or beaten want to see the perpetrator behind bars. So do I. But it's not that simple. Sometimes the police don't get the right guy. Sometimes they get the guilty party, but they don't get enough evidence to prove his guilt. I often hear people say, "Everything in the justice system favors the criminal." Well, that's true. The burden of convicting someone of a crime is great, maybe too great. But that's the system.

Of course, it's impossible to explain that to the victim. Telling a rape victim that you are going to release the defendant for lack of evidence is a most unpleasant job. But that is what a prosecutor often must do in the name of justice.

Prosecutors sometimes forget that they are supposed to seek justice. Under Florida law, the state attorney has to show all the evidence to the defendant before the trial begins. A lot of prosecutors try to weasel out of it. They apparently think they'll have a better chance of winning a conviction if they ambush the defendant. That ticks me off. I never pulled that crap. I figured it didn't matter if the defense lawyers knew what caliber bullet I was going to shoot them with. I was still going to shoot them. So I always let the other side see everything I had.

When a trial started, though, I was no longer nice. Then I wanted a conviction. To hell with getting a lesser verdict: I wanted to win. The spirit of competition took over and I turned into a raging she-devil. I took the defendants' crimes personally. When a guy mumbled on the witness stand, I would shout, "Speak up, pal! I can't hear your head rattle." In prosecuting cases, I used every advantage I could muster. And with lots of men on the jury, I found that short skirts and low necklines gave me quite an advantage.

Early in 1965, a *Miami Herald* reporter named Jo Werne wrote an article about me. The headline said, simply, SHE'S AN ASSISTANT STATE ATTORNEY. Werne asked me how the criminals felt about me.

"Well," I said, "when I step into the courtyard by the jail, first I get wolf whistles from the prisoners. When they recognize me, the whistles become four-letter words.

"They hate my guts."

The most enjoyable job I ever had was not prosecutor, fashion model, secretary, radio talk-show host, civil lawyer, nor even judge. It was den mother.

Dale joined the Cub Scouts early in 1963, Dean a short time later. When I was asked to lead one of the groups, or dens, I naturally accepted. At age thirty-three, I would at last get the opportunity to be a little boy.

If you ask me, the Cub Scouts program is the greatest thing that ever happened to little boys, save for little girls. Each den was supposed to have only five or six boys, but my den—Den 5—always seemed to have eight, ten, or more. I collected kids the way eccentric old ladies collect stray cats. (Which, come to think of it, is also something I do.) I often wore my den-mother uniform under my suit so I could be ready for action right after court. There is no such thing as a den mother today. Now they're called den leaders. I do not consider that progress.

We had loads of fun. Once a week we would all pile into my car and go on some great adventure. I had an interesting job and I knew some influential people, so my boys got to see some things the other Cub Scouts never dreamed of. Once, we went on a tour of the United States nuclear-missile bases in the Florida Everglades. I kept a close eye on the boys there. I didn't want one of them to press a button and accidentally eliminate Cuba.

Sheriff Tal Buchanan, my old boyfriend, once gave us a tour of the Dade County Sheriff's Department. The boys got to look at blood under a microscope, which is the kind of thing most boys live for the chance to do. We were in the crime lab when I noticed that my boys were playing near several bags of evidence from a recent sensational murder. I almost had a heart attack. Very quickly, I got the boys out of the lab and into the car. I shuddered to think what would happen if I'd had to tell Dick Gerstein that we couldn't try the case because my Cubs had monkeyed with the evidence.

But if the boys got me into trouble, they also kept me out of it. One week, I took them to the Dade County Youth Fair to go on the rides, eat cotton candy, and pet the livestock. While we were there, we ran into Jack Headley, with whom I was still conducting a torrid and not very well disguised romance. Jack was with his daughters. We exchanged pleasantries for a moment, then parted ways, hoping the kids had not paid any attention to us.

They had. When Jack got home, the first thing his little daughter said to his wife was, "Mommy, Mommy, we met a friend of Daddy's. A pretty lady!"

Mrs. Headley's back stiffened, and her face grew hard. "Oh, really?" she said, and Jack knew he was in for it.

"Yes," the girl said. "And guess what? She has eight children!"

End of problem.

I remember these things because, as a good and diligent den mother, I documented everything that happened at our meetings. Each week, I would sit at the typewriter and tap out a few sentences for posterity. The record of the first meeting, on March 30, 1963, is as straightforward as a court transcript: "The first meeting of Den 5 opened with the Lord's Prayer, Pledge of Allegiance, and Scout promise."

As time went by, simply recording what had happened no longer provided me enough stimulation. So I began to expand on the week's events, often providing editorial comment where I saw fit. The Cub Scout log became less a record of the den's activities than a sort of truncated diary of Ellen Morphonios. As these excerpts show, I wasn't always thinking about the best way to tie a slipknot.

Oct. 5, 1963

The 18th meeting of Den 5 was a complete drag. John Samuelson [who is now an outstanding police officer] was absolutely impossible. He upset the whole meeting. I hope no more den meetings are as bad as this one. I won't stand for it.

Nov. 30, 1963

We discussed what fees were due. This sometimes becomes a real problem for me as I am not made of money, contrary to the kids' belief. I have a headache trying to figure out my own budget, and have to complain about something so it might as well be this. I can't get in a fight with a typewriter, but I can if I go argue with Alex.

Dec. 28, 1963

This meeting was called off because I had a lovely case of the flu and didn't feel it quite right to share my good luck with the boys.

March 7, 1964

Alex packed the boys into the car and brought them down to the Justice Building to see me in action. I just wish they could have seen some real fireworks, as during this particular trial the defense lawyers and I have had some real knock-down, drag-out arguments. But on the other hand, maybe it's better if the boys don't see their Den Mama showing her claws.

April 18, 1964

I spotted an ad in the newspaper for a special children's movie called "Puss 'n Boots," which was playing downtown, and decided to take the boys in the afternoon to see it. The boys were as good as gold in the movie. They were so quiet I thought they might have gone to sleep, but they seemed to be thoroughly enjoying it. Personally I thought it smelled.

June 6, 1964

For some reason I got the bright idea to take the kids to the Hialeah stock car races at night. It started out as a good idea.

My nephew Donald Wright is working off a phase now, and drives one of the fool things on Saturday night for the fun of it. This, of course, gave the kids a real personal interest in the whole thing because Donnie sat with us most of the time when he wasn't out there on the track trying to commit suicide.

Time began to go by. The seats to me were especially hard and for the sake of my sadly deteriorating nerves I desired to depart. The kids desired to remain and see that which is called a destruction derby, where the drivers deliberately crash into other cars. The boys thought this a delightful way to spend an evening. I thought the whole idea stunk. But the kids are hard to turn down when they want something so badly. So sit there we did, while my tailbone became gradually numb and my nerves taut.

When it was all over, we left, and the hour was late. The kids were scared half to death that their parents would draw and quarter them for being so late. I was quite sure this was a needless worry, but felt quite certain that the parents would draw and quarter me instead. It did not occur. Perhaps parents are more understanding than I thought they would be. Whatever medieval torture thoughts circulated through their minds for me they never voiced.

The kids may forget the experience, but I doubt that I ever will, and if I never see that track again it will be all right with me.

July 25, 1964

We decided to go in the paddle boats on the lake. I stayed on shore. They were supposed to have the boats out 30 minutes. Time came and the young man in charge very kindly called on the loud-speaker for Den 5 to bring their boats to shore. There they sat. He called again. There they sat. The next thing I knew, I heard this voice on the loudspeaker say, "Den 5, you'd better get your boats in before your den mother beats you to death with her whistle strap." The boats started in as fast as those little feet could peddle.

Sept. 5, 1964

I often wonder what the boys really think I do for a living. I sometimes wonder if they have some kind of mental idea that I stand in the courtroom with a machete, slicing off the heads of criminals.

Feb. 9, 1965

We gained admittance to the target range at the Miami Police Department for a demonstration in the proper handling of firearms.

The den mothers of Den 5 and Den 7 (Betty Kennedy) both fired the guns. We each fired several volleys for the benefit of our admiring respective dens. My own sons kept telling me I was missing the target, but it didn't happen to be the first time I had held a gun, and I knew darn well I was hitting. I'm no marksman to be sure, but I sure as heck wasn't missing any target. When I finished, this was confirmed by the police officers present.

Still, I didn't find that a machine gun is just the thing every little woman needs around the house. I couldn't move my shoulder for two days. That thing is powerful, no matter which end of it you're on. I'd prefer the sore shoulder to the ventilation, though.

My days as a den mother ended soon after that. Dale, Dean, and the rest of "my" kids were growing older, and their interests were changing. I could no longer easily amuse them with the traditional Cub Scout activities. I knew things were beginning to change the day my cubs met a gorgeous young lady who worked in my office. We were at a parade. When I introduced the boys to the woman, whose name was Judy, their mouths fell open. "Is she a movie star?" they said. On the way home, they talked more about her than they did about the tanks in the parade.

You know a boy is growing up when he thinks sex is more interesting than war.

I made my share of mistakes in my days as a prosecutor. Taking testimony from the Swedish Angel was one of the worst.

That was the nickname we had for a cop who worked in Sweetwater, a city just west of Miami. His real name was Wilmur Nash, but we called him the Swedish Angel because he resembled the big, burly guy who wrestled professionally under that name in the fifties. Old Wilmur stood way over six feet tall, weighed more than two hundred pounds, and had a head as hard and bald as a trailer hitch. He had a reputation as a tough guy, someone who would do almost anything, even things nobody wanted him to do, in his zeal to protect and serve. Consequently, the state attorney's office had to bail him out of trouble a lot. But this much was certain: People tended to pay attention to him.

But not everyone did. One Sunday morning, the Swedish Angel was patrolling his city, which in those days consisted of a church, a couple of bars, and a dusty road, when he came upon a couple making love in the backseat of a parked car. Normally this would not have bothered the Swedish Angel much, but these particular people had chosen to park directly across from the church, which was just now ringing its bell to call in the faithful. Worse, the woman in question was having her period, so the cop couldn't tell immediately if the guy was just screwing her or perhaps killing her too. It looked like war had broken out in the back of the sedan.

The Swedish Angel ordered the guy to get out of the car. The man, who had other things on his mind, not to mention something large between his legs, ignored him. The cop insisted, and after further delay the man finally hiked up his trousers and opened the door.

The Swedish Angel was angry now, sad to say, and he showed it in the way he effected the arrest. He pulled from his belt a device called the iron claw, which essentially was a single handcuff that a police officer could snap on to the wrist of a subject to get control of him. In court, the cops always called the things single handcuffs, because the term *iron claw* made them sound like instruments of torture, which basically they were.

The cop, in a sour mood, vigorously snapped the claw onto the suspect's wrist—almost. Instead of slipping over his wrist the way it was supposed to, the sharp part of the clamp caught ahold of the fellow's wrist bone and just about shish-kebabbed him. The defendant, in ecstasy only moments before, was now in serious pain, and was likely wondering whether he would ever again be able to prop himself up for sex with that wrist. It was a pretty bad injury.

The Swedish Angel charged the man with indecent conduct, resisting arrest, and a few other things, and I got the case. I had a couple of strong incentives to win it. First, I thought the couple had shown extremely poor taste in screwing next to a church on a Sunday morning. They needed to learn a lesson. Second, I knew that if I didn't convict the guy, he would almost certainly bring a brutality suit against the cop, and would stand a good chance of winning.

At trial, the defendant testified in great detail about how the bald-headed cop had shish-kebabbed him. I didn't want him to win the sympathy of the jury, so I called the Swedish Angel to the stand and asked him to demonstrate what had happened.

"Officer Nash," I said, being careful not to call him Officer Angel, "please take out the single handcuff and place it on me exactly as you placed it on the defendant."

A truly awful idea.

I extended my wrist to him, and he did as he was told. I thought I was going to die. He didn't shish-kebab me, but the force of the thick metal hook snapping down on my skinny forearm was enough to shatter granite. The pain screamed inside my arm from the tips of my fingers to my shoulder. It was horrible, and for a moment I was sure I would faint.

Fortunately, I had my back to the jury box, so the jurors couldn't see the tears welling in my eyes. But they could easily see that I was massaging my wrist. I came up with a fast excuse. That day, I happened to be wearing a dress I really liked—a pink dress with a high neck and long sleeves. I pretended that I wasn't massaging my wrist, but rather checking the sleeve of the dress for stains.

"You better not have gotten any grease on my pretty pink dress," I told the Swedish Angel.

I got away with it. The jury didn't convict the defendant on every charge, but they came back with enough guilty verdicts to provide the Swedish Angel with an adequate defense against a police-brutality suit. Just another great day in law enforcement.

By the way, the Swedish Angel's wife killed him with a .357 magnum about ten years later. I don't know if he asked for it, but I wouldn't be surprised.

The case of the Swedish Angel should have taught me not to give courtroom demonstrations, but it didn't. I continued to do re-enactments, with disastrous results.

In the mid-sixties, three young men were arrested in Miami with enough Molotov cocktails to blow up the Orange Bowl. The police believed that the men, all avowed anti-Castroites, were planning to incinerate the homes of Communist sympathizers. This was not uncommon. For some radical Miamians, figuring out ways to kill or maim Communists and then reclaim Cuba was a major preoccupation. We prosecuted lots of them.

The three men in this case—two Cuban exiles and a Miami native—were charged with illegal possession and transportation of explosives, and were facing twenty years in prison. After I rested my case, the very smart defense lawyer, James Whitmore Miller, asked a question of the judge.

"Are the bombs explosive? The state has had them for ten months, and no effort has been made to set them off." Miller quoted my expert witnesses as saying there was "a possibility" that the bombs would explode if ignited. That wasn't good enough for him, and he said so.

That was when I piped up. I was sure the things would explode. I had seen it on TV lots of times. On TV, you can blow up a Sherman tank with a Molotov cocktail. Why couldn't you do the same thing in real life? "We would be glad to test," I said. What I didn't know when I said it was that Miller had worked his way through law school as a fire fighter, and that he knew a lot about explosives.

Judge Carling Stedman welcomed the idea of a demonstration. He had to sit in the courtroom day after day and listen to mind-numbing testimony, so he jumped at the opportunity to go on a field trip. Somebody located a condemned house in a poor part of town, and we all headed over there to see if we could detonate the neighborhood.

The house turned out to be an old pine structure with sagging floors and a buckling roof. The place was as dry as sunburned grass. I figured that sucker would go up like a piece of flash paper. We certainly were prepared for that possibility. The county's bomb experts were on hand, along with a half-dozen police and fire trucks and a hundred assorted spectators who had heard what we were going to do. It figured to be a pretty good show, and no one wanted to miss it.

Everyone stood back. Then the local bomb expert, Tom Brodie, lit the wick of one of the bombs and threw it at the house. There was a poof, a flash, and then a tiny fire that quickly extinguished itself. Brodie tried another one, with the same result. The third and fourth bombs also fizzled out. By now, people who had been ducking behind cars were standing next to the house, laughing.

We threw seven bombs at the place without lowering the property value in the slightest. I was depressed. I was really hoping for a tremendous blast. "I had to open my big mouth," I said. Judge Stedman just shook his head. He dismissed the charges against the three inept arsonists, who were once again free to plot the overthrow of Fidel Castro.

The defense lawyer, having snookered me, was graceful in victory.

"If you want to make Molotov cocktails illegal, you've got to make a special law. They don't always explode."

I took his advice. When the case was over, I went to work with some state legislators to change the law pertaining to bombs. A law was passed in the next session. From that day forward, a Molotov cocktail did not actually have to explode to be considered a bomb.

NINE

"HI, ELLEN.
THIS IS JACKIE GLEASON."

If you think abortion should be illegal, you should have known the amateur abortionist I called the Ugly Old Lady. She would have made you think twice.

I know I'm not supposed to say that. I'm conservative. I'm supposed to believe that it will rain fire on us all if we do not do away with the sin of abortion. But I have never thought what other people wanted me to think, and I'm too old to start now. I don't like abortion. I think it's tragic and unnecessary, and though I might have considered it, I never would have chosen it for myself. Abortion is murder. There is no way you can say it is not murder. But I know women will always want abortions, and I would rather they get them from qualified doctors than from wire-wielding back-room quacks. To hell with the right-to-lifers. I have seen too many young women with their insides torn out to look at it any other way.

Back-alley abortion operations can be almost medieval in their ways. As a prosecutor working before *Roe* v. *Wade*, the 1973 United States Supreme Court decision that legalized abortion, I put away my share of abortionists. Some were doctors who were doing what they felt compelled morally to do. But most were opportunists—greedy people who learned everything they knew about anatomy in high school biology class.

The Ugly Old Lady—that's what we called her—was such a person. I'll never forget the face: big nose, acne scars, wirelike gray hair. She was a real hag. The police found out about her when she botched an abortion on a young woman. The girl, who wound up in the hospital with severe infections, provided a phone number and a description. That was all the cops needed.

To catch abortionists, the police drafted a female officer and sent her in under an assumed name. The cop would start by dialing the abortionist's number. She would be told to stand holding a newspaper on a certain street at a given time. The "doctor's" helpers would then come along in a car and pick her up. Often they would blindfold her, and sometimes they would make her lie down in the backseat so no one would see. Meanwhile, an unmarked police car would follow. At the house or clinic or whatever, the officer would be examined and told she was pregnant, even though she knew she was not. When she at last got onto the abortionist's table, wherever it was, the other officers would burst in, guns drawn, and make the bust. It usually worked like a charm.

Usually, but not always. Once, the cops and some people from the prosecutor's office decided to use one of Richard Gerstein's secretaries as the fake patient. Her name was Virginia Jimenez. The place the cops wanted to bust was a sophisticated one with lots of security and lots of patients. When Virginia got into the car with the abortionists, she felt secure knowing that a police helicopter was following.

Then the copter lost track of the car.

Virginia Jimenez was now in serious trouble. The cops on the ground radioed the license number to the helicopter, but it was too late. The abortionists were gone. They brought Virginia to the clinic, which unlike most was fairly well equipped, and examined her. Then they put her feet in the stirrups to begin the procedure. When it seemed they were about to start, she jumped off the table and shouted, "Police! You're under arrest!"

But the police did not burst in. The cavalry did not come.

The abortionists beat her to within an inch of her life. It was lucky they didn't just kill her and dump her in a canal, because if they had, the cops probably never would have found her. Instead, they drove her to a deserted area and dumped her in a field. She stumbled to a nearby house, where a Good Samaritan allowed her to call the police. At that point, a bad situation got worse. The cops, who were hysterical and rightly so, thought Virginia was calling from the abortionists' place, so they stormed the Good Samaritan's house as if Public Enemy No. 1 were holed up inside. Virginia managed to stop them before they did too much damage. The whole day was a disaster, and it could have been worse.

The arrest of the Ugly Old Lady went more smoothly, thank heaven. The evidence the police found was convincing—and horrifying. Her home was the picture of abortion hell. Like her, it was dirty and badly cared for. She had an awful metal tool that she used for examining women; God knows where she got it, or what mayhem it wreaked on a woman's insides. The cops found her abortion tools in the yard, under a big tree, soaking in Donald's water bowl.

Donald was not her dog. Donald was her duck.

It was the kind of case that outraged me, that brought out my zest for what I did. It was easy to sense the conscience of the community in such a case: People, even proabortion people, would want this woman locked up for a long time. After presenting the evidence, I argued vociferously for her conviction, and I did not leave out the part about the duck's water bowl.

The jury found her guilty. The maximum sentence she could have received was five years, and that was what she got.

I don't mean to alarm you, but I think you should know: In no city are children safe from perverts and deviants.

I learned that when I was a prosecutor. I specialized for several years in child prostitution and child sexual-abuse cases, and I learned that all children are susceptible to the tricks of an abuser. No matter what color they are or how much money their families have, all children are essentially the same, and all are terribly vulnerable.

Child sexual-abuse cases are among the most difficult for a prosecutor to win. In most cases, kids make bad witnesses. They forget a lot of important things, and they often don't answer the questions they're asked. When they do answer, they tend to give the answer they think will satisfy the questioner. A prosecutor may think he has extracted a pretty good story from a child—until the defense lawyer gets a chance to ask questions. Then the whole story changes. Suddenly the bad man who hurt the little boy is a nice man who bought him candy. To convict a defendant, juries must believe that he is guilty beyond a reasonable doubt. Child sexual-abuse cases often create nothing but doubt.

I won my share of kiddie-rape cases, but I lost some too, more than I would like to remember. Among the worst defeats was the case of the Man Behind the Screen.

The case involved the children of a police detective. One of the cop's daughters, a child about six years old, had a habit of twisting her hair around her finger. At first, it seemed like a simple nervous habit, nothing serious, just a quirk like thumb-sucking or nail-biting. But then the detective and his wife noticed that the child was twisting so hard that she was pulling the hair out of her scalp. She was actually getting bald on one side of her head. Clearly, something was wrong.

It took time, but the couple finally got the girl to tell them what was bothering her. It came out slowly, a little bit at a time, but soon the parents began to understand what was happening. Living near the detective's family was a middle-aged man. The cop and his wife didn't know the man well, but they thought he was a nice enough fellow. He sometimes came by to say hello, and he was friendly to the children.

Too friendly, as it turned out. The neighbor, it seemed, had somehow convinced the children that they had to do as he said, no matter what he wanted. I wasn't surprised that he had been able to—kids are easily led, and some adults are master manipulators. What the man had done was horrifying. He had cut a hole in his back-porch screen, and then he had stuck his penis through it and forced the kids to perform oral sex on him. Every child in the family had done it, but only the little girl had begun to show the emotional strain.

The family filed a complaint and the man was arrested and put in jail. The case was assigned to someone else in my office, but I was asked to help in interviewing the kids. The thinking was that they might talk to me more easily than they would to a male prosecutor, and that turned out to be true. I became great friends with the children, and persuaded them to tell me, in painful detail, what had happened and when it had happened. When it was time for trial, we felt we had an unshakable case.

The other prosecutor was to handle the trial. But things didn't go well. After a day or two, I received word that I would have to go to court and help. The children had clammed up. They wouldn't tell the prosecutor a thing. The case was about to go down the drain: Without a reliable witness to testify, you can't convict a person of jaywalking.

I was an awful failure. I said to the little girl, "Honey, do you remember how we talked in my office, and how you told me all about what happened?" She nodded yes. But when I asked her to tell me again so the jury could hear too, she froze. The judge gave me every opportunity to get her to talk, but nothing worked. It was frustrating, but I couldn't blame the kid. I have met hundreds of grown-ups who were terrified to talk to a judge and a jury. How could I blame a six-year-old?

The man was found guilty only of disorderly conduct. He was out of jail by the end of the day. I'm sure he never bothered the neighbor children again, but I'm not so sure he didn't go off and abuse someone else.

There were many other tragic cases. One of my high school classmates had a child who was abused. She was a sharp woman, her husband a sharp man. They were sitting on the front porch one night, just enjoying the evening, when one of their sons came out to talk to them. He was in his early teens, a Boy Scout and a good kid. He had just returned from a camping trip to Fisheating Creek, a place in rural central Florida. He hemmed and hawed for a while, then he told his parents he didn't want to go on overnight trips with the other scouts anymore.

"Why not?" his father said.

"I don't know," the kid replied. "I just don't like the sleeping arrangements."

The man, who had already begun to think something was wrong, had his arm around his wife. When his son mentioned the sleeping arrangements, he tapped her on the shoulder and said, "That's it. Something's going on."

After further prodding, the kid revealed that the scoutmaster was crawling into the scouts' bedrolls with them at night. "It's cold," the creep would say, and the kids, respecting authority as scouts are trained to do, would not refuse him. He had neither performed oral sex on the boys nor asked them to perform it on him, but he had fondled them as they lay in their sleeping bags, which confused them terribly and also scared the hell out of them.

My former classmate came to me with her story. I was outraged. This scoutmaster, this upstanding citizen, had assumed a position of great responsibility, and then had abused it in the worst way. Besides violent people, this was the kind of jerk that infuriated me the most—a calculating, skulking, two-faced criminal. My school chum and her husband had enough information at least to arouse suspicion, so I ordered an investigation.

We quickly found several other children who told stories similar to the first kid's. The stories seemed strong, the kids' memories clear. But there were problems. Many of the illegal acts had taken place in other counties, which meant they could be prosecuted only in those counties. The crimes were not investigated as vigorously there because, frankly, the victims lived far away and the local prosecutors had their own criminals to worry about.

We made one good case in Dade County, but it fell apart at trial. I had prepared a bill of particulars that said the molestation had taken place at a certain time and in a certain place. But when the victim testified, he gave a different time and a different place, and that was the end of the case. I don't know what happened. Maybe I made a mistake in preparation, or maybe the kid's memory failed him. Anyhow, that ended that case. We embarrassed the scoutmaster, but never really stripped him of his merit badges.

What could I do? Losing a case on a technicality always hurts. But there is little time to mourn the one that got away. I knew that a hundred more cases would be filed the next day, that a hundred more victims would be crying for justice.

Many of those cases, I knew, would involve child prostitution. If there was an expert on the subject in the state attorney's office, I guess I was it. Possibly because I was a mother and could be very sympathetic when I had to be, the boys who got involved in the trade found it easy to talk to me. They told me stories they would tell nobody else.

The story was always the same. The names changed and the faces changed, but the story didn't. The boy would start at age thirteen or fourteen with all the feelings a kid that age has. He would have a girlfriend, someone he wanted to impress and please. Then a grown-up would come along—a family friend, someone from the church, maybe a stranger—and befriend the boy. The grown-up would take the kid camping or to the movies, and maybe give him some money to spend on his girlfriend. The kid, having no other source of income, was understandably grateful for the dough.

Then the adult would try to capitalize on his friendship with the boy. He would put his hand on the boy's thigh and then gradually begin closing in on the crotch. Eventually, the grown-up would offer a deal: "If you let me do such-and-such to you, I'll give you some money." Usually it was a pretty good sum of money, at least to a thirteen-year-old. Some kids would turn the guy down flat, and the guy would make the whole thing seem innocent by pretending he had been joking. But a larger number of boys would think, Okay, I'll let him do it once, and then I'll never see him again.

One part of the story never changed: After the grown-up had done his thing, the kid always threw up.

The kid would think he would never do it again, but then he would run out of money. And there the chicken hawk would be, offering cash in exchange for a favor. Soon the young chicken would be seeing more and more of the chicken hawk and less and less of the girlfriend. Usually the kid got involved only in oral sex, but some of the hard-core boys had anal sex too. Many of them eventually became chicken hawks—depraved grown-ups cruising the streets for young flesh. The crime went full circle.

I made a lot of speeches in my prosecuting days. The job of state attorney is very much a job of public relations. People want to be reassured that crime is under control (even when it isn't), and that law-enforcement people have the same concerns they do. The speech I gave most often was the one about chickens and chicken hawks. I used to go to the Rotary and Kiwanis clubs at lunchtime and deliver the talk, and I included everything, even the detail about what the chicken hawk wanted to do with the chicken. So the Rotarians and the Kiwanians would be sitting there eating their lunch and thinking, Yecch.

It was the reaction I was hoping for.

I have a reputation for never giving anyone a break. I guess I deserve it. Going on *60 Minutes* and shooting a machine gun at a target does not build a person's reputation as a softy. But I would like to say, for the record, that there have been many times when, as a prosecutor and as a judge, I did give someone a break, or at least tried to.

Early in my tenure, I was assigned an armed-robbery case involving a kid from South Carolina. One day this kid got bored, borrowed his brother's car, picked up a couple of his girlfriends, and headed for Florida. Sometimes I think *Florida* must be a synonym for trouble, because that's what so many people are headed for when they come here. This kid certainly was. He was a nineteen- or twenty-year-old with no money in his pocket and two very demanding young ladies in the front seat. Not a good combination.

The three of them had fun for a few hours before the kid went broke. This, clearly, was a problem. Then the kid remembered that his brother's rifle was in the trunk. He figured he might be able to use the rifle to persuade someone to lend him some money. So he and the girls picked out a gas station, cruised up to the pumps, and stuck up the attendant. The attendant turned over some money, but the kid never got a chance to spend it because the cops arrested him ten minutes later, easy as pie.

That was when I got the case. I knew from the start that this guy was no Al Capone. He was a nice kid, at least when he wasn't pointing guns at people and taking their money. He had never been in trouble in his life, and I thought it would be best if he just got back in his car and went back to South Carolina before someone got hurt. I told his lawyer, Marco Loffredo, that if the kid pleaded guilty the judge might go easy on him—as long as we didn't let on that the rifle was loaded. The lawyer said he thought that would be just fine.

When the court date came, the kid entered his plea of guilty. But that wasn't good enough for him. He had a guilty conscience, and he wanted to tell the judge every terrible detail of what he had done, especially the part about how he just knew that gun was loaded, and how easily he could have killed someone. What a dope! Marco and I were doing all we could to shut him up. We were standing on either side of him, kicking his shins and trying to talk over him. Sometimes it's best not to tell the whole truth.

Everything worked out all right. The judge placed him on probation and he went home none the worse for wear. Except in the shins.

Later, I decided to go easy on another guy who was charged with armed robbery. When it was over, I wished I hadn't. He did too.

The evidence against this guy was very weak. I really didn't think the jury would convict him. I didn't even want to try the case, but the victim was insistent that I not drop the charges. So I had to go with it.

It was just before Christmas, and this guy, who was in jail awaiting trial, had a big family. So I figured I would push the case to trial, lose it, and let the guy go home for the holidays. I could have chosen any number of cases to try, but I specifically chose this one because I thought it was a loser. We went to trial a few days before Christmas.

The jury found him guilty. I couldn't believe it. I was horrified. Worse, on Christmas Eve the judge sentenced him to state prison as his whole family sat in the courtroom, watching. If I ever wanted to cry after winning a case, that was the time. I still think of that guy and wonder where he is.

Wherever you are, pal, I'm sorry.

As one of the senior prosecutors in the state attorney's office— by the late sixties, that's what I was—I was called upon not only to make public speeches but also to represent Richard Gerstein on radio talk programs. Every time a broadcaster did a show about crime and punishment, I was there, promoting Gerstein's views and supporting his work.

I enjoyed it. I had plenty of experience in radio, so I had no fear of the microphone and I knew my way around a studio. I liked to argue back and forth with the listeners, trying to sway them to my way of thinking. Not all the callers liked me, but I think most respected me. Even on the radio, I always said exactly what I meant, though perhaps not as colorfully as I might have in private. There are some words you just can't say on radio, and, unfortunately, I use them a lot.

One day I received a telephone call from Bill Smith, the vice-president of radio station WKAT, which called itself "The Talk of Miami." WKAT is no longer the dominant station in the market, but in those days it aired the most challenging and consistently interesting programs of any radio station in town. I had appeared on various shows and had met Bill Smith, who had a show of his own. Smith told me he wanted to get together with me for a chat.

"About what?" I said, with a tone of cross-examination in my voice. Lord, I can be a suspicious person.

"About your career in radio," he said.

I met him for lunch the next day. He told me he had been listening to me on various shows, and had decided I would make a good broadcaster. Finally, after buttering me up some more, he offered me a job as Saturday night talk-show host on WKAT. I could talk about anything I wanted, be it the justice system or the war in Vietnam. It didn't matter. He just wanted me on the air, he said. The pay would be twenty-five dollars a show.

I couldn't think of a reason to say no. I certainly enjoyed doing radio. The boys, now both in their teens, didn't need me around on Saturday night. My marriage had deteriorated so badly that I looked favorably on any excuse to get out of the house at night. And my long-lasting romantic ties to Jack Headley were beginning to loosen. Already we were seeing less of each other. So why not try talk radio?

I would have accepted the offer on the spot, but first I had to check with Mr. Gerstein. I wanted the broadcasting job, but I wasn't about to give up a career in the state attorney's office for it. The boss said it was all right with him. He was campaigning for reelection at the time, and he had drawn a difficult and contentious opponent. It could only help to have one of his most loyal assistants receiving public notice.

My show made its debut in 1968. I broadcast only Saturday nights at first, but soon agreed to work from ten P.M. to one A.M. six nights a week. I went by my own name, but I soon found that listeners had trouble pronouncing Morphonios. Lee Vogel, the talk host who was on the air just before me, took care of the problem. I used to sit in the studio and knit while waiting for his show to end and mine to begin. Well, Lee recalled that in one of Shakespeare's plays there is a woman who knits the names of those she is planning to behead. So when Lee would see me, he would tell the audience that Lady Ellen was in the studio, plotting the executions of a few more knaves. Soon the callers began to call me Lady Ellen. It was more manageable than Morphonios, and besides, it suited me.

I got to know the callers well. Many people who listen to daytime talk radio take only a casual interest in it. They're salesmen on the way to the next client, repairmen on the way to the next job. Many of them never call the program, never express an opinion. I got the feeling that my audience, a nighttime audience, was somehow more obsessed with my show. It was a small but fanatical group. My listeners were fringe people—insomniacs, lonely widows, night security guards, old folks, fire fighters, drunks. More than the daytime listeners did, they needed someone to talk to, and I was happy to be the one.

One lonely woman called me almost every week. She told me she was caring for her mother, who was elderly and very frail. One night, this woman called and said, "My mother died."

I said I was sorry and asked her when it happened.

"Just now," she said. "I don't know what to do."

Now, that was a surprise. I went to a commercial and then got back on the phone with her. I told her to call the police and an ambulance, and she did. It was remarkable. Here was a woman so alone that when her mother died, she could think of no one to call but the faceless voice on the radio.

That experience taught me what a great responsibility I had as a broadcaster. Many listeners, I found, would do almost anything I told them to do. Others could get terribly insulted when I meant no harm. So I always went easy on people—much easier than I go on them in the courtroom. I always spoke in even tones, always conducted a reasonable debate, not a fistfight. I don't believe in nasty talk radio. I think some of Miami's best-known talk-radio programs are insulting and degrading. I can't listen to them.

I might have been gentle on the air, but that didn't keep some people from hating my show. My husband was one of those people. My radio program drove Alex crazy. I was broadcasting at a time when blacks were rioting in the streets in many cities. I have never approved of violence, but I expressed support on my show for the blacks' fight for freedom and equality. Alex, no friend of Dr. Martin Luther King, Jr., hated that. I often came home at one-thirty A.M. to find him not only awake but pacing the floor in a fury.

"If you like blacks so much," he said one time, "why don't you go marry one?"

This of course touched off a volcanic argument, which woke Dale and Dean and probably everyone else in the neighborhood. Things got so bad that the boys and I called a family meeting to talk about it. Everyone agreed, for starters, that I was not going to give up my radio show, and that Alex was not going to cease being a bigot. Knowing those things, we suggested that Alex no longer listen to the show. Alex, who really was trying to be reasonable, at least for the moment, promised not to listen anymore. But he immediately broke the promise, and the fights continued.

I was often surprised at who was listening. At the time, the late comedian Jackie Gleason had a home in Dade County. He had been a fixture in South Florida since the days when he broadcast *The Honeymooners* from Miami Beach. One night he called my program just to shoot the breeze. It turned out that he was an insomniac and a conservative, which made him perfect for my show. I was delighted. He stayed on the air with me until the end of the show. He called every six or eight weeks after that. I often asked him to come to the studio so that I could meet him in person, but he always said no, he'd rather lie in his bed with the phone in his ear and a glass of booze in his hand. He was quite a drinker, and a nice guy.

Martha Mitchell, the wife of former U.S. Attorney-General John Mitchell, called me once in 1972. She told me she was vacationing in Florida when she happened to turn on the show. Jack Anderson, the Washington columnist, had just published a story saying that International Telephone & Telegraph had paid the Republican party $400,000 in exchange for favorable settlement of a federal antitrust suit. The story made the Republicans look like slimeballs at best, and thieves at worst. Martha Mitchell told me she thought the whole controversy had been cooked up by Senator Edward M. Kennedy.

"It has a very strong odor of politics about it," she said. She went on for quite some time, never saying anything flattering about the Democrats.

Some people suggested later that the caller wasn't really Martha Mitchell. They thought the call was just a prank. Maybe. But it sure sounded like Martha Mitchell. And the newspapers checked it out and learned that Mitchell had indeed been in Miami at the time.

I thoroughly enjoyed doing my radio show, but in 1970 I decided to give it up for a while. It wasn't because of the long hours or the crazy callers. It was because I had decided to spend my evenings another way.

I was going to run, once more, for judge.

TEN

WINNING THE GREEK VOTE WAS NOT A PROBLEM

If Nathaniel Pressley had not killed so many people, I might never have run for judge.

Pressley, a ruthless criminal, had been a defendant in Judge Everett Dudley's court. He was charged with murder, but his lawyer wanted him set free on the grounds that the police had gathered some of the evidence illegally. Like most people in the state attorney's office, I felt the defense lawyer was wrong. But Dudley didn't. He ruled in favor of the defense and set Pressley free.

Within a month, Pressley went out and killed five people. He wounded seven others and left an eighth paralyzed for life.

I thought Dudley's decision was wrong, and I was damned angry. I now know that I should not have been. Dudley, who happened to be a nice guy, had made the decision based on the law as he saw it. He was trying to do what he felt was the right thing, not the expedient or popular thing, and it had blown up in his face. I have learned since then that it can happen to any judge. I have made decisions to free lots of defendants other people thought were dangerous. I have just been lucky in that none of them has ever walked out of the courthouse and gone on a murder spree. Yes, I thought Dudley was wrong in that decision. But more than that, he was unfortunate.

At the time, though, I was furious. So was my friend and fellow prosecutor Al Sepe. Al had already decided to run for judge against Carling Stedman in the November 1970 election. One day he came into my office and proposed an idea to me.

"I think you should run in Dudley's spot," he said. "You could beat him."

I liked the idea. Normally it is damned hard to defeat an incumbent judge, but I thought Dudley might be vulnerable. Governor

Claude Kirk had appointed him only sixteen months earlier, so he wasn't all that well known to the voters. And he was a Republican in what was then a strongly Democratic state. That alone could cost him a lot of votes.

I knew too that I would be a much stronger candidate in 1970 than I had been in 1960. By then, Richard Gerstein had made me his coordinator for the criminal courts, which meant I floated from courtroom to courtroom offering help to whichever prosecutor needed it. It was a highly responsible position, one I was sure voters would respect. Also, my radio show on WKAT had made me a celebrity in Miami—a very, very minor celebrity, but a celebrity all the same. Most judges get elected not on their qualifications or their positions on the issues but on name recognition. And my name, though hard for some to pronounce, was very well known by then.

One day I stopped into Richard Gerstein's office to talk about a case. On the way out, I stopped in the doorway and said, "Dick, what do you think about the idea of me running against Everett Dudley?"

"I think it's a great idea," he said. "You'd make a fine candidate."

That did it. By the time I had closed the door to his office I had made the decision to run.

In June 1970, Gerstein called a press conference and announced my resignation. (I could not work as a prosecutor while seeking elective office.) It was the last day in what had been a thrilling and, I think, successful career as a prosecutor, and I would be lying if I said I didn't shed a tear. I hated to leave that office, judgeship or no judgeship.

Not long ago, I found my state attorney's commission, the document that officially made me a prosecutor. It was funny: By some oversight, the effective date had never been filled in. Technically, I never really was an assistant state attorney. A lot of people in Florida's state prisons might find that amusing.

So now I was a judicial candidate. Big deal. It was just a fancy way of saying I was out of work.

It was going to be a long campaign, and I had to earn a living somehow. So I went into partnership with Mike Hacker, who was then an up-and-coming defense lawyer in Miami. Mike and I had worked closely together in the state attorney's office in the mid-sixties. Because of my work with the Cub Scouts, he had taken to calling me "Den Mother." (He still calls me Mother when he comes to court, and he doesn't mean it as half a word.) In the late sixties, he had tried repeatedly to get me to leave Gerstein's office and join him in private practice. Now, finally, I had agreed to do it.

It didn't take me long to learn that the private practice of law wasn't for me. As I've said, I didn't like representing people who were guilty of things. And I hated to separate people from their money, especially people who had a relative in trouble and were half-crazy with anxiety as it was. But I must have done a good job, because Mike constantly pressured me to quit the judicial race and become his partner permanently. For years I have accused him, jokingly, of voting for someone else.

In the beginning of the campaign I went to see Don Petit. After many years of marriage, he had gotten divorced from Jean and had married a lovely lady named Marie. Our romance, of course, had ended years earlier, but I still counted on Don for advice whenever I was making important decisions in my life. When it came to politics, I wouldn't have dreamed of doing anything he didn't know about. But when I met with him, I knew that our campaigning days were over, and that his master plan for me had been forgotten. He wished me the best of luck in the campaign, and told me he would do anything he could to help. But I knew by the way he said it that I was on my own. Maybe, I thought, his new wife didn't want him to get involved in my campaign. People paid Don for his political advice—that was how he made his living then—and I wasn't a paying client.

I considered hiring another political insider, but decided against it. Don had taught me everything he knew about politics, and that was a lot. This time, I was going to be my own public-relations person.

I knew just what needed to be done and how to do it. I designed my own bumper stickers, choosing fuchsia and black as the colors because I thought they made an impression. I designed the palm cards, found a printer, and wrote the copy for my TV ads, which were only ten seconds long because it was all I could afford.

Though I quit my radio show during the campaign, I used WKAT's studios to tape all my radio commercials. Don Russo, once a big football star at the University of Miami, let me borrow his white van during the campaign. We painted my name on the side and made sure it hit every corner of Dade County. We even painted a number on the side of the van so people would think we had a fleet of them. It worked.

People couldn't help noticing that a woman was running for judge in the felony courts. Charles Whited, a columnist for the *Miami Herald,* said in one column, "If Ellen Morphonios wins her shot at the Dade criminal court judgeship in November, she'll bring to the bench something we've never really had before: glamour.

"In her years as an assistant state attorney, Mrs. Morphonios not only was the prettiest prosecutor we ever had, she also was one of the toughest. Somehow, I could never get used to the idea of a hard-nosed prosecuting attorney coming on with ribbon bows and frilly dresses.

"For that matter, neither could the men she's sent to Raiford. Mrs. Morphonios has more admirers in the state penitentiary than any prosecutor in the county."

I knew that that writer wasn't the only one who had reservations about someone wearing ribbons with a black robe. So I did my best to make my gender an asset instead of a liability: I printed a picture of Lady Justice in my campaign brochures. "A woman," the brochure said. "The very symbol of justice itself!" Sure, I was stretching things somewhat. But in politics, anything goes.

I had two opponents in the Democratic primary election. One was Norman Haft, the defense lawyer who had shoved me during the Vivian Walsh trial. Boy, it sure was nice to see old Norman again. He was a flashy, backslapping guy, and he had a real funny way with words. When the newspapers asked him about his qualifications, he said he could rule on cases "regardless of outside pressures against black, red, white or any color in God's bouquet." He was also a little reckless. Once, I saw him walk through a restaurant in downtown Miami, pounding people on the back and saying, "More graft with Haft!" It was only a joke, but some people didn't consider it appropriate behavior from a judicial candidate.

Norman Haft almost managed to defeat me before the campaign even began. When I entered the race, I paid a qualifying fee of several hundred dollars. The amount was based on a percentage of a judge's salary, which at the time was about twenty-six thousand dollars. What I didn't know was that state legislators had raised judicial salaries to the grand sum of thirty thousand dollars, which meant that the qualifying fee had also gone up. Most people running for judge didn't know it, either. But Norman knew it. He filed a suit asking to be declared the winner because he was the only one who had paid the proper fee. It was the campaign equivalent of a good, hard shove, but it didn't work. The courts ruled against the flamboyant Mr. Haft, and we all were allowed to stay in the race.

My other opponent was a defense lawyer named Marty Saxon. He was forty years old, overweight, and not nearly as flamboyant as Norman Haft. He was a former police officer, detective, and municipal-court judge. A few months before the election, he hired a research firm to determine his chances of getting elected. I had already announced my candidacy, so Saxon asked the firm to ask the question, "Can a woman be elected judge?" The answer, overwhelmingly, was no. But Saxon asked the wrong question. He should have asked, "Can Ellen Morphonios be elected judge?" If he had asked that question, I think he would have received a different answer. Some people might have had reservations about electing a woman to the bench, but I wasn't just any woman. I was a well-known prosecutor and a radio personality, and a lot of people I had never met felt they knew me personally. If Saxon had realized that, he might not have run against me.

I believed I was much better qualified than either of those candidates, and I was confident that the voters would see that. But I wasn't taking any chances. Not only was I female, but I also had a long, foreign-sounding surname. To win, I assumed I would have to work harder than Saxon and Haft, and I was prepared to do so. So was my family. Daddy was retired by then, so he devoted all his time to the campaign. Lord, he worked hard. He distributed leaflets and bumper stickers all over the county, and he made Dale and Dean do the same. Once, Daddy and the boys put fliers on all the windshields near St. Sofia's, the Greek Orthodox Church. One guy approached Daddy and asked if he was planning to put notices on every car in Dade County. "I'm sure as hell going to try," Daddy said. With a name like Morphonios, winning the Greek vote was not a problem.

Daddy must have lost fifteen pounds during that campaign, and he didn't have fifteen pounds to lose. Shortly before the election, he took me aside, wiped his brow, and said, "When this thing is over with, I'll know I've done everything in my power to get you elected." He couldn't have been enjoying the campaign any more if he had been running for judge himself.

My campaign strategy was the same as it had been ten years earlier—be everywhere. Bruce Neuman, a friend and fellow lawyer who worked with us on the campaign, drove me all over the county. We went to the airport, the garbage dump (a pretty good place for a politician, some people thought), the plumbers' meetings, condominium meetings, you name it. I wasn't supposed to attend Kiwanis and Rotary meetings because they're nonpolitical, but friends got me in anyway. Any good politician knows that every Rotarian is a registered voter.

At the time, Dade County was facing what it considered a serious drug problem. In 1964, the state attorney's office had prosecuted 156 drug cases, and not one person had died of an overdose. Five years later, there had been 2,221 drug cases and 37 deaths by overdose. Those numbers are chicken feed by today's standards. The cops tell me that 90 percent of the arrests they make are drug-related, and dozens of people, including many children, are killed each year in Dade County's crack cocaine wars. Crack has driven the city completely mad. But in 1969, 37 deaths by overdose constituted an epidemic. People thought society was going to hell.

In my campaign, I promised to do what I could to set it right. "The Morphonios Court," my brochures said, "will be a formal court, a fair court, a strict court, a court that will provide speedy trials, a court that will render common sense decisions not blinded by senseless technicality." I also promised to impose "realistic" sentences against people convicted of crimes, which of course meant that I would lock them up and throw away the key. I also said there should be no probation for drug dealers, even first offenders, a position I no longer hold simply because the jails can't contain them all anymore. I did not say anything to discredit my opponents, simply because I didn't want to do them the favor of making their names better known. Besides, I didn't have anything too awful to say about Norman and Marty, and probably wouldn't have said it if I had. Daddy would have killed me.

It was Al Sepe's judicial campaign that was generating all the heat. This was a bitter feud between one of Richard Gerstein's most loyal assistants and a judge who had feuded with Gerstein for years. Sepe cast the first stone by accusing Carling Stedman of holding high-publicity trials just before election time. In one, the judge sentenced a holdup gang's girl decoy to ninety-nine years. In another, he handed a second life sentence to the notorious robber Jack "Murph the Surf" Murphy. To this, Stedman said only that he dispensed justice "regardless of the self-serving demands of the state attorney." When the newspapers wrote their stories, it was always Sepe's campaign that made the headlines, which was all right with me.

Just before the election, the *Herald* and the *News* came out with their endorsements. The *Herald* endorsed me, but the *News* said that it had not made up its mind and would wait until the general election to endorse a candidate. I was satisfied with that. Studies had shown that the *Herald*'s endorsement alone was worth about thirty-nine thousand votes in those days. I sure hoped the studies were right. I also received the endorsement of my old political opponent Dr. Ben Sheppard. I suppose he endorsed me partly because he felt sorry about creaming me in the juvenile court election ten years earlier.

The primary election was held on September 8. I got up early that morning as usual to campaign at the airport. I felt confident, and rightly so. When the early returns came in, I was ahead, and when the later returns came in, I was farther ahead. In the end, I got 54,580 votes, Martin Saxon got 18,502, and Norman Haft received 12,209. There would be no need for a runoff election.

The next day's *Miami News* had one of the most ironic sentences I had ever read in a newspaper. "Mrs. Morphonios," it said, "discounted claims that her sex may have helped her win so big." If anything, I thought, it kept me from winning bigger.

Ah, it was nice to be on the winning side for a change. I had backed a lot of losing campaigns—my own in 1960, Richard Nixon's 1960 presidential bid, Barry Goldwater's 1964 presidential bid. But now I was a winner, and I found that it felt better than I imagined it would. I began to think I was finally going to fulfill Don Petit's dream for me, at least in part. And I was going to do it myself, without Don's help. I would never be the Supreme Court justice that Don wanted me to be, but I would be the felony court judge I thought I should be, the judge I felt Dade County needed.

*   *   *

I knew, though, that I would first have to defeat Everett Dudley in the general election. I had the advantage of being a Democrat in a strongly Democratic county, but he had the edge of being the incumbent, the one with experience on the bench. I could say I was every bit as qualified as he was, but he had the one thing that helps a judge more than any other—experience.

So, like any good politician, I avoided the subject. I stressed the work I had done as a prosecutor, saying I had won more than 85 percent of my cases. I really didn't know the exact percentage, but I thought that was a fair estimate. I also stressed my view that the courts should be harder on people who persistently violate the law. I did not, however, criticize Judge Dudley for his decision to release the killer Nathaniel Pressley. Once, near the end of the campaign, I called a press conference for just that purpose. The night before the press conference, I told one of my friends what I was planning to do.

"That's fine," he said. "Go ahead and do it—if you can live with yourself."

I canceled the press conference the next morning.

I will confess to having pulled one dirty trick during that campaign. Actually, one of my campaign workers did it. This worker was out putting up MORPHONIOS FOR JUDGE signs when he came upon one that said DUDLEY FOR JUDGE. In his partisan zeal, he reached up and ripped it down, then replaced it with my sign. Unfortunately, he got caught—by Judge Everett Dudley, who happened to be in the neighborhood posting signs.

The campaign worker, incidentally, was my dear friend, now a Dade County Judge.

In all, I spent only $20,000 on my campaign, most of it donated $5, $10, or $20 at a time by WKAT listeners and other individuals. Today, in the era of $500,000 campaigns for judge, $20,000 would buy you a couple of newspaper ads, a television spot, and lunch at McDonald's. But in those days, it was enough to buy a pretty good campaign. I never let on that I was only spending $20,000, of course. I let word get out that I had amassed a campaign war chest, that I was going to spend Everett Dudley into retirement. It was a blatant fabrication, I'll admit. That's politics.

Ten days before the election, The *Miami Herald* came out with its endorsement, and thirty-nine thousand votes went down the drain. The paper went for the incumbent. It said that Dudley had shown leadership by working with a drug-education council and called him "a tireless worker for the salvation of the addicted." As for me, the *Herald* said I was "a competent lawyer," which I must say I considered an understatement. "The margin," the *Herald* went on, "is in Judge Dudley's promise of continued usefulness, with the power of the bench behind him, to a sorely besieged community.

"Judge Dudley's candidacy is a singular one, and so it is singularly endorsed," the paper concluded. "We trust the voters Nov. 3 will keep him where he is."

I panicked on the day of the election.

I had used money wisely throughout the campaign, spending small amounts on newspaper ads, radio spots, brochures, bumper stickers, and the like. But on November 3, I went overboard. Maybe it happened because I had lost the *Herald*'s endorsement. Maybe I just had a case of the jitters. Whatever the reason, I did something really dumb, something unnecessary.

I hired a plane to tow a MORPHONIOS FOR JUDGE banner over the beach. It cost three hundred dollars.

What a waste of money. Three hundred dollars was a hell of a lot of money to blow on something that would do me absolutely no good. I wasn't going to win the election by appealing to sunbathers and hot dog vendors. A lot of people laughed at me for doing that, and rightly so. It was the act of a political novice, a woman nervous about her prospects.

My desperation surprised me, because until then I had never been afraid to lose. I knew that if I did not win, I could always get another job as a prosecutor, perhaps with Mr. Gerstein's office or the U.S. Attorney's office. If I had learned anything from my years with Don Petit, it was that in politics, someone always loses. It's part of the business, the way shoplifting losses are part of running a dime store. No good politician should stake his self-esteem on a campaign, for God and registered voters work in mysterious ways. I wanted to be a judge as much as I had ever wanted anything, but I knew it was possible that I would never become one.

I spent that morning greeting workers at the airport, as I had ten years earlier. I watched the first returns that night on television with a friend. That evening, Daddy, Mama, Alex, the boys, the campaign workers, and I went to my campaign headquarters to wait for the late results. I was expecting a long, difficult night, but I didn't get one. When the early returns came in, I had a small lead. When the next ballots were counted, the lead got larger, and it kept getting larger as the night went on. A few hours after the polls closed, Judge Dudley called to congratulate me.

Lydia Ellen James Morphonios was a judge. The final tally: 158,890 votes for me, 81,770 for Dudley.

My picture appeared in the next day's papers next to a picture of Al Sepe, who had also been elected. The *Miami News* quoted Dudley as saying, "I feel I was beaten by a label. How can you fight a label? I knew when I was appointed what the odds were against my being elected as a Republican. I did my best and feel badly for all those who worked so hard on my campaign." In a way, he was right when he said people had labeled him. It was damned hard for a Republican to get elected. But it was just as hard for a woman to get elected, especially a woman with a name like Morphonios. I can't honestly say why people voted for me instead of Dudley, because I don't know. But I think that, party affiliation aside, the best man—er, the best person—won.

The swearing-in ceremony was scheduled for January 5, 1971. I would take the bench the next day. When the day came, I was much more nervous than I had been on Election Day. Everyone I knew and cared about was there—Daddy, Mama, the boys, my niece Carole, even Don Petit. Al Sepe was there to be sworn in with me. Richard Gerstein presided over the ceremony, which was fitting. Al had worked for him for fourteen years and I had worked for him for ten. There was no one we respected more, no one we would have chosen to perform the ceremony instead. The room was full of our friends and relatives, who applauded lustily when the occasion was over.

I appeared to be wearing a judge's robe at my swearing-in. I was not. The county had not been able to order a robe my size before the ceremony. But I did not want to be sworn in without one; the robe is the symbol of the judge's position and authority. So I drove to a church supply store near St. Mary's Catholic Church in Miami and bought a black choir robe. It had large, open sleeves that hung from my elbows instead of cuffs that hugged my wrists, but I'm sure no one noticed that. I wouldn't have cared if they had. I was in choir-girl heaven. If I had had the talent, I would have belted out a song of praise.

"Judge Ellen James Morphonios," it said on my office door at the Metro-Justice Building. The first time I walked through that door I smiled and said to myself, "Well, how the hell do you like that?"

Young Ellen, posing
amid the kindling

A modeling pose from the forties. If I
look uncomfortable, it's probably
because I have fire ants crawling up my
spine.

Don Petit, shown in the mid-sixties, was my Svengali—he created me as a politician. When the picture was taken he was working for a Miami mayoral candidate—behind the scenes, as usual.

Courtesy of *The Miami Herald*

This picture was taken in the 1960s when I was running for juvenile court judge. I am wearing the look of a woman who *knows* she is going to lose.

Courtesy of *The Miami Herald*

Top left, former Florida governor Fuller Warren was my first law partner. He was also a whole lot more.
Courtesy of *The Miami Herald*

Top right, Dade State Attorney Richard E. Gerstein, shown here in 1970, gave me my start in criminal law in 1960. To me, he will always be "The Boss."
Courtesy of *The Miami Herald*

Left, by 1966, I had become the chief assistant to the state attorney. Trust me—there was nobody on the other end of the phone line.
Courtesy of *The Miami Herald*

Above, Judge Jack Turner swears me in as a judge. That's Daddy standing behind me. We couldn't find a judge's robe in my size, so I wore a choir robe.

Courtesy of *The Miami Herald*

A picture taken in 1971, in my first days as judge

Right, me and my pet chimp, Toto, in my days as a talk-radio announcer. Eventually I gave up the job—and, sadly, the chimp.

Courtesy of Jim Annan Photography

Below, Judge Al Sepe performing the ceremony at my marriage to John Rowe, the dog trainer. Anne Cates, my secretary, was maid of honor. You could tell from the looks on our faces that the wedding wasn't such a good idea.   Courtesy of *The Miami Herald*

A family outing at the shooting range. Dean is in shorts, Dale in long pants. You'll notice I'm wearing flat shoes. I wore heels to the range once—and almost bagged an Australian TV cameraman.

Photograph by Acey Harper

My desk would be a lot messier, and my life a lot crazier, if not for my friend and assistant Shirley Lewis. Whenever I need something, Shirley brings it to me, usually before I know I need it.

Photograph by Acey Harper

Dean's daughter, Kimberly, six, assisted me on the bench one day. I think she was a lot more interested in the gavel than she was in the parade of bad men trooping past her.

Photograph by Acey Harper

Back in chambers with Kimberly, who is keeping us cool in the Miami heat. You'll notice the sweepstakes letter lying on my desk. I didn't win.

Photograph by Acey Harper

A recent picture

Courtesy of Marice Cohn Band, *The Miami Herald*

ELEVEN

A ROBOT IN
A SHINY BLACK ROBE

I took the bench on the morning of January 6, 1971, and realized when I got up there that I didn't know what to do first. I had been in dozens of courtrooms and watched dozens of judges, but I had never paid much attention to what the judges said to begin the proceedings. Before me was a roomful of lawyers, court personnel, and defendants, and I hadn't the slightest idea what to say. Nor was there anyone to help me. At that time, the courts didn't provide an administrative judge to help rookie judges on their first day. I was on my own.

I didn't know what else to do, so I said, "All right. Who's first?"

It worked. The prosecutor spoke up. "Judge, the first defendant is Jean Wilks." The charge was prostitution.

"All right, Miss Wilks, step forward," I said.

But no one came forward. I waited a moment, then called again for the defendant to step to the front of the courtroom. Still no one appeared. I tried one last time, but Miss Wilks obviously had not come to court. Maybe she had decided she couldn't take time away from work. Whatever the reason, I issued a warrant for her arrest and went on to the next case.

One defendant, one arrest warrant. Not a good start.

I was elected into a justice system that had gone completely out of control. It doesn't work very well now, to say the least, but it functioned even more poorly then. It was a broken machine, the worst bureaucratic nightmare imaginable. And it got worse before it got better.

When I took the bench, my division had a backlog of 1,700 cases, a number that positively boggled my mind. That meant that, somewhere in Miami, 1,700 crime victims were waiting to find out if justice would be done in their cases. Add to that 1,700 defendants and you've got 3,400 people who deserve a resolution to their troubles. And my problems were small compared to Al Sepe's. His court had a backlog of 3,000 cases. For two judges who had taken the bench on promises of swift justice, the problems seemed insurmountable.

The backlog existed for a couple of reasons. First, Miami had only five criminal court judges, simply not enough for a city of that size. In the previous ten years, the city had changed from a quiet Southern town into an international city with thousands of new residents. Things had changed, but the court system had not kept up with the times. Second, judges were not processing cases quickly enough. If a prosecutor couldn't find his witnesses in a certain case, he didn't have to drop the charges. He simply asked for a continuance so that he could look a while longer, and the judge almost always granted it. The system was slow because judges let the lawyers get away with murder. I know: I was one of the prosecutors who got away with it. As a result, defendants, witnesses, and victims were being forced to wait as long as two or three years for their cases to come to trial. Clearly, something had to give.

It did. Shortly after I took the bench, the Florida Supreme Court introduced what was known as the speedy-trial rule. The court could not tolerate such long delays, so it ordered that each defendant be tried within 180 days of arrest. If the defense filed a speedy-trial demand, the defendant would have to be tried within 60 days. It's simple, the court said. Either try these guys within this period of time or drop the charges and let them go. It didn't matter if the defendant was a burglar or a murderer. If the trial didn't start on time, everybody walked.

There was pandemonium in the Metro-Justice Building. The Supreme Court had told us what to do, but of course it hadn't told us how to do it. That was our problem, and it was a doozy. Suddenly, there was intense pressure on the judges. The taxpayers didn't care about our big backlog of cases. They only knew that if we judges didn't work hard, robbers and rapists and killers were going to be released from the Dade County Jail in bunches. The thought, not surprisingly, caused quite an uproar. I had not created this awful situation, but it was sure as hell up to me to fix it.

First, I seized complete control of my courtroom. When I became a judge, the assistant state attorney in each courtroom generally called the calendar. That is, he or she decided in what order the cases would be heard. I had done it myself when I was a prosecutor. Now I decided to take that job away from the state and do it myself. The prosecutors didn't appreciate it. When they called the calendar, they could simply skip over any cases they weren't ready to try. I had used that tactic many times. Now, with the judge doing it, they had to be ready for anything. Many of my former colleagues in Dick Gerstein's office considered me a backstabber, I'm sure, but I was doing what I thought was best. Today, all judges in Miami call their own calendars, and most of them don't know how the tradition started.

Now that I controlled the calendar, I began to set for trial as many as three hundred cases a week. There was chaos in the Metro-Justice Building. Today, we simply put witnesses on notice and then call them if their cases go to trial. But back then, anyone whose case was set in a given week had to be at the courthouse on Monday morning, just in case. So, at the beginning of each week, my courtroom overflowed with the lawyers, defendants, witnesses, and loved ones involved in three hundred Dade County felonies. It was a weird, teeming mass of humanity: Felons mixed with cops, victims with defendants' wives, defense lawyers with other defense lawyers. My friend Al Sepe was cutting his caseload the same way I was—we had discussed strategy together—which only added to the throngs in the courthouse.

I cleared out a lot of cases by calling the calendar myself. On Monday mornings, the prosecutor would say, "Judge, the state is ready to go on John Jones," or whatever. To which I would always say, "That's fine, but I want you to try"—and then I would pick a name at random from the long list of cases set for trial—"Joe Smith." If the state was ready to try Mr. Smith, I started the trial. If not, I forced the state to try the case anyway. Soon, the prosecutors came to court prepared for almost anything.

It soon became easy to tell which cases the lawyers were ready to try and which they were not. Each time I called a name, the clerk handed me a case file. If neither the state nor the defense had asked for a continuance—a delay—I knew there was a good chance we could try it. But if the prosecutor had asked for a couple of con-tinuances, it generally meant that the state couldn't locate its wit-nesses and was stalling until they turned up. As a former prosecutor,

I was well aware that lost witnesses rarely turn up. The Good Samaritan who promises to testify after witnessing an armed robbery may reconsider after realizing how angry the defendant may be about his testimony.

On the other hand, a couple of defense delays often meant that the defense lawyer thought he was going to lose at trial. The more damning the evidence against a defendant, the less likely he is to want to stand trial. Every good defense lawyer knows this scientifically proven fact: The defendant who doesn't get tried doesn't get convicted.

I gave the lawyers another reason to dislike me: I made their witnesses stand up and face the jury while testifying. My thinking was that witnesses would better be able to describe what they had seen if they could move their bodies and their hands. What's more, it speeded things up. Some lawyers seemed reluctant to keep asking needless questions to witnesses who looked like they were late for a bus. I was reasonable about it: If a witness was elderly or handicapped, for God's sake, I let him sit down. I also let the witness sit if the testimony was expected to take a long time.

But the lawyers still griped. When prosecution witnesses testified, defense lawyers had to leave their seats so that they could make eye contact with the witnesses. They said this kept them from immediately discussing the testimony with their clients. Oh, come on. All they had to do was stroll over to the defense table and whisper into the defendant's ear. It wasn't so far. But I couldn't convince them of that. Early in my tenure, the office of the public defender appealed a client's conviction on the grounds that I had skewed the case against the defense by making the witnesses stand. The appeals court, as it would on many issues for many years to come, ruled against me.

"In the event that the witness should be required to stand for direct examination longer than a few minutes, that person would likely become tired and at a disadvantage by the time he is turned over for cross-examination," the court said.

"Extended questioning of an obviously fatigued witness would engender in the jury otherwise unwarranted sympathy for the witness and antipathy toward counsel conducting the examination. Additionally, the witness may be more circumspect in his answer to shorten his appearance at 'center stage.'"

Did the court's ruling faze me? Not at all, sir, not at all. It was, and still is, my policy to do what I felt was right. If the higher courts wanted to decide I was wrong, that was fine with me. They'd have to live with it. Anyway, the battle over the standing witnesses would not be my last great fight with the appeals courts.

In those first few months on the bench, I worked at a killing pace. My goal was to have no caseload whatsoever—simply to try cases as they were filed by the state. To reach the goal, I was working late every night and often on weekends, and it was beginning to wear on me. Late that year, I told *Miami Herald* columnist Charles Whited, "This is a numbers game. You're dealing with masses of humanity, with no time to devote to individual trials. I feel that I've ceased to exist as a human being. I've become a robot. And that's not the way things ought to be."

I may have been a robot, but at least I was an effective robot. The *Herald*, concerned about the effect the new speedy-trial rule would have on the system, kept track of how many cases each judge handled in those difficult months of 1971. By late September, I had tried 196 cases—an average of five a week—and taken 1,590 guilty pleas. All told, I had cleared 2,682 cases. Only one judge, Al Sepe, had disposed of more.

It was assembly-line justice, but it was better than no justice.

Oh, yes, the media were watching. Six months after I took office, the *Miami Herald* published an article under the headline THIS DADE JUDGE IS A TOUGH COOKIE. I think it will be best if I quote directly from the story.

"The Honorable Ellen J. Morphonios, who a decade ago became Dade County's first female prosecutor, has been its first female Criminal Court judge for six months now.

"And almost from the time she took the bench there have been waves of controversy throughout the legal system over the woman with the ski-tilt nose and slightly slangy way of speaking.

"One of Miami's well known criminal defense attorneys says, 'She is prosecution-oriented and predisposed to burn everybody. Her attitude is really lousy and she is arbitrary as hell. She has no compassion and doesn't temper justice with mercy.'"

You'll notice, astute reader, that the respected criminal defense attorney didn't have the balls to put his name in the article. But of course the critics never do. To answer his complaints, let me say that I deny everything. I was not predisposed to burn people, my attitude was not lousy, and I was as consistent as the sunrise. I had some compassion and I tempered justice with mercy in the rare cases that warranted it.

Was I prosecution-oriented? Guilty as charged, Your Honor, guilty as charged.

It's true. I was prosecution-oriented. I couldn't help it. When I took the bench, I found it hard to suddenly be objective. My mind was saying, "Ellen, you've got to give this nice fellow a fair trial, because he is presumed innocent." But my heart was saying, "The bastard is guilty, and the sooner this jury knows it, the better." I couldn't immediately put aside ten years of training as a prosecutor. A couple of times I tried to help the prosecutor by suggesting what question he might ask next, or by telling him how to introduce a piece of evidence. During one trial, I butted in once too often. "Your Honor," the prosecutor said, "if you don't mind, I'll handle this one myself."

I don't think my leanings to the prosecutorial side affected the outcome of any cases. When I slipped and favored the prosecution, it was always on a relatively small matter—the introduction of a minor piece of evidence, something like that. When it came to the big issues, I always managed to be fair. In nonjury trials, for example, I was often harder on the assistant state attorney than I was on the defense lawyer. If a prosecutor came to court unprepared or presented his case poorly, I often dressed him down for it. And when the state's evidence was weak, I didn't hesitate to throw the case out of court and set the defendant free. I may have been prosecution-oriented, but I also had that huge backlog of cases. If there was a good legal reason to get rid of one, I did it.

Some lawyers say I'm still prosecution-oriented on some issues, and that may be so. Old habits die hard. But they also say, almost unanimously, that Morphonios gives a defendant a fair trial.

In the late sixties, my marriage to Alex finally went to the dogs. Greyhounds.

Alex loved greyhound racing. At first, he was just a bettor. He went to the track near our house and bet on race after race. He never went overboard; he was just enjoying himself. Then a friend gave him a greyhound named Little Gossip. She didn't run anymore, but she could still have pups, and she soon did. Alex was convinced that the money in greyhounds was in raising them, not in betting on them. I didn't think there was any money in them at all, but never mind. We were now in the greyhound business whether I liked it or not.

Now, I loved dogs—we already had one—but this was too much. At one time, Alex had as many as thirty-two greyhounds eating, sleeping, running, and, yes, shitting in the backyard. (Sometimes they did all those things inside the house.) The smell of our home was gaseous, choking. It was like living in a colony of skinny gray yelping rats. Alex, who was then working as a teacher at the local community college, took care of them himself. But the boys and I still had to live with them. We all quickly learned the correct angle at which to place shovel to surface to pick up feces.

When the job became too much for him, Alex rented a kennel in Hialeah and hired a greyhound trainer to help him. Then he moved the dog trainer into our house with us. It was the last mistake he would ever make in our marriage. John Rowe was a tall, tough Southerner with thick hands and long sideburns. He had begun training dogs when he was a kid in St. Petersburg, Florida, and had never been anything but a dog man.

John quickly made friends with my boys. (Dale, Dean, and I thought later that he may have been trying to get to me through them. It certainly would have been an excellent way to get to me.) He listened to Dale and Dean in a way that Alex never did. Alex wouldn't spend ten minutes with his sons if he could help it, but John would stay with them for hours, playing carpet golf, throwing a football, or just horsing around. When they had something on their minds, they felt they could talk to him.

I also found John interesting, which complicated things mightily. For one thing, I was married to the man who gave John his living. For another, I already had a boyfriend—a lawyer I'd met at the Metro-Justice Building. I was not in the market for a second secret boyfriend, but when, one fine day, rugged, good-looking John suggested that he and I meet at a certain Miami motel, I said, "What time?"

It was a hectic time for your local circuit court judge. I never fooled around with John at home, so he always wanted to drop in on me at work. Trouble was, so did my lawyer boyfriend. I can remember times when I had the lawyer in my inner office, John in my outer office, and Alex on the phone, on hold. As quickly and as courteously as I could, I would kiss the lawyer and escort him out the back door, then ask Anne Cates, my secretary, to usher John in. I got to Alex when I could.

Alex had never had a great disposition, but by now he was getting even meaner than even I had ever seen him. (Not that I blame him.) Having long since lost his ability to push me around, he tried to overpower the kids. Nothing they did was good enough for him. He watched every move Dale made, and when he found a mistake, no matter how slight, he called him a stupid ass. Soon, Dale began avoiding him. After school, he went to the home of his girlfriend, Gina Gathings, and stayed there until Alex went to sleep. Weeks went by when Alex didn't lay eyes on his eldest son. With Dale in hiding, Alex naturally laid into Dean.

One night John Rowe came into the living room when Alex wasn't around and said he had to talk to me.

"The boys don't want me to tell you this. They told me not to, but I have to," he said. "They're leaving. They can't take it around here anymore. They're getting their stuff together to go live with their aunt in North Carolina."

I couldn't believe my ears. My boys were leaving? Without me? I immediately went to confront them. I had never seen Dale and Dean so sure of themselves. They said they cared for their father, but they couldn't live with him anymore.

"We want you to go with us," Dale said. "But we're leaving—with you or without you."

It was, I assure you, a damned easy choice to make.

We planned our departure carefully. We did not simply go to Alex and announce that we were leaving. He was by then so emotional, so consumed with the idea of controlling me, that we thought it best just to disappear. Dale's girlfriend, Gina, lived near the south end of town, and Dale wanted to be near her. So he, Dean, and John found us an apartment at a complex called Wellington Manor. John rented it in his name. The kids took money from their small bank accounts and bought everything we would need in our new home—dishes, silverware, glasses, bathroom items, and so on. Each day when Alex was at work we moved some clothes and things from the house to the apartment, always taking care to spread out the clothes in the closet so that it would look as if nothing were missing.

On the last day, February 28, we loaded up the rest of the clothes, Jeff the dog, and Fatso Joe the hamster, and then we left. Alex came home that night to a dusty, ransacked house, with nothing but empty closets to remind him of us. I wanted only the kids, the pets, my clothes, and a few personal things. I left everything else. I figured I had made it by myself once and I could do it again. I asked only that Alex leave me alone.

I did not file for divorce. Nor did I have any plans to do so. I assumed that when the boys grew up and went out on their own I would return to Alex and we would resume our miserable marriage. I really thought that. Remember, being married to Alex was like not being married at all. I still did whatever I wanted with whomever I wanted. But none of my other boyfriends could tempt me with offers of marriage because I was already wearing a little gold ring. "Can't," I'd say when they proposed. "I'm already married." I liked it that way. Being married to Alex had soured me on marriage. Staying married to him was the only thing that kept me from entering an equally unsatisfying union with somebody else.

But in the end, Alex gave me no choice. I had to divorce him. Another man in his situation might have come home, found me gone, and decided that was it, the marriage was over, time to forget about it. Alex did not do that. My departure made him crazily possessive and pathetic. He had no idea where the kids and I lived—we kept it a secret for more than a year—so the courthouse was the only place he was sure to find me. He followed me all over that building, alternately begging, threatening, and haranguing me, until the only thing I could do was insist that it was over and then file for divorce.

He did not take it well, not at all. One day he came to the courthouse and banged his head against the wall outside my office until I consented to talk to him. Another time I talked to him in my office. He got so furious that he began to bang his head against the side of my desk. Well, the desk had a glass top, the sharp edge of which quickly opened a gash in the bridge of his nose. His face was streaming blood when he walked out.

One day things got out of control. Alex came to talk to me in my office, as he often did in those difficult days. Alex's nephew Donnie Wright, who was my bailiff, stayed in the office because he knew of the trouble between Alex and me. Alex and I talked for a while, and everything seemed to be going fine, so Donnie left. There was nothing wrong with leaving me with Uncle Alex, right?

Wrong. After Donnie left, Alex suddenly became unfriendly. He wanted me back, he said, and if he couldn't have me, he would make it so no one could. Pretty soon he was trying to get across the desk so that he could get his hands on me, and he clearly did not wish me the best of health. I slipped out the back door and ran toward Al Sepe's office. Alex was close behind me, hell-bent on killing my ass, or at least maiming it somewhat.

Breathless, I grabbed Sepe's door. It was locked. Damn. I was about to make a run for Judge Jack Turner's office at the end of the hall, but Alex caught me. He grabbed me and pushed me up against the wall as if I were a poster he was hanging. He had me by the throat and was beginning to lay into me when I heard a door open down the hall. Then I heard a voice.

"You all right?" It was Sailor Burke, Judge Turner's bailiff.

"No," I gasped.

Then Sailor, a tough old man with hands like granite, addressed a question to Alex. "Something going on here, mate?" Sailor called everybody "mate."

Alex turned to tell Sailor to mind his own business. I slipped away and ran to Judge Turner's office. There, I was given cigarettes and soothing words while Sailor escorted Alex out.

I was a basket case. It had been, to say the least, a very embarrassing, not to mention dangerous, scene. But it wasn't over yet. I still had to compose myself and get back to my own office. I was a judge, for God's sake. I couldn't go back to my office looking like a sniveling female worn down by a domestic argument. Finally, I got my makeup straightened out and began the walk to my office. When I came around the corner, I found myself faced with three or four TV cameras and a couple of newspaper reporters. They wanted an interview—not about my crumbled marriage, but about some damned case I had handled. What could I do? I took a deep breath and answered all their questions, and I'm sure it looked great that night on the eleven o'clock news. How could they know they were talking to a woman who had just seen the end of her marriage of twenty-one years?

Yes, that was the end of it. The divorce became final shortly thereafter. I have seen Alex only once since then, at Dean's graduation from fire college, and even then we did not speak. Dean still speaks to his father, who no longer lives in Miami, and sometimes visits him. Dale does not. Dale and Alex tried to speak for a while after the divorce, but when the subject turned to me, as it inevitably did, Alex always spoiled things by asking, "How's the bitch?" Dale couldn't take it anymore, and gave up. As for me, I still blame Alex for much of what went wrong in our lives. He was, in far too many ways, an impossible man, and he bears responsibility for that. But I am not bitter, not about anything. It all happened a long time ago. I wish Alex well, wherever he is, and hope he is happier with himself now.

I also acknowledge my own responsibility. I was not, I admit, the Good Housekeeping Wife of the Year. Do I think we would have been happier if I had been eternally faithful to Alex? Do I think our marriage would have worked? No, I do not. He and I had problems quite aside from the other men in my life, and they would have done us in sooner or later. But my behavior didn't help matters any. I am not going to sit here and tell you that it was all Alex's fault, that the things I did had no effect whatsoever on his state of mind, or, for that matter, on mine. I was honest with myself then, and I'll be honest now. Some mistakes were made, some sins committed.

For mine, I will not blame Alex.

TWELVE

THE MONKEY TOOK
MY NEIGHBOR HOSTAGE

Charlie Smith, an old man from central Florida, was the inspiration for some of my longest sentences.

In my first year on the bench, the death penalty was still illegal. The harshest punishment any criminal could receive was life in prison. I didn't agree with it—I was, and am, a strong proponent of the death penalty—but I had to live with it. I was sworn to uphold the law.

I sentenced several people to life in prison during my first year. But I soon realized that life might be a longer sentence for one person than it would be for another. So, to be fair, I decided to assign a number of years to the sentence. That was where Charlie Smith came in.

Smith, who said he was born into slavery in Florida in the mid-1800s, was still alive when I took the bench in 1971. He gave his age as 130, which meant he had lived to see the harnessing of electricity, much of the Industrial Revolution, and the birth of baseball. It also probably meant he never got carded in bars.

Soon after I heard about old Charlie, I made use of his name in court. While sentencing a particularly nasty defendant, I mentioned how long Smith had lived, and then sentenced the guy to the equal number of years in prison. Then I wished him the best of luck in living that long. After that, 130 years became my standard life sentence. I still use it today, and I still explain why, even though Smith has by now gone to the great hereafter.

How did the bad guys take it? In December of my first year, I received a Christmas card from Larry Cole, whom I had sentenced to 130 years for robbing a truck and then shooting a gun at police. The card did not tell me to drop dead. The card did not say,

168

"Have a lousy Christmas, bitch." It did not tell me to go to hell. Said the card: "Best wishes for the upcoming year."

I had been on the bench only six months when I began to consider quitting. It wasn't that I didn't like the job. It was just that I had received another offer.

Before the election, I had made an agreement with the management of WKAT that, win or lose, I would return to my six-nights-a-week talk-radio show. I loved radio and didn't want to give it up just because I had a day job. Nor did I feel that being a judge precluded me from discussing the issues of the day, so long as I didn't discuss any case pending before me. Some people didn't see it that way. Jim Kukar, a columnist for one of the local papers, once wrote, "As I see it, there is still little justification for a supposedly neutral guardian of the judiciary spending her nightly hours saturating the airwaves with right-wing propaganda. It just seems to lessen the sanctity of the bench a little more and further erode the American judicial system. Frankly, she should probably be off the air or off the bench. And since her performance as a talk show moderator could be considered superior to her judicial performance, perhaps she should stick to talking." I certainly respected Mr. Kukar's point of view, no matter how pompous, fatuous, or witless he was in presenting it. But I wasn't about to quit radio just because some liberal columnist didn't see things as I did.

I got to do some exciting things on the air. One night at WKAT, I got a call from a talk-show host named Jim White in St. Louis. White worked for KMOX, the CBS-owned and -operated station in that city. He wanted to know if I would join him in doing a show that would be broadcast to listeners in both cities. It was a simple matter of hooking up telephone transmission lines. He was offering to pay the bill, so I said, "Why not?"

That show went so well, we got together to do several more. Then, shortly after I took the bench, Jim called to say he was going on vacation for a week and wanted me to come to St. Louis to do his show while he was gone. Not only would the station pay to put me up in the Stouffer Hotel, it would also pay the airfares and other expenses of Dale, Gina Gathings, and Dean, whom I wanted to accompany me. On top of that, KMOX was going to give us eleven hundred dollars in spending money for the week. What person in her right mind would say no to an offer like that?

KMOX was, and is, a great radio station. One of the few fifty-thousand-watt clear-channel stations in America, its signal can be heard for miles and miles. On one of my first nights there, I got calls from twenty states, including one from a neighbor in Florida. Because of the sheer number of listeners, I never had to wonder if I would receive calls when I was on the air. And because of the long reach of the signal, I always knew I would hear from a diverse group of people.

My shift started at eight P.M. and ended at three A.M.—seven hours of uninterrupted talk. It was a long time, but it passed quickly. I never lingered on a single subject for long. I would start each show by giving my opinion on something that was happening in the news—say, Vice-President Spiro Agnew's problems with the press (I agreed that he was being mistreated). Then I would jump to, say, social security, and then maybe to snakes, and then to the Miss America pageant, and then back to Spiro Agnew, if anybody had something new to say. For accuracy, I always kept a copy of the Constitution of the United States in my briefcase. A good broadcaster, like a judge, is often called upon to interpret that document.

Before the week was over, Robert Hyland, the regional vice-president of CBS, offered me a job at KMOX. He wanted me to move to St. Louis and take over a regular shift. "You have natural ability," he said. "Whatever you're making as a judge, I'll pay you more."

Now, that was a damned inviting offer. I think the world of Mr. Hyland. He is a brilliant, meticulous man, and I respect him completely. A devout Catholic, he went to mass early every morning and then went to the station before the sun rose. I know because I had a clear view from my hotel room of his car pulling into the garage across the street. He knew everything that happened at his station, and he had the utter devotion of everyone who worked for him. I could not imagine working for a kinder or more decent boss.

Nor did I have anything but good things to say about St. Louis. I particularly admired the love and caring St. Louis residents had for their city. They believed there was no place greater than their hometown, and I liked that. Once when I was there, the city government closed off the streets and the people held a gigantic bicycle rally called the Midnight Ramble. It seemed everyone in St. Louis was there, pedaling around and enjoying the event. The sense of community spirit was powerful and inspiring. Granted, the city had some problems, but that was to be expected.

Dale and Dean were ready to go. They liked Miami, but they also liked the idea of getting a new start in St. Louis. For Dale, getting a new start would be easy: Anne Gathings, Gina's mother, was talking about selling her house, climbing into the car with Gina, and going to St. Louis with the rest of us. Dean wouldn't have it so easy, but he didn't seem to mind. The more I thought about the job, the more I wanted to take it.

But in the end, I couldn't. I just couldn't walk away from the bench after such a short time. The people of Dade County had elected me to sit there and try cases, and that was what I felt obligated to do. How could I spend months wooing the people into voting for me and then, after they did, just walk away? It would be like romancing a handsome man night after night and then, when he finally asked me to dinner, telling him I was busy. My parents didn't raise me to go back on my word, and they didn't raise me to be a tease, either.

I told Mr. Hyland I wanted to finish at least one term on the bench, and then I would take the job. But by 1974, the first time I came up for reelection, I was so accustomed to my job as a judge that there was no leaving it. In later years, Mr. Hyland would often say, "If I could just get you to come to St. Louis for a month, you'd never go back." He may have been right. But I never gave him a chance to find out.

I went back to KMOX a couple of times, just to fill in. One night when I was on the air, the news came over the wire that a school bus full of children had disappeared in California. Soon it was revealed that a couple of guys had hijacked the bus and buried it in a mountainside. This was a major national-news story, the kind that KMOX prided itself on reporting. Shortly after the story broke, Mr. Hyland called and told me to switch exclusively to coverage of the story. The news people and the producers were already lining up interviews with people on the scene. All I had to do was conduct the interviews. I was dumbfounded. "I've never done a news show," I said. "You'll do fine," the general manager said. And then he hung up. The red light went on and I was on the air.

I was at a loss. How the hell do you interview someone for a news story? I had no idea. I also had no alternative but to do it. So I decided simply to cross-examine the people I was interviewing as if they were witnesses in a criminal case. When a source gave me a piece of information, I asked question after question designed to challenge that information. The more questions I asked, the more people filled in the blanks of the story. Soon, people in California began calling the KMOX newsroom to learn the latest details. We knew more about the story than anyone in the country. Man, the adrenaline was flowing. When the show ended at three A.M., I called Dean in Miami and tried to explain the thrill to him. "Yeah, Mom," he said. "G'night, Mom."

Becoming a judge also prevented me from keeping my radio job in Miami. Shortly after I took the bench, I realized it was going to be too tiring to hear cases all day and then work at WKAT for three hours at night. I also got tired of the critics who said it was unethical for me to do the show. I couldn't spit on the sidewalk without somebody complaining about it. Normally, I would have fought it out, but I was too exhausted. In 1972, I quit WKAT for good.

Liberals everywhere celebrated, I'm sure.

Jose Martinez gave himself a much harsher sentence than I ever intended for him.

He appeared in my courtroom late in the summer of my first year on the bench. He was a forty-four-year-old carpenter from Hialeah, a family man with two children. He had never done anything wrong in his life, at least nothing he had been caught at. But a couple of years earlier, he had suddenly gone bad. He had sexually molested the ten-year-old son of a neighbor, a neighbor who had considered him a friend. It was a terrible crime, one that had upset the neighborhood and had destroyed the child emotionally. Martinez had pleaded guilty at an earlier hearing.

Now he was before me for sentencing. His lawyer recommended probation, as I expected he would. The probation officer who conducted the presentence investigation also thought he should receive probation. But I did not think so. Normally, I go easy on a person who has committed a first offense. But this was a crime of violence, a brutal sexual assault on a child. Jose Martinez, I thought, was a danger to the community, a criminal in need of punishment. He was a child molester. I sentenced him to four years in prison. Afterward, the court officers brought the sobbing man to a jail holding cell, where he was to stay until they took him off to prison.

Just after noon, an officer went to the holding cell to bring Martinez a sandwich. But there would be no lunch today. Martinez was dangling from the bars of his cell. He had taken off his shirt, rigged it around his neck, and tied the other end to the bars. His feet were hanging a foot above the floor when he was found. The officer dashed upstairs to get a cell key, then quickly came back and cut Martinez down. When the paramedics arrived, they attached Martinez to a cardiac compressor and tried to get him to breathe. A passing doctor joined in the effort.

Too late. The defendant was dead on arrival.

A newspaper reporter called me that afternoon to ask me about it. She wanted to know how I felt. Well, I felt awful. The man had died needlessly, had left behind a family that would have needed his support when he finished his sentence. The reporter asked if I felt responsible. No, I did not. I had sentenced Martinez to four years, a sentence I considered fair and reasonable under the circumstances.

The carpenter sentenced himself to death.

If she isn't careful, a divorced woman can wind up married. I wasn't careful.

After my divorce, I continued to date John Rowe. He had a lot to recommend him. He was handsome. He had helped me to free myself from Alex. He was good to the kids. And he was always there, always ready to romance me and fulfill my needs. I needed that. I had left my parents' home as a very young woman and had never really taken care of myself. So when John asked me to marry him, I didn't say "Yes" so much as "Why not?"

In November 1971, I returned to St. Louis to do a week of talk radio on KMOX. John and the kids came along. The plan was that John and I would get the marriage license when we arrived, then, a couple of nights later, have an intimate wedding ceremony before a justice of the peace. It was all going to be very quiet, very lovely. Our plans changed when we went to get the marriage license.

The man who issued the licenses signed us up and said, "Do you want to get married right now?" He was about as romantic as a turnpike toll collector. It was as if he had asked us for the correct time.

I wasn't exactly dressed for a wedding. I was wearing purple slacks, a purple blouse, and a purple vest. For John, it would be like marrying a grape. I had planned at least to wear a nice dress and have my hair done before the ceremony. But vanity didn't seem like a good enough reason to say no. So I said, "Oh, what the hell."

The fellow at the marriage-license bureau gave us an address in East St. Louis where he said we could get married immediately. So we all piled into the car—I had driven my Lincoln from Miami—and headed over there. It was a perfectly lovely building, nicely kept, the sort of place any blushing bride would be proud to be married. Except for one thing.

It was a funeral home.

My wedding day was growing stranger and more fun every moment. We went inside and met the funeral director, who, lucky for us, was also a notary public. He conducted the ceremony in a lovely chapel that, on less festive occasions, housed the grieving relatives of the dead. Fortunately, the funeral director read from the correct service. He did not say, "Ashes to ashes, dust to dust." (Though, as we will see, he might as well have.)

During the ceremony, Dale asked John, "Are you going to put a cigar band on her finger?" John, who had of course bought a ring for me, apparently wasn't in a joking mood. When the funeral director pronounced us man and corpse, John gave me a peck on the lips and said, "All right, let's go." The wedding of Charles and Diana it wasn't.

The honeymoon lasted a couple of days, tops. The next day, the kids took the bus to Nashville to meet a girlfriend. John and I spent a couple of pleasant evenings in St. Louis, then drove to Tennessee to meet the boys. On the way, John developed a toothache. Not just a normal, annoying toothache, either. This, judging by John's behavior, was a monstrous, agonizing, practically life-threatening toothache. Suddenly, he was not the nice guy I had married forty-eight hours earlier, but a snarling, complaining, angry person who behaved as if I were the decay that had caused the inflamed nerve ending in his tooth. In Nashville, he was bedridden with the toothache and I was beginning to think, I have made a very large mistake.

Coming into Atlanta the next day, I missed the turnoff for our hotel. We were wandering around in circles while, in the backseat, pained John was beginning to bitch. At last, I pulled into a service station to get directions. John shoved the seat forward violently, jerked the door open, and said, "Goddammit, I'll find out where we are and see what the fuck is going on." Then he slammed the door behind him, leaving me and the boys sitting in the quiet aftermath of his outburst.

Dale filled the silence. "I've got to hand it to you, Mom," he said. "You sure know how to pick 'em."

We had a family conference right there on the side of the high-way. Dale wanted to peel out of there and let John find his own way home. Dean was on the fence: He could live with it if I drove away, but he wasn't sure it was a good idea. I decided to give John another chance. A minute later, he came back to the car with the directions. At the Holiday Inn, John and his tooth went to bed while the boys and I discussed what a dope I was. I drove us back to Miami the next day, doing 110 miles an hour most of the way. That was a good Lincoln.

Back at home, John, who tended to overreact to problems, took care of that toothache, but good. He had all his teeth removed.

When you're a judge, you expect people to criticize you. People demand a lot from judges. They expect them to be saintly, infallible, above reproach, all of which, in my opinion, is too much to expect. But I know they expect it, and I understand that when they're disap-pointed, they say so. I can accept that. But I can't accept the kind of criticism I got from a man named Jack Orr. He was a crybaby.

He was also a prosecutor. Early in my tenure, Assistant State Attorney Jack Orr handled a corruption case against a Miami Beach constable and a credit-card investigator. The state said that these two men accepted one thousand dollars to fix a case involving a stolen credit card. The men were charged with compounding a felony, conspiracy, and grand larceny. It was a weak case—the state had precious little evidence—but Orr, aware that the media were watching, was intent on winning it. He was determined to put this constable in jail.

Orr presented the state's case as best he could. When he was done, I dismissed the charges of conspiracy and compounding a felony. I simply didn't hear anything in the evidence to support the charges, and I wasn't going to send the jury to deliberate on baseless charges. But I left the grand-larceny charge intact because I thought a reasonable jury might convict the constable and the investigator of that crime.

This reasonable jury did not do that. It found both men not guilty. The two defendants walked out of that courtroom free men. Orr simply had lost his case.

But he was still determined to get a public official: me. Shortly after the trial, he sent a letter to Governor Reubin Askew saying that I had deliberately sabotaged the state's case. He said that I "patently" showed friendliness to the defendants by calling them by their first names in front of the jury. He said my rulings during the trial were biased against the state and "made a mockery of any concept of a fair trial." He even said I winked at the constable when the jury came in with the verdict. When he sent the letter to the governor, he made sure to call the newspapers so that they would have the story too.

What an unprofessional thing to do. I knew the constable well enough to shake his hand at social functions, but he was not a friend. I called him and the investigator by their first names because, hell, I call everyone in court by his first name, and always have. I called Jack Orr by his first name too. It was simply not true that my rulings had favored the defense. In fact, the defense lawyers felt so strongly that I was ruling for the state, they filed papers with the appeals court to have me removed from the case. (It didn't work.)

Did I wink? Yes, I did. But not at the constable. I winked at my friend Harvey Shenberg, now a judge himself, who happened to be walking into the courtroom when the verdict came in. I would not wink at any defendant during a trial.

Orr's charges were absurd and ironic—the usual complaint against me was that I was heavily biased toward the state, not against it—but more than that, they were stupid and offensive. He was angry because he had lost a big case, and he had taken it out on me. It was unforgivable. He should have known better than to jeopardize my reputation that way. He would get a chance to try more cases, but I had only one professional reputation, and I didn't care to have it trampled.

Normally, I am not a vindictive person, but I did not forget that insult. Years later, when Jack Orr died, my old boss Richard Gerstein took up a collection to buy a memorial for him. I was surprised at first that Gerstein would ask me to contribute, considering our bad history. I decided to contribute anyway. I wrote a check for fifty dollars.

And then I made a copy of Orr's insulting letter to the governor and attached it to the check, just so everyone would know I had not forgotten.

I learned early on as a judge that any decision I made—even one that seemed routine and harmless—could be a life-or-death decision. Each time I decided to give someone a second chance, I risked the possibility that the person would go out and do something far more hideous and destructive than what he had done in the first place. As a politician, I knew that that sort of misjudgment could destroy me. The press would certainly find out about it, and the terrible headline would read, MAN, FREED BY JUDGE, KILLS THREE CHILDREN IN SCHOOL YARD RAMPAGE. More important, as a human being I knew that an innocent person could be hurt as the indirect result of a decision I made. I tried always to act wisely—to avoid making the kind of mistake that could get someone killed.

In one awful case, I had no choice but to free a dangerous man. And when I did, my worst fears were realized.

It was a case of child abuse. The defendant, a man, had severely beaten his girlfriend's very young child. Someone had called the police and the man had ended up in my courtroom. Now, child-abuse cases are ordinarily very difficult to prove. In many cases, the only witness is a terrified and traumatized child who may be too frightened to give reliable testimony. In this case, the child might have been strong enough to testify, but the mother would not allow it. As often happens, she didn't want to jeopardize her relationship with this monster who had hurt the child. So the chances were good that an abuser was going to go free for lack of evidence.

The prosecutor, unable to bring a decent case, decided to swing a deal. He said he would recommend a term of probation if the defendant would agree to plead guilty to a reduced charge. The guy took the deal. And I reluctantly imposed the sentence the state recommended: probation. If I rejected the plea, the state would have to drop the charges altogether. This way, at least the authorities would keep an eye on him. "I hope this is the last I hear of you, sir," I told the guy.

It wasn't. Lord, it wasn't.

In those days, my mother and father lived on a pretty street in northwest Miami. It was a modest neighborhood, nothing fancy, but people got along very well. There was a store on a corner not far from Daddy's house. Evenings, people in the neighborhood used to walk there to pick up the two or three things they needed to put dinner together. On the way, they would stop in front of other people's houses to chat.

Daddy liked to sit on a lawn chair in front of the house and see who passed. When I visited, I sat with him and he introduced me to the neighbors. One I particularly liked was Mrs. Williams, who lived down the street. She was a kindly, gentle woman who always asked me about my work and about how the boys were doing. In turn, I asked her about her daughter and her grandchild, both of whom lived in the house with her. Our talks were always brief and always superficial, but pleasant.

One day, Daddy told me that Mrs. Williams had given him some terrible news. Her daughter had taken the child and moved in with her boyfriend. And the boyfriend, an angry, frightful man whom Mrs. Williams feared and disliked, had, in a fit of rage, beaten the child to death.

The boyfriend, of course, was the man I had set loose.

I had made a decision and a child had been killed. No, I was not responsible. Under the law, I could not have done any more than I did. If the state had gathered enough evidence to convict this man of a serious crime, I gladly would have sent him to a place where he wouldn't have bothered anyone for a long time. So no, it was not my fault. But I felt responsible anyway. I blamed myself. And I thought of poor Judge Everett Dudley, my opponent in the judicial race, whom I had faulted because he had freed a man who then committed terrible crimes. It was a hard lesson, but I learned it well: A judge can never know what effect a decision, no matter how routine, may have. I am paid to make those decisions, paid to accept the consequences. But how I cried for that child.

Later, Mrs. Williams saw Daddy in front of his house. She knew I was the judge who had freed the man who had killed her grandchild. Was she angry? Did she curse my name? She did not.

"She was doing her job," Mrs. Williams told Daddy. "No hard feelings."

About the time I married John, my boys were growing more and more interested in girls. They already had a convertible sports car— an MG Midget. But that apparently wasn't flashy enough to attract young women in the numbers they wanted. To catch exotic women, it seemed, you needed exotic bait.

So they decided they wanted a lion.

I do not know where boys get their ideas. Maybe Dale and Dean saw a lion on an episode of *Wild Kingdom* and agreed it would be just the thing to attract females. In any case, they presented the idea to me completely seriously, as if they were expecting my full approval.

They didn't get it. I love cats, but there are limits. To begin with, I didn't think our dogs would appreciate meeting a 250-pound housecat with claws like razors and a roar like a steam engine. An experience like that could give a dog serious psychological problems. Besides, we were still living in a rented apartment in the Wellington Manor development. The lease didn't exactly say we couldn't keep a lion in the apartment, but I think the landlord would have frowned on it. Would you let Elsa the lion use your floorboards as a scratching post? I wouldn't. Nor did I want a pet who could eat me for dinner. Was I going to let Dale and Dean get a lion? No way. But I'm a reasonable woman, so I suggested an alternative.

That's how we ended up living with a monkey.

His name was Toto and we just adored him. A chimpanzee, he was nine months old when we bought him from an animal importer in Miami. He was a wonderful pet, loving and unpredictable. Especially unpredictable. At night, he would lie in bed with John and me and watch television. During commercials, he often ran into the kitchen to grab a monkey biscuit. He was always back by the time the show started again.

Toto also liked to jump up and down a lot, which was distressing to the law student who lived one floor below us and was trying to study. Soon the little apartment began to feel cramped, so we bought the home where I still live today. (Toto was the first pet for whom I bought real estate.) The house is in a suburban section of Miami— perfect for a homebody judge, a dog trainer, a couple of active boys, and a chimp.

Toto lived with us not as a pet but almost as a member of the family. He was smart, but not smart enough to use the toilet, so he wore a diaper around the house. At first, this was sort of amusing. It became less amusing when we began to understand that, in Toto, we were raising a baby who would never grow up. As long as Toto lived with us, the Pampers people would never go broke.

The monkey got along fairly well with all of us, but he was

especially fond of John. My second husband may have been at his cutest when spending time with the monkey. Each morning, John would get up, shuffle into the kitchen, and sit in his favorite chair. Then he would open the sports section of the newspaper, pour himself a cup of coffee, and light a cigarette. He would add cream and sugar to his coffee and stir it so vigorously that it would always spill on the table. Dean, who is very neat and tidy, couldn't stand this.

Dean might not have minded so much if the monkey had not done it too. Toto always got up in the morning when John did. Then he would follow him into the kitchen, where John would pour him a cup of coffee and give him a section of the paper. Toto would stir in his cream and sugar, spilling coffee everywhere, then, while seeming to read the paper, drink from the cup just as John did. He would also take a cigarette from the pack and put it between his lips, but John wouldn't light it. I emerged from the bedroom every morning to find my husband and my monkey having breakfast. Sometimes I wasn't sure who was imitating whom.

Toto became so attached to John that sometimes the monkey wouldn't come when I called. He was a jealous little guy, and he didn't like it when I spent time with his best friend. Toto treated other people the same way. He loved Dean, but didn't like Dean's first wife, Karen. He didn't like Dale worth a damn, which was funny because getting an exotic pet was Dale's brainstorm to begin with. I never knew when the chimp would suddenly become jealous of me. One night, John and I were lying in bed when John leaned over and gave me a kiss. The kiss might have led to further adventures if Toto had not sprung onto the bed and, in a fit of jealousy, bit me on the nose. There was no permanent injury. It was one of the few times Toto showed any real dislike for me. And at that particular moment, I could have done without that bite—and the red nose it caused.

Not all our odd experiences with Toto were so intimate and private. It's hard to keep a monkey secret. For one thing, when Toto got upset he screamed so loudly that you could hear it not only in the neighborhood but probably in Key West and Havana too. Anything might spook him. If he was approached by someone he didn't know or made to do something he didn't like, he screamed like a dozen dainty women in a roomful of mice. This was a jungle scream, the terrified howl of a little savage. We didn't find his screaming so unusual—not much more unusual than having a monkey, that is.

Toto ate fruit mostly. He liked bananas, peaches, and especially canned pineapple. Going to the supermarket was always fun in those days. We had two dogs then—Lady Bug and Fluffy White Fang. When I went to the store, I always bought a large bag of dog food, several bunches of bananas, a dozen or so peaches, and enough canned pineapple to raise the stock price of Dole. Having filled one shopping cart with food for the animals, I could then begin to load another with human chow. The girls at the checkout counter used to do all they could to stifle their curiosity. But usually they couldn't help asking what I was doing with a case of pineapple a week.

Nights, Toto stayed in a large cage we built for him in the garage. The cage, constructed to zoo specifications, was nearly as large as the garage itself, so he was comfortable. Which is not to say he liked it. Like any of us, Toto enjoyed his freedom. He hated to be locked up while everyone else was out having fun. As soon as you closed the door, he began to cook up new and interesting ways to get out. He was quite good at it. At first we had a simple latch on the cage, but it took Toto only a couple of hours to figure out how to lift it. Soon he was back in the house, wandering around. After that, we put a somewhat more complicated spring latch on the door, but he figured that out too. We progressed to a padlock, but the little guy managed to get the key and let himself out. It often made me wonder who was really the monkey.

Toto's ingenuity made his hairy face well known in the neighborhood. People couldn't help noticing him when he went for one of his unsupervised strolls in the neighborhood. Fortunately, everyone seemed to think he was pretty cute. And if people got concerned that he had been away from home too long, they would call and tell us to come and get our monkey. There was never any confusion about whom to call. It wasn't as if the rest of the families in the neighborhood had monkeys.

Toto had a rather embarrassing habit of taking a piece of cloth—a rag, an old shirt, whatever he could find—and holding it over his private parts. I don't know why he did it, and don't really care to know. The name we gave to this piece of cloth was, appropriately, I think, the dick rag. One of the things he used as a dick rag was an old sweater. Nobody was wearing it anymore, so we gave it to him to use as he wished.

One afternoon when I was out of town, Toto got loose. Dean

stopped by the house about six P.M. that day to find a neighbor waiting for him.

"I saw your monkey around here somewhere," the neighbor said. "You're not going to believe what he's doing."

Just then, Toto came around the corner. Instead of holding the sweater over his private parts, he was wearing it tied around his shoulders, the way people do. But that wasn't the best part. Behind him as he walked down the sidewalk were the dogs, Lady Bug and Fluffy White Fang. After escaping from his cage, Toto had gone into the house and decided to take the dogs for a walk. The neighbors nearly died laughing. If Toto had bothered to get leashes, they would have. Dean said he looked like a hairy old lady wearing that sweater and walking those dogs.

He was great for imitating people. One day, Toto got loose when the mailman happened to be coming through the neighborhood. I was at work, hearing cases. The mailman was not alarmed. Toto had escaped and introduced himself to the fellow before. But this time Toto didn't just say hello to the postman. He joined him on the job.

The mailman had stopped his truck near our house when, uninvited, Toto jumped in. When the fellow went to the back of the Jeep to sort some letters, Toto followed him. The monkey picked up a stack of letters and began to shuffle them around, just as the mailman was doing. The guy thought it was cute, so he took Toto along with him for a few minutes. Soon, though, the fellow decided it was best to send Toto home. At the time, the postal union was in some intense labor negotiations with the government. The postman told me later that he was afraid people would see Toto and say, "Hell, any monkey could do that job."

But when he asked Toto to leave, the chimp wouldn't budge. He enjoyed working for the U.S. Postal Service, and he wasn't going to be kicked off the job by someone only a notch or two higher on the evolutionary chart. So he sat in the back of the Jeep, sorting mail and baring his teeth. Fortunately, this was a resourceful postman. Neither rain nor sleet nor hail nor stubbornness of monkey could keep him from delivering all those bills. He called me at work and told me to come and get my damned monkey.

It was not the last time I would get a monkey-related distress call. Living across the street from me was a nice lady. She was, and still is, a terrific neighbor. For some reason, Toto just adored that lady. Whenever he saw her standing in her driveway or walking in the neighborhood, he just had to run over to her and say hello. Maybe it was a perfume she wore, or maybe, like everyone else, Toto could sense that she was a good person. I don't know. Who can really know the motivations of a monkey?

One afternoon when I was at work, Toto once again got out of his cage and out of the house. About that time, our nice neighbor was walking to her car to go shopping. When Toto saw her, he raced across the street on all fours—he walked upright, but didn't run that way—and jumped into her arms. It didn't bother her at all. She knew Toto wasn't trying to hurt her. So she gave him a big hug and then told him, "All right, honey, you'll have to get down now. Say bye-bye."

But he didn't let go.

She tried and tried, but Toto would not loosen his grip on this poor woman. She tried to pry him off, shake him off, and talk him off, but that monkey was stuck to her like sap on a tree. From a distance, it must have looked like she was carrying a very homely baby, or perhaps as if she had developed a terrible, hairy growth. Finally, in desperation, she called my office.

I was on the bench when Anne Cates, my close friend and secretary, came into the courtroom to speak to me. She had taken the call from my neighbor. Her eyes were red and watery, and when she tried to speak she could only gasp. She was laughing so fitfully I was afraid she might hyperventilate and keel over right next to the bench. She tried several times to speak, but had to give up each time because of the laughter. I was laughing too, but I didn't know why. Finally Anne choked out a sentence.

"The monkey," she said, "took your neighbor hostage."

That unusual sentence, I would like you to know, is forever noted in the records of the Dade County, Florida, courts.

Laughing even harder now, I staggered off the bench and called Dean on the phone. I explained the situation to him, and he said he would see what he could do for our neighbor. When he got there, Toto was still clinging to her. She was doing her best to look unperturbed, as if our dog had merely tipped over her garbage cans. Dean, who had quite a good friendship with the chimp, called him, and he finally let loose. Our neighbor was not hurt, but her clothing was. Her beautiful yellow linen dress was covered with monkey prints.

It was not as if our neighbor could simply have lifted Toto off her torso. As he got older, our pet grew increasingly big and strong, until it got to the point where he was not only stronger than I was but also a lot stronger than either of my strapping sons. His great advantage in strength became a real problem for me one particular Saturday morning.

I was alone in the house that weekend. Everyone else was out of town doing business or visiting people. When I woke up that day, I put on my light nightgown and stumbled into the garage to hose down Toto's cage. He did not wear a diaper at night, so this was an important job. I opened the lock as always, then stepped inside, grabbed the hose, and went to work. When I finished, I tossed the hose aside and started toward the door of the cage.

When I got there, Toto was in the way.

"Look out, Toto," I said, "Mommy has to go into the house."

Toto didn't move. He just stood there, grinning his monkey grin. I took a step forward and Toto screamed. I knew right then that he meant to keep me in that cage as his playmate. If I tried to get past him, he might push me to the floor, or maybe even attack. There was no question that he didn't want me to leave.

The situation called for calm. I needed to think analytically, to figure out exactly what to do to divert Toto's attention to something besides me. It should be easy, I told myself as the hairy critter guarded the door. He may be stronger. But you're smarter. I looked around the cage and noticed that, for whatever reason, Toto didn't have a dick rag. He must have tossed it aside someplace and forgotten to take it back to the cage with him. That's it, I told myself. Give the monkey a dick rag and you'll be free. I had no choice. I would have to take off my nightgown, toss it into the corner, and slip out of the cage before he got back to the door.

I slipped out of the nightie and tossed it with all my might. The monkey was not only stronger than I was. He was faster. By the time I had taken my first step to the door, he was back—holding my nightgown.

I was now stark naked in the cage with a monkey.

I am not normally a betting woman, but I would be willing to wager that few if any other circuit court judges spent that morning naked with a chimpanzee. While wearing the nightgown, I had been uncomfortable with my predicament. Now that I didn't have it, I was downright rattled. Not that Toto ever would have done anything unseemly. He just stood by the door, using my favorite nightie as a dick rag and laughing at me in his own monkey manner. I was in for the long haul now. So I sat down in a corner of the cage and waited.

An hour went by. Toto kept watching me. Two hours passed. Nothing changed. The third hour was the same.

Sometime into the fourth hour, Toto got bored with me. He wandered over to the far corner of the cage and sat down. He hardly moved when I sprang up, unlatched the door, and made my way to freedom. When I got over the embarrassment, I told all my friends what had happened. If it had happened to anyone else, they might not have believed it.

It was a funny story, but after that I knew I could no longer live with Toto. He was just too strong. By 1974, the boys were busy with other things and my marriage to John was over. There was nobody to tend to Toto but me, and I couldn't handle him. So the boys and I decided to find him a new home before I got hurt. After visiting several zoos around Florida, Dean decided the best place for him would be the Central Florida Zoo in Sanford. The staff was young and dedicated and eager to have as fine an animal as Toto. So, in June 1974, we chartered a plane and flew our pet to his new home. It was a heartbreaking day, as you can imagine.

I hear from the zoo people from time to time. They tell me that Toto is doing well, and that he seems to enjoy his new home. Dean has visited him a few times, but I myself have done so only once. To go more often would only make me sadder about his loss. The one time I was there, I stood outside his cage and talked to him. I couldn't tell if he remembered me. He just kept swinging around his cage, full of life and fun.

"Hi, Toto," I kept yelling to him. "How are you, Toto?"

A little girl and her mother were standing next to me. "How do you know the monkey's name?" the child said.

"Because I'm his mommy," I told her.

The girl looked confused. Her mother looked alarmed.

"Come on, honey," her mother said, grabbing the child's hand and looking at me as if I were some kind of weirdo. "We have to go."

COURT IN RECESS
Letters from the Public
(Part Two)

Maria Hernandez was twenty-six years old and in love. One night, she had a quarrel with her boyfriend, Luis Duenas. He slapped her across the face, but hard. She looked at him, surprised and hurt, and told him never to do it again. In an article in the *Miami Herald*, writer Edna Buchanan reported what happened next.

"'What are you going to do, kill me?' Duenas asked, and he handed her a gun. 'Here, kill me,' he challenged.

"She did."

Yes, she certainly did. Dropped him with a single shot. The case ended up in my courtroom. Hernandez looked more like a child than a woman. She was scared out of her mind, still astonished at what she had done. She came before me to plead guilty to a charge of manslaughter.

Everybody had an opinion about what the sentence should be. The dead man's family wanted her locked up for fifteen years. The parole and probation people thought seven years was about right. At the most, I could have given her thirty years. That's probably what she was expecting. I am Maximum Morphonios, after all.

In most cases, it's easy to know the right thing to do. People who kill other people usually need to go to prison for a long time. But this wasn't one of those cases. I sat there looking at Maria Hernandez for a full minute without saying a word. Nobody in the courtroom uttered a sound, not so much as a cough or a breath.

Then I sentenced her to fifteen years—of probation.

Yes, she had killed him. But Duenas, a nasty man, had pushed her to it. Court testimony proved he was often rough with her, just as he was the day he slapped her and dared her to kill him. He was a bad guy, and she was a frightened young girl.

Edna Buchanan quoted me in the next day's paper.

186

"It was just a terrible tragedy and there was nothing to be accomplished by sending that little girl to prison. It was just an awful,
awful, awful tragedy. I understand how extremely upset the family
of the victim is. If it was my son, I would want blood. I had really
been thinking about this case and worrying about what I would do.
She is not a criminal. I'm convinced she'll never commit another
crime."

Oh, the letters I got. Two stood out. One came from the ex-
wife of Luis Duenas, and boy, was she angry. It seems Duenas had
supported her even after their divorce. Now that he was dead, she
had no way to provide for her two-year-old son. Maria Hernandez
had taken away her livelihood, and, in her opinion, I hadn't done
anything about it. To emphasize her point, she sent me a picture of
her baby boy. I wrote this letter back to her.

Dear L.:

Thank you so much for your kind letter regarding your
deceased husband.

I can certainly understand that you are upset over the
sentence I imposed on the person that killed your husband.
There is no easy answer when it comes to sentencing. I
imposed the sentence which I believed to be the proper
one. If I were in your position, I am quite sure I would not
understand that sentence any more than you do.

You have a beautiful son. I am returning the picture to
you as it is too precious to wind up in a court file.

I wish for you all the best.

Very truly yours,
Ellen J. Morphonios

The other memorable letter I got about that case came on white
lined paper, and was written in lovely script.

Dear Judge Morphonios:

You must be the stupidest human being in the world.
That girl took a gun and committed murder and you say
you know she wouldn't do it again. Only an idiot would be

guilty of making such a statement. And to make the basis of your opinion on such flimsy evidence shows what a stupid judge you are. No wonder everyone has no respect for criminal justice.

Only the criminals are treated well. The poor, dead victims and their families are slapped in the face by stupid judges like you, who slap the wrists of murderers.

I hope you can sleep at night, judge. We taxpayers don't sleep so well knowing we could be killed on a whim and you would do practically nothing to the criminal.

That girl got away with murder. Hopefully you will be her next victim. Surely that would be justice.

> Signed,
> A very worried taxpayer

Crackpots never have the balls to sign their letters.

I like cops. I think they do a fine job under tough circumstances, and I appreciate it.

Some of them appreciate me too. Few things make a police officer happier than seeing some creep he has busted go to prison. I often hear from police officers who have ushered a defendant into my courtroom. Sometimes they are happy with my decisions, sometimes not.

Here is a letter from one who was.

Dear Judge Morphonios:

Recently a case was tried in your court with defendants Maria Valdez and Arsenio Leal being charged with several narcotics violations.

Sgt. Scott Forsyth, who is in charge of our Crime Suppression Team, and who headed the investigation which led to the defendants' arrest, has advised me that you saw fit to place the defendants in prison for two-and-a-half and three years respectively.

As the chief of police of Miami Beach and in representing the citizens of this community, I would like to personally thank you for taking this very appropriate action.

Although the actual amounts of contraband being distributed were never of great proportion, these individuals were helping to create a blight in the community.

It is through hard-working and conscientious judges such as yourself that efforts to rid this community of its problems become successful.

Sincerely,
Ken Glassman

The fellow who wrote the following letter also liked me. I am not going to publish his letter in exactly the form he wrote it. This book could get into the hands of children.

Hello, Dear:

Dear, rise up, lift your skirt. I wish to see your thighs. I wish to have you in bed, on your [BLANK], I am on top of you. I wish to [BLANK] my [BLANK] into your [BLANK]. Oh dear, I wish to [BLANK] with [BLANK] the whole night. To [BLANK] you, to [BLANK] you, and to have you the whole night. I need your [BLANK], dear. I think of you, your legs, your tummy, the whole night.

He didn't sign it. He drew a picture instead. I can't reprint it.

For the victims of violent crime, the pain never goes away. It may lessen with time—the initial shock may fade and the wounds may heal—but the memory of being victimized never completely vanishes. I am reminded of this every time I meet a victim in my courtroom. I can tell by the hardness in their eyes and the quivering in their voices that they have been through something the rest of us could never begin to understand.

In 1983, the newspapers published an article about a man I had sentenced for rape in the mid-seventies. He had been released early from prison, and now he was wanted in a killing in another state. He was also wanted for more crimes in Miami. After the story hit the paper, I got the following letter. It reminded me of the pain victims feel.

Dear Judge Morphonios:

Enclosed is a copy of an article that appeared in the Miami Herald.

I hope you remember this waste of human flesh. About eight years ago he was arrested for rape. The victim was an 11-year-old girl, my best friend.

I will never forget the hell he put her through. Did you know that for the longest time she refused to leave her house? I used to take her school work to her house every night. I made excuses to other schoolmates. She was humiliated and hurt. We have lost touch over the years, but she finally got back to her friendly, sweet self.

When this jerk pleaded guilty and we were told that he'd be put away, I was glad to hear it. I was able to breathe easier knowing that the judicial system really works.

Well, what the hell happened?! Why was this guy released from prison? If he is extradited to Miami, will he again get a slap on the wrist?

He is obviously not fit for society.

My faith in our judicial system is slowly diminishing. I respect you as a judge. I did eight years ago and I still do today.

But it scares me to know that this guy and garbage just like him can walk the streets of the country. I fear for myself, I fear for the children that have to grow up in this world. I am from a small town up north and maybe what we need is some backwoods law and order. Or maybe our judges and attorneys should take a long hard look at the system and improve it. At least let the people of the country feel safe again and give them a judicial system they can have faith in.

Otherwise, we all might as well just stay in our homes and not come out.

Why should the police officers across this nation do their jobs, making the arrests, if the people in the justice system are not going to do theirs?

Sincerely,
Jane Doe

She didn't give her real name for fear the bad guy would come and find her or her friend.

What could I say to her? She was absolutely right. My mother used to have a saying that she used when she was thinking about someone she particularly disliked: "I hope he gets the dribblin' shits and lives to be a hundred." (My mother was not dainty.) That was how I felt about this guy. I wrote a letter back to Jane Doe saying I understood her frustration. I also pointed out that I had no say in what the parole commission did with prisoners. I'm sure that did not satisfy her. Hell, it didn't satisfy me. I had done everything possible to put that guy away. And now all I could do was throw up my hands.

The young woman was scared to testify. She had been in her real estate office one night when a man had come in and tried to rape her. Eventually she would take the stand and tell how she had somehow found a gun and managed to shoot him—in the groin.

This was the woman to whom I said, "Nice shot."

But before the trial, she was afraid to take the stand. Most people are. So I soothed her the best I could, speaking to her in my gentlest voice and my kindest terms. Then she got up there and testified like a pro. The guy was convicted. I got this letter.

Dear Judge Morphonios:

Just wanted to drop you a note to say thank you for being so fair at my trial. It was quite an experience for me to endure, but you instilled me with such a state of confidence when I took the stand that I believed justice would prevail.

I am so proud to have met you. Once again, many, many thanks for making me believe once again in the judicial system.

Sincerely,
[The victim]

A tremendous wave of relief and exhaustion always washes over criminal defendants when their cases are resolved in their favor. It's no wonder. I have never been on trial and expect I never will be, but I'm sure it's a lot like sitting down on a hot plate in nothing but your skivvies. If you get out of it without getting burned, you're grateful.

Often, defendants who narrowly escape serious trouble in my courtroom are moved to write letters of thanks to me. One of my favorites came from a star soccer player who got into—and then got out of—some trouble in South Florida. It was a serious charge, but he was acquitted.

Judge Ellen Morphonios:

Have a very nice day!

Lady Morphonios, I have a very humble vocabulary, but I want you and your staff members and the six-person members of the jury for my trial to know how thankful and grateful I am for your fairness and honesty in the judgement of the cases against me.

I pray that almighty God reward you all accordingly in the fields of study, work, love and family.

Please forgive the misspelled words and poor writing style.

Your debtor and friend for life,
J.

I couldn't find anything wrong with the spelling. Or the style. Seemed to me J. could handle a phrase as well as he could a soccer ball.

This letter, which I received late in 1989, also came from a former defendant. I do not want to embarrass this young man needlessly, so I will not list the charges he was facing when he appeared before me. Suffice it to say that I could have sent him to prison for much longer than I did. This letter makes it clear that he appreciated the sentence I gave him, and that he has learned from it.

Dear Judge Morphonios:

Hello, and how have you been? I suppose that you are wondering who I am and why I am writing. Well, I would first like to begin by saying thank you for your concern and caring for the younger generation. Thank you, too, for saying to my friend and myself, "Good luck" as we stood before you after you had sentenced the both of us, K. and D., to seven years, with three mandatory.

K. and I were both 18 years of age and I cannot explain, nor do I think you can understand, the impact it had on the both of us, spiritually and mentally, to face life in prison, appear in front of who was said to be the worst judge by all criminals, and be sentenced to only seven years with three mandatory. Then, to top it off, you wished both of us, "Good luck." I cannot speak for K., but for myself, I can say that the experience was one I could not forget and one I would not trade for the world.

I do not think you were aware of the fact that I had a full-time job and was attending school in the evenings. I was addicted to a variety of drugs and was simply lost and confused. Around the time when I had turned 18, my eyes were beginning to open up to reality. I started to realize that I was heading nowhere, that I was not progressing or becoming a successful human being in life. I began to disassociate myself from the people I hung around with. I began praying to God and asking Him to help me change my life. I did not know how to pray, nor did I even know God at that time, but I gave it all my heart for I sincerely desired to change my life.

On Feb. 22, when I was arrested and brought to the Dade County Jail, I tried figuring out a way to commit suicide. I was too much of a coward to do it. Then, on Feb. 26, I was transferred to another facility, where I met a number of people, basically your common drug addicts and thieves. But there was one individual there by the name of Herman Minor, who seemed at first to be just another inmate. The way he looked at me when I carried my things to the back of that cell made me feel we were going to be enemies right off the top.

I boasted of the marijuana joint I had smoked in the holding cell. He asked, "What do you want to do with your life?" I looked at him and said, "I don't know." He then began telling me about someone who could help me change my life if I would give Him the chance. He told me all about God and how He let His only begotten son, Jesus Christ, die on the cross for the sins of the world.

He explained to me for about two hours how the Lord wanted to help me change my miserable life. I was then led in prayer, and my life did change! For the very first time in my life, I had a relationship with my Lord. I had understanding, peace and love. I never mentioned it to the court because I knew that whatever happened from there on out would be God's will. When I called my mother and explained to her what had happened, she cried with joy and accepted what I was saying because she knew I was telling the truth. I was crying too, as I told her that my life had not come to an end, but rather a fresh, new beginning.

I am now 21 years of age and have grown much wiser and smarter. I have left my childish ways behind me and am planning for a bright future ahead in society. I have accumulated a number of hard-won certificates in Narcotics Anonymous, Bible studies, psychology, etc., and am presently working toward my GED. Afterward, I would like to enter college. I will eventually write the governor and ask for a pardon so I will be able to join the military.

I am even considering helping my local police department fight against drugs, so that little children, as well as my own future children, do not have to go through what I went through.

At the present time, I am working at the Union Correctional Institution School as an academic/vocational clerk, where I share a rather large office with another clerk. I am improving my typing skills and picking up on a number of new office skills as well. I know it will not be easy for me in the future but I will continually strive to succeed and fulfill my dreams.

Once again, I would just like to thank you for using correct judgement. God bless and keep you.

Most sincerely yours,
D.

What a great letter. True, among criminals I am "said to be the worst judge." But that young man's letter makes me think I'm not such a horrible old lady after all. Here is a young man who has taken the opportunity to better himself, who has managed to stop his life from twisting down the toilet. Hallelujah! Sometimes it seems there are no success stories in my business.

I only wish I could hear otherwise more often.

THIRTEEN
THE COPS PULLED THEIR GUNS ON SANTA CLAUS

Like so many in Miami, Ramon Donestevez died violently. Sometimes I blame myself for what happened to him.

Donestevez, an intense man with narrow eyes and flecks of gray in his black hair, was a great hero to many in Miami's Latin community. Exiled from his native Cuba when Fidel Castro took power, he dedicated his life in the United States to freeing the island of Communist rule. A lot of people in the Little Havana area of Miami despised Castro, but few hated him as much as Donestevez did. And few went to the extremes that Donestevez did to try to overthrow him.

He was a fanatical Cuban patriot. Donestevez, a boat builder by profession, made at least a half-dozen boat trips to Cuba in the sixties and seventies. On several occasions, he said he was trying to arrange for the freeing of political prisoners, and he even managed to free a couple of them. Another time, he claimed he was on a mission to bring food, medicine, and used clothing to the island. He might really have been doing those things, but he was also doing something illicit, something dangerous. He was running guns to the rebels.

His base of operations was a boat-building warehouse south of Miami. He used the place, called Piranha Boat Corporation, to construct beautiful pleasure boats and to store the incredible arsenal of guns he was building to use against the Commies. In another part of the building, he built fully armed attack vessels—floating tanks with enough firepower to cut down half an army of Castro loyalists. If the United States government couldn't liberate Cuba (and by then it had pretty well proved that it could not), he would do it himself. He was risking his life in the effort: On five different occasions, bombs either exploded or were found in his boatyard. The perpetrators, presumably Castro agents, were never found.

His fanaticism got him in hot water several times. In 1973, the

196

cops charged him with threatening to dynamite the home and car of
a Cuban exile businessman if the man didn't give eight hundred dollars to his operations. This, clearly, was not a good way to raise
funds. Donestevez pleaded guilty and was sentenced to probation,
which was a pretty good deal considering he could have gotten fifteen years in prison. But when Donestevez turned around and made
another unauthorized trip to Cuba, the judge got annoyed and sent
him to jail for two months. I might have given him a longer sentence if I had been the judge.

Well, pretty soon I was the judge. In 1975, the police found
four semiautomatic rifles and three pistols in Donestevez's office. Ordinarily this would not have been a problem, but Donestevez was on
probation at the time and was not supposed to have guns. Besides,
nobody thought he was going to use them to hunt quail. He was in
jail awaiting a hearing on charges of violating his probation when
the case was assigned to me.

I found out quickly that it was not going to be an ordinary case.
Soon after it showed up on my calendar, I began to get telegrams by
the dozen urging me to set Donestevez free. What's more, I knew the
man's family. His son, also named Ramon, was a friend of Dale and
Dean. I didn't know it until later, but Donestevez once had even
asked my boys to accompany him on one of his gun runs to Cuba.
The boys thought it over a long time before finally saying no, bless
their hearts. In court, I told the lawyers about my connection to
Donestevez and offered to take myself off the case, but they said they
didn't see any need for that. Later, I would regret that—and so
would they.

The evidence at the probation-violation hearing was clear: Donestevez had not only broken the law, he had thumbed his nose and
stuck his tongue out at it. I supported what he was trying to do—I
hate communism, especially Castro's oppressive and cynical brand,
as much as the next guy—but I could not take that into consideration in making my decision. I had to find Donestevez guilty. So I
did. And then I sentenced him to seven years in jail. Donestevez's
fellow rebels in the courtroom hollered at me like hell as they led
him away, and for a moment I thought there might be trouble. Fortunately, the court personnel kept control.

I went home that night with a police escort. All through the
night, the cops kept a close watch on my house. It was a good thing.

Dean and his then-wife, Karen, spent the evening at my house, watching television and taking it easy. They had their two poodles with them. Late that night, someone pulled up outside the house and rang the bell. Karen went to the door and found young Ramon Donestevez, the son of the great rebel, standing in the yard, looking very, very angry. He told Karen, "Let me see your mom. Now."

Karen went bananas. Not only was she afraid that Ramon was upset enough to hurt me, but she also thought he might take out his anger on her two poor little poodles, who had ventured outside to see what was happening. I was in the bathroom taking a shower when Karen burst into the room screaming, "Ramon's outside. He's demanding to see you and I don't know what to do!"

I shot out of that shower like a greyhound out of the gate. Bare-assed and dripping wet, I ran to the phone to call the cops who were standing by. "This is Ellen Morphonios," I shouted into the phone, and if the dispatcher could have seen me he probably would have fainted. "You'd better get your guys over here goddamned quick." He did not ask me to explain why. Then I called Dale and told him to get the hell over to my house. Then I went and got a towel to put over myself.

A dozen police cars pulled up in front of the house at the same time. Ramon wasn't anywhere in sight. The officers fanned out around the house, keeping their heads low and their eyes peeled for any sign of Ramon. It was close to Christmas, and I had a blinking Santa Claus on top of the house. The first time that Santa blinked, one of the cops jumped up and, apparently expecting an army of anti-Castroites, yelled, "Christ, there's one on the roof!" Poor old Santa Claus nearly got blown away. It didn't take long after that for the police to figure out that Ramon was long gone.

Later, Dale went to Ramon's house to talk to him. The police talked to him too. Ramon was a nice kid, really, and he never wanted to hurt me. He was just upset that I had put his daddy in jail, so he flew off the handle. I never held it against him or his father.

The lawyers for the elder Donestevez came to my courtroom sometime after that to ask me to release their client while he appealed my sentence. The court was full of Donestevez backers, all of them anxious to have their hero rejoin them. I decided to give him a chance. He was interested not in harming innocent people, but only in getting rid of Castro any way he could. I set a bond of $125,000 and placed one important condition on his release: I insisted that he have no weapons. No grenades, no rocket launchers, no .22-caliber pistols, nothing. He posted the bond and got out of jail shortly after that.

He never got to file the appeal. At eight-thirty one Tuesday morning, Donestevez called one of his employees, Antonio Estrada, and told him to come to the boat factory immediately. Donestevez said he had to talk to Estrada about something very important. It couldn't wait. When the employee got to the office, he found his boss slumped face-first on his desk, the blotter too small to absorb all the blood. Ramon Donestevez was dead.

Someone had shot him five times at close range. Four bullets hit him in the upper torso. The fifth took off half his face. It was a vicious, violent murder, obviously committed by someone Donestevez trusted. Donestevez hadn't even stood up when his killer walked in to plug him. There was no sign of a struggle. The killer was never found.

There were many rumors surrounding Donestevez's death. Some believed the assassination had been carried out by agents of Fidel Castro—not so much because Castro thought Donestevez was a real threat to his rule, but because he liked to discourage such efforts any way he could. Others believed that Donestevez was actually a Castro agent, and that he had been found out by the anti-Castroites. I myself do not subscribe to that theory. The man was nothing if not a patriot.

In a way, I blamed myself for his death. I never regretted sentencing him to prison. He was breaking the law, and no matter how much I supported what he was doing, I could not condone that. A crime committed out of principle is still a crime. But it was a shame that I had to order Donestevez to steer completely clear of weapons. He was a sitting duck when the killer came into his office that day. If I hadn't given that probation order, and if he had not been so careful to obey it, maybe, just maybe, he would have been able to defend himself.

I was not the only one who saw it that way. The day after Donestevez was killed, a young man picketed the justice building, saying I was responsible for Donestevez's death. When Daddy found out, he wanted to go straight down there to punch the guy out. I had a hell of a time calming Daddy down. When he got it in his head to go somewhere, you almost had to shackle him to a signpost to stop him. The guy picketed for a couple of days, then stopped. I didn't think of him for a long time after that.

But that fellow eventually reappeared in my life.

The mid-seventies were a time of great political turmoil in Miami. In those days, the anti-Castro movement was at its fiercest. All over the city, exiles were plotting different ways to reclaim control of their homeland. I supported their cause entirely, except when it meant breaking the laws of this country. It often did.

In the spring of 1976, three men were arrested while trying to bomb Libros Para Adultos, a dirty bookstore in the Little Havana section of Miami. The three defendants were Jesus Corbo, a Pennsylvania prison escapee, Antonio de la Cova, a graduate student in history, and Gary Latham, a brilliant physics student who lived in Fort Lauderdale.

The key witness against them was Miguel Angel Peraza, a thirty-five-year-old Bay of Pigs veteran and anti-Castroite. Peraza testified in trial that he had met Antonio de la Cova at a funeral in late January or early February. He had told De la Cova that he was a terrorist who worked against communism and other evil influences.

De la Cova and Latham, who was his brother-in-law, agreed with Peraza completely. Eventually, De la Cova and Latham told Peraza of their plan to bomb the adult bookstore. They asked Peraza if he wanted to get involved, and Peraza said he certainly did.

What Peraza didn't mention was that he was an FBI informant.

At one-thirty A.M. on May 6, De la Cova, Latham, Peraza, and Corbo, the prison escapee, went to the dirty bookstore to do the dirty deed. These guys were well prepared. They had a .38-caliber revolver, some wigs, surgical gloves, dynamite, fuses, black powder, notes in which they claimed credit for the act, and, of course, the pipe bomb itself. This much weaponry could have blown up Rhode Island, never mind a little porno house in Little Havana.

They never got to use any of it, thank God. Peraza had tipped off his friends at the FBI, who were there in force when the gang showed up. Thirty FBI agents and police officers arrested De la Cova, Latham, and Corbo after they dropped a brown paper bag containing the pipe bomb. Peraza, the informant, conveniently was allowed to "escape."

There was no end to the surprises. A couple of days before trial,

Gary Latham appeared before me to enter a plea of guilty in exchange for a twenty-year sentence. I had no problem with the arrangement. I was ready to accept the plea. But at the last minute, Latham changed his mind. He was about to make the deal when he learned that if he pleaded guilty, he would have to testify against De la Cova. He wasn't willing to do it.

He was back the next day. This time he wanted to plead no contest. Since he was no longer admitting that he had a part in the crime, he was of no use as a witness to the state. But there was a price for his loyalty: If he wasn't going to plead guilty, the state wasn't going to let him off with only twenty years. Now the sentence would be thirty-five years. He entered the no-contest plea anyway, and I slapped him with thirty-five years.

I got a lot of heat for it, but it really wasn't my fault. If Latham was so sure that he didn't want to testify against De la Cova, that was his decision. The state insisted on thirty-five years and he accepted it.

What I didn't realize until after the case was over was that I knew Gary Latham, sort of. He was the guy who had picketed the building after the murder of Ramon Donestevez. He was the fellow my father had wanted to punch out. Small world.

In the trial, the FBI informant told the jury all about the bombing plot. His testimony was pretty convincing. The defense lawyers did the best they could under the circumstances—they came up with some story about how Peraza had set up De la Cova and the others for an arrest by the FBI. They said their clients were guilty of illegally possessing guns and dynamite—but said they weren't guilty of the attempted bombing.

While the jury deliberated, De la Cova sang "Cuba Libre" and the Cuban national anthem in his jail cell.

The jury apparently didn't hear, or didn't care. It convicted De la Cova of all the charges against him. Corbo, the prison escapee, had really just gone along for the ride, and was found guilty only of conspiracy. I gave him five years in prison and never saw him again. De la Cova got hit harder: I gave him sixty-five years in prison. He had set that pipe bomb to go off forty seconds after he put it down. It easily could have killed an innocent civilian walking by.

Outside the courtroom, De la Cova's parents were in anguish.

"I don't understand," his father told the newspaper. "He is so smart and I am so dumb. But he is in jail and I am out here."

De la Cova didn't serve the whole sixty-five years. He got out on good behavior after a few years. It was one of the rare times when I wasn't sorry to see a guy get out early. One day after they released him, he came to my office for a visit. He introduced me to his wife and told me how well he was doing. He had moved to Puerto Rico, where he was publishing a newspaper or a magazine. He even spoke about how misguided he had been in his days as a bomber. Well meaning, but misguided.

There was nothing even vaguely threatening in the way he spoke to me. He was a complete gentleman. He and Gary Latham may have hated me for sending them to prison. But De la Cova said they always respected me anyway.

I never had a normal marriage with John Rowe, the greyhound trainer. First John went to the dogs. Then the marriage did.

It was strange from the start. John and I had been married on November 22, 1971, but I didn't want my parents to know that. I hated to have them think that I had run off and gotten married in St. Louis without telling them. So I didn't tell them. When John came back, we began to live together, but we didn't let on that we were husband and wife. The way I figured it, we were the only couple in Dade County who were married—but who were pretending to be shacking up.

The marriage was doomed from the start. John was and is a smart guy, but we came from different worlds. He had tried, on several occasions, to do something other than train dogs, but it never worked out. He was a trainer through and through. Since the dogs often run at night in Miami, he often had to stay out until two A.M. I didn't like it. I hadn't gotten married with the idea of being asleep when my husband finally got home and came to bed. I wanted John to be a house-husband.

Now, that is a marvelous way to emasculate a man. I don't recommend it to anyone. If you marry a man, you have to let him have his profession, or he'll lose his sense of self-worth faster than you can say North Dakota. For a while, John tried to stay home, but he hated it, and he probably hated me for asking him to do it. He had, as I have said, an awful temper, and it was at its worst when he was sitting home, sulking.

In 1973, John's boss transferred him to Jacksonville, a city several hundred miles north of Miami. For a while we tried hard to maintain a commuter marriage. Some weekends he would drive to Miami to see me. Other times I would go to Jacksonville. When I went north, I usually spent a lot of time helping him with the dogs, who of course require daily care to survive. I spent a lot of hours shoveling greyhound dung, and a lot of hours asking myself, "Gee, what are the other judges doing this weekend?"

Distance does bad things to relationships, and it certainly hurt ours. The more John was away, the more I resented it, and the lonelier I got. So I did what I had always done when I felt abandoned by a man: I found another one.

This time, my boyfriend was a well-known criminal defense lawyer in Miami. This fellow, whose name was Ben, was best known for defending mobsters. A lot of people—including some federal prosecutors—didn't especially like him for it, but he didn't care what anyone else thought. He went about his business in a professional way, never associating with his clients socially or even acknowledging them if he saw them in public. He gave them the defense that they were entitled to under the Constitution and he left it at that. Once, when he was out with his wife, some hood stopped at his table to socialize. That really pissed Ben off. After dinner, he escorted his wife to the car, then went back into the restaurant and grabbed this big thug by the lapels. He was a little man, but a tough one.

"You son of a bitch," Ben said, "if you ever recognize me in public again when I'm with my wife, I'll kill you."

I knew who his clients were—everybody did—but I never met any of them, and I never knew him to do anything illegal whatsoever. He was a good man who defended not-so-good men. He was a good attorney, conscientious and completely ethical. His word was his bond.

I should note here that Ben is dead now. I went to his funeral, which was attended by hundreds of people. It was a mob scene— literally. He was loved and respected by people in all walks of life.

I had known Ben for several years, but we first got to know each other after he defended a client—not a mobster—on a minor charge in my courtroom. (It was, incidentally, the last case he ever handled in my courtroom. He never would have dreamed of appearing before me after we developed a personal relationship, for being ethical was as important to him as it is to me.) He came in, did his job for his client, and left. Later that day, he called my office and asked me to join him for a cup of coffee. I agreed, but since I didn't know him well, I asked my nephew Donnie to join me. I had no idea what Ben wanted, and I wanted to play it safe.

The three of us went out and enjoyed a cup of coffee and some light conversation. When we parted, I still didn't know what Ben wanted. He soon asked me out for another cup of coffee. This time I took Dale, and again I drank lots of coffee but never found out what the hell this guy wanted with me.

The third time he asked me to join him for coffee, I couldn't find anyone to join me, so I went alone. As he drove me back to the courthouse, he put his hand on my knee and said, "You sure are a beautiful woman."

When I got back to the office, I said to my secretary, Anne Cates, "Now I know what he wants."

I dated Ben for some time. He was an extremely kind, generous man. Our relationship really was no secret at the courthouse, but naturally we tried to be discreet because we were both married. Ben's wife knew, I'm sure. But far from being bitter or resentful, Ben said she used to defend my decisions when people criticized me at cocktail parties.

She had class. Once, she and Ben walked into a breakfast restaurant where Ben and I used to go. The cashier said to Ben, "Judge Morphonios isn't with you this morning?" Ben was about ready to lose his breakfast, but his ever-dignified wife just said, "Oh, no, Judge Morphonios couldn't be with us this morning. She's a good friend of ours. Thank you so much for asking."

I was in the midst of this relationship when my husband, John, was sent back to Miami to work. This created something of an inconvenience. When he was gone, I had been living as a single woman. Now I would have to adjust back to being known as Mrs. Rowe, a title I hadn't much cared for since I got it. I didn't think I could do it. I didn't feel as opposed to a second divorce as I did to the first.

My cavalier attitude cost me in the end. I knew John had a temper, but I didn't know how bad it could be until the weekend Dean and Karen left town to visit Karen's folks. I sensed that John was upset, but I couldn't get him to talk about it. The kids asked if they should hang around, but I told them to go ahead. "I'll be fine," I said.

John started in on me as soon as they left. He claimed he had been following me. He said he had come to see me at work only to find that I wasn't in the building. I wasn't surprised to hear that: Ben and I took some awfully long lunches. John said he knew what I had been up to.

"You've been to some mighty interesting places with some mighty interesting people," he said.

It occurred to me that he might be full of shit—that he didn't know a thing and was just trying to trick me into a confession. But in a way, I didn't care. I was in a dangerous mood. I had a feeling he was going to smack me if I said the wrong thing. I know just how far I can stretch a rope before it will pop, and John's rope was pretty tense. But I couldn't help myself. We were sitting at the kitchen table. When John accused me of fooling around, I looked at him in my most casual way and shrugged my shoulders.

Bad idea.

John came across the table like a panther on the pounce. "You bitch," he said, "you don't even bother denying it." And then he slugged me in the face, but hard. He grabbed me by the hair and dragged me into the other room. In the next few minutes, I developed a healthy respect for spouse-abuse cases, because he beat the pure shit out of me. I can't really say it was a fight, because he was the only one swinging. I was on the floor, screaming and trying in vain to cover my face. It seemed it would never end. I felt I was rolling down a steep hill in a steel barrel, rattling against the sides as it tumbled. The noise and the pain were incredible. I thought John was going to kill me. Soon I hoped he would, because I didn't think I could live with the agony of the beating another second.

Then he stopped. For a minute, I lay there wheezing and swelling. Then John said, "Call Mike Hacker. We're getting a divorce."

So I did. Half-consciously, I moved to the phone and called my old law partner. I told him I needed him to come over right away. Just then, John started to realize that he was in a world of trouble. He got his things together and went to spend the night at the kennel, where he had a cot. Suddenly he didn't seem so interested in a divorce. He wanted only to get out of there.

I couldn't seem to get a grip on myself. I was confused, acting irrationally. When Mike Hacker arrived, I told him that everything was fine, that John and I had worked things out. Here the man had just beaten me to a pulp, and I was telling my friend that I was all right. It didn't make sense. When Mike left, I decided I had to get out of the house, just in case John came back. I put my things in an overnight bag, looked out at the driveway to make sure John wasn't lurking there, then ran toward my Lincoln. On the way, I fell and smacked my knee so hard my eyes watered. It brought me to my senses.

"I'll be goddamned," I said to no one, "if I'm going to be scared out of my own home."

Dean and Karen came home the next morning. For reasons I still don't understand, I was still trying to keep the whole thing a secret. I put on my heaviest makeup, probably an inch deep, and stayed in my room so Dean wouldn't see me. Later that day, I took Karen aside and told her what had happened, but I asked her not to tell my son.

The next day was Monday, a work day. My face still looked like it had been run over by a Jeep, so I had to cake on the makeup again. When I got to work, I told my secretary, Cindy Shelton, and my nephew, Donnie Wright, about the fight. They swore they wouldn't say anything about it, but everyone in court could see that something had happened to me. Someone from the state agency that watches over children asked me what was wrong, and I said I had ridden my bicycle into a tree. I have never been able to ride a bicycle, much less into a tree, but somehow everyone believed me.

I stayed away from Ben for a couple of days. I feared, probably irrationally, that one of his clients would find out what had happened and fit John with a pair of cement shoes. It was bad enough that a circuit court judge had been in an ugly domestic dispute. The last thing I needed was to have my boyfriend's buddies do away with my husband.

Ben eventually found out anyway. Dean soon noticed that John wasn't around the house anymore, and he mentioned it to Ben.

"Did he hit you?" Ben asked me.

"Nah," I said. "He just slapped me once. I told him to get out. It was no big deal." The man had damn near killed me and I was saying it was no big deal.

The next time I saw John was Valentine's Day. I came home that day to find some candy by the back door. John had put a card in it. At first I thought of throwing the candy away, but it looked so good I couldn't bring myself to do it. The kids and I had eaten much of it by the time John appeared at the door a few nights later, saying he wanted to talk.

He must have known he was in serious trouble with me, because he was more conciliatory than I had ever seen him. He said he was sorry about hitting me, and wanted to know if we could work things out. What he wanted was to be let off the hook, but I wasn't about to do that. We were sitting at the kitchen table having a drink when I began to lay into him. I screamed at him for not being home enough. I screamed at him for once slamming the sliding glass door on the dog's neck. I hollered at him for forgetting to give me a Christmas present. No transgression in the entirety of our blissful union went unmentioned, I promise you.

It was more than John could take—more than any man could take, probably. Somehow we wound up standing in the front hallway. It was there that John slugged me. I was out like a light by the time I hit the terrazzo floor.

I remember having one thought in my half-conscious haze: This is a second-degree murder on its way to happening, and I'm sending it an engraved invitation. Karen, meanwhile, was standing over me, screaming, "Mommy, Mommy, are you all right?"

Dean was in the house this time. When he heard what had happened, he went after John with murder on his mind. He chased him down the street, throwing kitchen items as he went. John outran him and went to spend the night at the kennel. He was in the doghouse again—literally.

The next day, Dean gathered all John's possessions and took them to the kennel.

"What do you want me to do with this stuff?" Dean yelled through the closed door.

"Ah, just shitcan it," John said, half-seriously.

So Dean drove to the apartment complex where we used to live and threw everything John owned into the trash bin.

The next day I flew to Panama City, Florida, a little town in the Panhandle, and had a judge give me a divorce. There would be less publicity that way. I felt no remorse about my second divorce. The only sorrow I felt was that I had gotten into the marriage in the first place.

I want history to note that, to some extent, I blame myself for John's violent outbursts. My friends tell me I shouldn't, but I do anyway. I can be, trust me, a very infuriating woman. I know just how far I can push a man before he loses his cool. I could see that John was getting angry with me, but I didn't back off. I kept pushing and pushing until he just lost his head and took a swing at me. Some might say that he was making all the choices—that he chose to hit me and bears the responsibility for it. That is partly true. But I think I was the one with the real control in that situation. I could have let the steam out of John with a single kind word, a single smile. But I didn't. I just kept adding pressure to that pressure cooker until it blew.

It may surprise some people to know that John Rowe and I are friends now. He lives outside Florida, and still works as a dog trainer. I hear from him every now and then. Where he lives, he can't get the Cuban black beans he used to love to eat when he was in Miami. So, from time to time he calls me and asks me to send him a couple of cans.

I always do, gladly.

FOURTEEN
THE MARKET CONNECTION

I can only think of one time in my career when I knowingly used my gender as a weapon. It turned out to be a mighty powerful weapon.

It happened the first time I came up for reelection. Incumbents have a natural advantage in any election, mostly because people tend to vote for people whose names they know well. That advantage may be even greater in judicial elections. Since most people don't follow judges' work very closely, they tend to rely on name recognition even more than in other races. It's hard to unseat a sitting judge. Most aspiring judges don't even try unless they think a particular judge is vulnerable for some reason. When my first term ended, I didn't feel I was vulnerable to a challenge. I had received some bad press, but almost every judge does. I was confident that I would run unopposed.

Too confident, as it happened. A few months before the election, I began hearing rumors that a certain prosecutor was thinking of opposing me. I knew the guy. I had worked with him and Al Sepe in the state attorney's office years earlier. He was a good guy, but at the moment I was not happy with him. I didn't want to run for reelection any more than I wanted to shovel manure with John Rowe. Campaigning takes time and, God knows, money. I had no interest in doing the endless, tedious work it would take to squash this guy on Election Day, and neither did my friends. So we decided to have a little talk with him.

Al Sepe did the talking. He met the guy somewhere for lunch and began to quiz him about his plans.

"Yes," the guy said, "I've been thinking of running against her."

"That's your prerogative," Al said. "But I want you to know that she has been building a pretty formidable war chest to use on anyone who might try."

What Al was doing here, with my complete blessing, was playing old-fashioned hardball politics. I hadn't been building any kind of war chest, much less a large one. But if I wanted to keep my job, and I did, I had to give the impression that I was ready for battle.

The prosecutor just nodded and said, "That's fine, but it won't influence my decision."

Then Al leaned forward, checked to make sure no one was listening, and said the only thing that could have changed this guy's mind.

"Look," he said, "you don't want to get your ass whipped by a woman, do you?"

I ran unopposed that November.

Beware the child you meet on the city streets, my friends. He may look like your son or your sweet young grandson. But he may have very unpleasant plans for you.

I was transferred to the courts' juvenile division in 1974. I had asked for the transfer. At last I would be fulfilling the dream I had had when I ran for judge in 1960. Indeed, when I made the change, Don Petit sent me a note saying, "Congratulations. You finally made it!" Yes, I had. And since I had a couple of kids of my own, I thought I knew quite a bit about them. That may have been so. But in the year and three weeks I spent in the division, I learned a lot more about kids—and about the way the justice system treats them—than I ever wanted to know.

Before I entered the division, I thought of most juveniles simply as young people—sweet, angelic little kids like my grandchildren. That image quickly changed. I soon began to think of many of them as big bruisers as mean as snakes, people without respect for me, the system, society, the police, or anything else. It is a dim view, I know, but trust me, it is a fair one.

I saw children charged with crimes that you wouldn't believe children could commit. The parade of misery and terror that I witnessed in my time in that division has stayed with me every day since then. I can't print the children's names here because the law won't allow it. But let me tell you about a few of the cases and a few of the problems in the system.

One day, a delightful old lady of eighty was walking down the street carrying her purse. Maybe she was on the way to the store or the bus stop, I don't know. I never found out. What I do know is that a "child," whom I'll call Michael, appeared from nowhere, grabbed the woman's purse, slugged her, and knocked her to the ground. He didn't kill her, thank God. But in the fall she broke both of her hips and was crippled for the rest of her life. The strain of it blew her mind—rendered her a vegetable until the day she died.

Oh, there were more, more than I care to remember. One day, an elderly woman in Miami opened her front door to tell a young man how to find his aunt's apartment in the complex. This nice woman once had a husband she loved dearly, but now that he had passed away she spent her nights alone. As she gave directions to the young man, he pushed his way into the house, dragged her to the bedroom, and threw her on the bed she once shared with her spouse. This "boy's" name was Antonio and he was fifteen years old. He raped the old woman viciously before finally striking a crushing blow to her skull and ending her last moments of hell on earth.

Do those stories sound terrible? Do they scare you? Well, I want them to sound terrible, and I want you to be scared. Because there is something wrong with some of our kids. And there sure as hell is something wrong with the way we treat the ones who commit crimes.

There is a theory in the juvenile justice system that it doesn't matter what the child did, but only why he did it. The do-gooders who think this way believe we should give the young offender training and therapy and guidance—everything but punishment. The idea, I suppose, is that if you catch a kid young enough you can turn him around, no matter what a menace he is. Maybe that is valid in some cases.

But we have been fooling around with that system for several decades now, and it has proven itself a failure. By offering heavy sympathy and light punishment, we have in effect condoned the criminal acts of children—and encouraged them to go out and commit some more. They have of course obliged us. The juvenile justice system is not a correctional system in the sense that it improves the young people who enter it. Rather, it is a highly expensive manufacturing plant that produces experienced, well-trained, capable violent criminals.

Now, I'm as interested in the welfare of children as anyone else. But I don't put the child's interests ahead of society's in every case.

Sometimes, so-called children commit acts that adults wouldn't conceive of committing. I myself find it difficult to use the word *child* to describe someone who would just as soon kill you as look at you. We are conditioned, when we hear the word *child*, to think of a pleasant, cheerful, and especially harmless being with wide, trusting eyes. We are not conditioned to think of a murderer, robber, burglar, or rapist. But that's exactly the kind of "child" the courts deal with.

When I first entered the system, a judge could do virtually nothing to discipline a terrible young hood. Any kid charged with a crime had to be dealt with in the juvenile system no matter what he had done. Fortunately, the state of Florida changed that a short time later. Now, under certain circumstances, a juvenile judge can treat a kid as an adult—and send him to adult court to stand trial. The judge in adult court can then send him to adult prison if he is convicted. This is only right and just. I know of one case in Florida in which a seventeen-year-old boy shot to death a couple who were camping in the woods. He was tried in another judge's court, convicted, and sentenced to death, a sentence he deserved.

One of my greatest battles in juvenile court involved a kid who was charged with murder. To put it simply and graphically, this kid had walked up to an innocent man and blown his brains out with a handgun. To me, this kid was a menace, as dangerous as Ted Bundy, Son of Sam, the Boston Strangler, or any other grown-up murderer you might know of. Florida's child-welfare people didn't think so—if they were thinking anything, that is. If they had a brain in their heads, it didn't show. These people felt it would be harmful to keep a child in detention longer than four months, no matter what he was charged with doing. I fought them the whole time I was in the juvenile division, and in the end they won. The law was on their side, and I thought that was wrong.

Our society has chosen the age of 17 as the cutoff line between adults and children. Well, my friends, there is nothing magical about age 17. We have selected it arbitrarily and then applied that arbitrary choice to criminal cases with complete disregard for common sense. Look at it this way: Why should a boy 17 years and 1 day old go to prison for several years for armed robbery when a boy 16 years and 364 days old merely plays Ping-Pong in reform school for a couple of months? It's ridiculous. I don't think the law lacks intelligence or even compassion. But too often it lacks common sense. Some kids deserve severe punishment.

Don't misunderstand me. I'm not against gentle treatment for a first offender involved in a nonviolent crime. But you don't teach a kid anything by condoning his misdeeds. I am very much of the philosophy that the only true deterrent to further criminal activity is a form of punishment—something that will make the kid wish he hadn't done what he did, something that will influence him not to do it again. The best education a young offender can get is to observe a court as a court, to see a judge in a scary black robe, to know that he is facing a serious charge, to understand that he has rights under the law, and to have a fair trial. In short, he should be given the impression that the trial of his case will be conducted exactly as trials are conducted in adult court.

Where did our society ever get the idea that people who rob, steal, and kill can be stopped with leniency, understanding, rehabilitative counseling, and probation? The only person probation changes is the person who would have changed even without probation. The fellow who wants to go straight will do so on his own. A one-million-dollar rehabilitation program won't do a damn thing for someone who doesn't.

So what should we do? Glad you asked.

With rare exceptions, children fourteen and under should be treated as juvenile offenders in our system. All others should be treated as adults. That way, the juvenile system could devote its full time to small children with relatively small problems. It is in those cases that the system does the most good.

Instead of sentencing minor first-time offenders to probation, I think we should never bring them into the system at all. The child, the police, and the victim should enter into an agreement whereby the criminal charges are set aside for a certain period of time. If the child behaves himself for that period of time, the charges will be dropped forever and the child will have no record. Florida's adult courts already have such a system; it is called pretrial intervention, and I think it's a fine way to ease the burden on the court system—and to rehabilitate people who are not criminals but who have simply made a dumb mistake.

I also think young people should receive mandatory terms of incarceration for certain crimes. Under my plan, a kid committing even his first armed robbery would go to prison or a place much like prison for a certain period of time. Most judges don't like suggestions like these, because it takes away their discretion as judges. I sympathize with them: I like to be able to wield power as much as the next judge. But I think kids need to know that if they stick somebody up with a pistol—even a toy pistol—they're going to be treated to summer vacation behind bars.

This last proposal will cost money. It costs money to build reformatories and to hire the people to run them. I understand that. But try to explain that to a grieving mother whose son has been disfigured by a fifteen-year-old criminal with four prior convictions who is released early because the state can't pay to keep him locked up.

Still concerned about the cost? Try telling that to someone who has lost her wedding ring and her grandfather's watch and her dead mother's tiny pearl brooch in a burglary. And what do you say to the family whose son's brilliant mind was destroyed by a drug dealer—a drug dealer who is released from detention because the system is full and his is considered a nonviolent crime?

What do you tell them?

The Bible suggests an answer to our problems. Leviticus says, "He who kills a man shall be put to death. He who kills a beast shall make it good. Life for life. When a man causes a disfigurement in his neighbor, as he has done it shall be done to him, fracture for fracture, eye for eye, tooth for tooth, as he has disfigured a man, he shall be disfigured. He who kills a beast shall make it good—and he who kills a man shall be put to death."

They didn't have much of a problem with violent crime in those days. Not with sentences like that.

When I entered the juvenile justice system, I decided to make it my business to clean it up—to add common sense where none existed. This was a fine and noble sentiment. It also was not worth squat. I failed to change the way people think about juvenile crime. I screamed and hollered and badgered and gave impassioned speeches in every Holiday Inn meeting hall in South Florida, and nothing changed. Nobody cared.

I suspect they're beginning to care now. The kids I saw in my days in the juvenile division were sweethearts compared to the little monsters that go through there now. This is largely because of the demon crack cocaine, which owns the hearts and minds of so many poor kids in South Florida it would make you sick to see it. It does me. These kids commit crimes absolutely without remorse so that they can get the money to feed their habits. And at last people are getting fed up with it.

Maybe now people will assert the public pressure that it will take to really do something about the problem of juvenile crime. Public pressure is the only thing that will do it. It's the only thing politicians respond to.

The worst scare of my life came a couple of years after I took the bench. I almost got indicted.

It all began with a nice old man named Frank Martin. Martin, who was seventy-one years old then, owned a filling station near Miami's Farmers' Market, a gigantic fresh-produce market in the northwest section of the city. Over the years, Martin had come to know a lot of people, including dozens and dozens of politicians. I first met him during the campaigns I worked on in the fifties. Today in South Florida, a candidate generally can't get elected without the support of the presidents of the various condominium associations. In the fifties, sixties, and early seventies, a person couldn't get elected without the help of Frank Martin.

He had great connections. He knew absolutely everyone at the produce market—the truckers, the shoppers, the vendors, everyone. Thousands of people did business there every day, and Martin knew all of them on a first-name basis. Naturally, every politician wanted Frank on his side. If Frank liked a certain candidate, he would take him from place to place in the market, introducing him to people and asking them for their votes. On the way, the candidate would be stepping over the rotten watermelons and crushed cabbages that invariably ended up on the ground during the day. But Frank didn't stop at introductions. Thousands of trucks left the market every morning and fanned out across South Florida. If Martin liked a candidate, he would make sure that person had a bumper sticker and a poster fixed to every truck.

I was fortunate enough to be one of the people Frank liked. During the 1970 campaign, Daddy and the boys brought a huge stack of posters and bumper stickers to the market. The next day, my name was being carried all over the place, courtesy of the truck drivers Frank knew and influenced.

He was a wonderful character. He seemed to have a phone attached to his ear all the time. Each morning he ate breakfast at a restaurant called Lindy's. Next to the table was a telephone reserved especially for him. I used to have breakfast with him every so often, just to see how he was. Often, when I was sitting across from him, he would suddenly stop the conversation and dial a phone number. When the person on the other end picked up, he'd say, "Guess who I'm sitting here with? Judge Ellen Morphonios. Yeah, that's right. Here. I'll let you talk to her." And then he would hand over the phone. I would end up talking to someone I had never met or even heard of. Frank got a kick out of it. He liked to impress his friends that way.

Often the person he called was his wife, Helen, who had been disabled by heart disease some years earlier. He adored her. He called her dozens of times every day. If you met Frank on the corner of Flagler Street and Miami Avenue in downtown Miami, he would take you by the hand and lead you to a pay phone so that he could call his wife and have you talk to her. I can't say I knew him well, but what I knew, I liked.

Frank was always happy to help a politician he liked, but he never asked for much of anything in return. Once in a while, when one of his employees was called for jury duty, he would ask a judge friend to get the person excused. Often, we would do it. Maybe we shouldn't have, but we did, and I'm not going to pretend we didn't.

But I certainly didn't do what the prosecutors would later suggest I did. I did not take Frank Martin's money to fix a case.

I will admit this—I will admit that it looked bad. About the time the authorities began probing the so-called Market Connection, I began thinking of putting an addition on my house. Dale and Dean were both married, and soon there would be grandchildren. I wanted to be sure I would have room for them when they came to visit. I couldn't afford to pay cash for the addition, so I began to shop around for a loan. For a while I considered taking a second mortgage, but when I heard what the interest rates were, I gave up that idea immediately. I would swear that some of those second-mortgage companies charge higher interest than the mob. I needed to seek financing somewhere else.

That was when I called Frank Martin. It seemed like the natural thing to do. He knew everyone in town. Surely he would know someone—a private individual or a banker—who could lend me twenty thousand dollars at a reasonable interest rate. There was absolutely nothing wrong with what I wanted to do. So I didn't hesitate to ask Frank to help me. The only thing I wanted, I said, was the right of prepayment. I don't like to carry a debt if I don't have to, so I always take loans I can pay off without penalty when I get the money.

Frank said he would see what he could do. The rest of our conversation was frivolous and unimportant. That's how I describe it, anyway. One newspaper reporter would later describe it, in print, as "a discussion of the merits of queen size and round beds." Let me see if I can explain. Frank mentioned during our talk that he had recently seen a round bed in a store window. He wanted to know if I had ever seen such a thing. I said I hadn't. Then he asked what kind of bed I had. A queen-size bed, I told him. We could not decide whether it would be easier to sleep on a round bed than a rectangular one. But we agreed that a person would not be as likely to fall off a round bed, as it provides more rolling-around space than a rectangular one. And that was the end of our ridiculous talk.

We did not know at the time that Frank's phone was tapped.

We found out in early February, when the Dade County sheriff served wiretap notices on 106 people, including me. Miami Mayor David Kennedy, Judge Jack Turner, and a couple of dozen other public officials also received notices. By law, the investigators had to tell us that our conversations had been monitored. The notices didn't necessarily mean we had done anything wrong. But when we got them, we knew we were under criminal investigation, and had been for some time. And that was bad enough.

Immediately I got a lawyer, someone I had known and respected for a long time. He told me not to discuss the investigation with anyone, which was easy because I wasn't sure why I was being investigated. I remembered asking Frank Martin for a loan, but I couldn't believe I could be in trouble for that. Besides, I had not taken any money from him. A credit union had made the loan to me, and I was in the process of paying it back. There were lots of rumors about the case, but it was some time before I knew what was really going on.

A television reporter for Channel 4 finally explained it to me. His name was Fred Francis, and he is now a network TV correspondent. Al Sepe put me on the phone with him and he told me the whole story.

It seemed that a defendant named Carlos Pinto had just been transferred from Judge Turner's division to mine. Turner had previously sentenced Pinto to eighteen months in prison for conspiracy to sell marijuana, but now he was vacating the sentence and sending the case to me for a new trial. I had never heard of Carlos Pinto, but there was nothing unusual about that. When you hear 150 or 200 cases a week, you don't remember names.

Pinto's mother, Mina Davidson, had written a letter to Turner asking him to reduce Pinto's sentence. She had also spoken to Mayor Kennedy, whom she had known for some time, about the case. Both Kennedy and Turner had been seen talking to Frank Martin. The investigators apparently believed that Martin was the middleman in a bribery scheme. They thought that Mrs. Davidson had paid the mayor and the judge to vacate Pinto's sentence. And they also apparently thought that Frank Martin had paid me, or was going to pay me, to go easy on Pinto.

This blew my mind. When I got off the phone with Fred Francis, my secretary, Anne Cates, and I read Pinto's file. Then I recused myself from the case. It was a hot potato, and I wanted to get rid of it as quickly as possible.

Naturally, the media were covering the case very closely. It was on the front pages and on the six o'clock news for weeks and weeks. For the most part, the media treated me fairly. They reported everything I had said in my telephone conversation with Frank, including the part about the round bed. It was embarrassing, but I couldn't complain. As long as journalists report the facts accurately and fairly, I won't complain—not even if the facts make me look bad.

I had trouble with only one news organization—Channel 7 in Miami. From the beginning of the case to the end, that station was rude, obnoxious, and unfair. The reporter covering the case was Brian Ross, a troublesome fellow who now works for one of the networks. He gave me a real pain in the ass. One day I got word that Channel 7 was going to air a story saying I had received a fifty-dollar bribe in a certain case. I was damned upset about it. So Anne Cates and I put together certified copies of the file showing that I had never presided over the case, not even for a day. Anne drove the copies to the TV station and explained what they were.

That night the station aired its little story anyway. When it was over, the anchor said something like, "A spokesman for Judge Morphonios denied she was involved." Alas, it was not my last encounter with Channel 7.

State Attorney Richard Gerstein began the investigation, but Governor Reubin Askew removed him because Gerstein, like every other politician in the county, knew Frank Martin well and had been assisted by him in his campaigns. To handle the case, the governor appointed an out-of-town prosecutor named James Russell. The grand jury investigation would take place not in Dade County but in Daytona Beach. In the months after the wiretap notices were served, a lot of us public officials logged a lot of highway miles between Miami and Daytona.

Alex's nephew Donnie Wright, who was the bailiff in my courtroom, was among the people called to testify. Apparently, the grand jury wanted to know about any arrangements that had been made for the treatment of Carlos Pinto in my court. Donnie didn't know of any, and that's what he said on the witness stand. When he was finished testifying, the news reporters chased him all the way to his car, as they did everyone. Now, Donnie is a terrific guy, but I wouldn't say he is mellow. If you rub him the wrong way, he'll let you know it. Brian Ross rubbed him the wrong way. Ross kept shoving his microphone into Donnie's face and Donnie kept pushing it away. Finally Donnie told him that if he put the mike in his face one more time, he was going to do such-and-such to him. Ross did it anyway.

That was when Donnie reached up and tweaked Brian Ross's nose, but hard. He just grabbed it and twisted it like a slice of lemon he was squeezing into a Coke. It was on all the stations that night. Ross's competitors had all gotten footage of the tweaking.

My attitude before the grand jury was the same as it was any other time: Ask me and I'll tell you. I wasn't about to hide behind my Fifth Amendment right to avoid self-incrimination. A lot of other people did that during that case, but I don't agree with it. A public official should never take the Fifth for any reason. It isn't right. So I sat there and answered the grand jurors' questions as best I could.

I got the feeling when I was on the stand that the grand jurors didn't want information about what I had done so much as information about what other people had done. For example, they asked me about the circumstances under which a judge might set aside a conviction and grant a new trial. Clearly, they were trying to get me to zing Judge Jack Turner, but I didn't do it. I didn't have anything to say about Jack, and still don't. I believed, and still believe, that Jack

Turner is straight. He's also a fine judge. The whole case was a bad rap, if you ask me.

At that time, I was frankly more concerned about my neck than I was about Jack Turner's. I was scared stiff that I was going to be charged with a crime—bribery or conspiracy or God knows what. If that happened, I would never live it down, not even if I was found not guilty of everything. An indictment would ruin my reputation and put an immediate end to my career. It would pretty much put an end to my life. The fact that I hadn't done anything wrong did not comfort me in the least. If that prosecutor wanted to charge me with something, I was sure he could get the grand jury to do it.

It didn't happen. Hallelujah, it didn't happen. The grand jurors indicted several people, including Frank Martin, Jack Turner, and the mayor, but they didn't charge me. What a wonderful feeling. It was as if someone had lifted a cruise ship off my shoulders. Until that day, I smoked four packs of cigarettes a day. I had a deal with my lawyer: If I wasn't indicted, the only thing he would ask of me in payment for his work was that I give up smoking. The day the indictments were returned, I smoked my last cigarette. I have never smoked one since. It was great to quit, sure. But if you are a smoker, I recommend that you find some other way. Nearly getting indicted is too stressful.

The case was not over, though. A few months later, I was driving toward my house when I noticed a car in the rearview mirror. The car followed me as I turned into my neighborhood. When I stopped in front of my house, it stopped too. I wasn't about to get out of the car until I knew who was following me, so I stayed put. Only when I saw a police officer I knew climb out of the car did I open my door. I met the cop in the street.

"Judge," he said, "we'd like you to come and testify in the trial of Judge Jack Turner."

I looked at him and held out my right hand. He put a subpoena in it, as I knew he would.

"Do you mind if I change my clothes and call my lawyer?"

The cop refused at first, but then he decided to give me a break. An hour later, properly attired in a conservative dress with a big collar, I met Dean, Karen, Daddy, and my lawyer at the courthouse. It was quite a scene. Someone obviously had told the press I was coming, and the TV people were in a frenzy to get me to say something. People had been speculating for months about my part in the Market scandal. Now they would find out. As I entered the building, the reporters and camera people surged at me so suddenly it scared me. Brian Ross's crew, always the first to do the wrong thing, crashed into my daughter-in-law, nearly knocking her over. Somehow we all got into the courtroom unhurt.

In court, I simply told the truth. I had called Frank Martin because I wanted a loan, not a payoff. I had never heard of Carlos Pinto before Fred Francis told me his name. And I had certainly never discussed Pinto's case with Judge Jack Turner. I didn't know anything about any conversations Martin might have had with Turner or with Mayor Kennedy. When I was done, I stood up and left the courtroom.

That was when I made my first big mistake: I ran from the press. Usually I don't run from anything. My only excuse is that I knew the camera crews would be in the hall when I got there, and I was afraid someone, especially my father, would get hurt this time. So when I emerged from the courtroom, I quickly ducked down a stairwell and ran to the basement. It was a foolish thing to do. The camera people naturally ran after me, and soon I was in the very undignified position, for a judge, of being chased like a jackrabbit by a bunch of news hounds. My father would later chew me out for making a bad decision.

Brian Ross was the first to find me. "Come on out, Judge," he said through the basement door. "I won't hurt you."

Oh, it was hell. But I could do nothing but open the door and walk out into the open. I said nothing to the press on the way back to the car. I merely held on to my father's arm, smiling happily on the outside and dying on the inside.

Nobody was ever convicted in the Market scandal, not Frank Martin, not Jack Turner, and not the mayor. Frank and his beloved wife both died some time later, and Turner and Mayor Kennedy went on to other things. No, they weren't convicted, but they were all made to look pretty bad, and a lot of people still think, wrongly, that they got away with something.

I'm sure there are some people who think the same of me. Once your name is connected in the newspapers with a criminal investigation, you never live it down. It doesn't matter if you haven't done anything wrong. People assume you're guilty, and mere facts don't change their minds. When the story was in the papers every day, people even harassed my sons, saying their mother was a thief. Say anything you want to me: I can take it. But when you say it to my sons, that's damned unfair. I always try to find the positive in things. I think the only positive in that experience was that I gained an appreciation for how it feels to be wrongly suspected. It wasn't worth it, not hardly. I have never recovered from the insult and indignity of the Market investigation.

And I resent it.

FIFTEEN

NEVER LIE TO SOMEONE
TAKING NOTES

It was St. Patrick's Day. Several of the jurors were dressed in green. One was more enthusiastic about the holiday than the others.

His name, I learned later, was Stan Ross. He was serving as a juror in a case I was hearing. The morning of March 17, I stepped up to the bench and greeted the jurors as I do every morning. Mr. Ross stood up.

"Good morning, Your Honor. As you know, this is a great and holy day for the Irish. Would you mind if I celebrated the day with a song?"

I laughed and looked at the lawyers and the court personnel. They all shrugged their shoulders. "Why not?" I said.

Then Mr. Ross took a deep breath and sang "My Wild Irish Rose" all the way through. The court reporter recorded every word. He was quite a fine singer. He had a beautiful baritone voice that rang clearly throughout the courtroom. When he finished, he took a small bow, blushed, and reclaimed his seat in the jury box. Everyone applauded. I thought it was a delightful way to start a day, and I said so. Then we went on with the trial.

Two days later, I got a letter from the crooner. "I want to apologize to you for exploding with a song on St. Patrick's Day in court," it said. "I guess being a singing guitarist and always on stage, it just happened. Yes, you were so nice about it. Hope to see you again— not in court." He enclosed a newspaper clipping that said he had performed at the wedding ceremony of John and Jackie Kennedy.

The fellow had nothing to apologize for. After years of seeing people come to court and lie or whine or swear or faint or complain, it was nice to meet someone who wanted only to sing.

Some judges are terrified of the press. I'm not talking about crooked judges, either. I'm talking about saints—people who wouldn't say shit if they had a mouthful. I'm talking about people who are so pure their children are probably adopted. And still they're scared. Part of the reason, I think, is that they don't know or understand reporters. Judges are like everybody else: What they don't know scares them.

Defense lawyers dread trying high-publicity cases in front of scared judges. When the press is watching, judges are extremely unlikely to go easy on a well-known felon. Even though some of them are soft on crime, they don't want to be seen that way. Enough bad-press notices could cost a judge an election. I've seen it happen. Naturally, I don't appreciate that kind of decision-making. A judge should rule according to the law and his conscience, not according to the size of the press horde in the courtroom.

I have never feared reporters the way some of my colleagues do. I'm sure that's partly because I was introduced to politics by a journalist—Don Petit. Don taught me how reporters operate, and how to have friendships with them without compromising my integrity or theirs. But even without Don I think I would have gotten along just fine with the press. I am a naturally garrulous person. And I don't distance myself from people the way some judges do. I think some of my colleagues view the bench as a high horse. Once they get on it, they're careful to associate only with people as high and mighty as they are. I have never done that, probably because Daddy wouldn't have tolerated it. I have always understood that everyone has a job to do, whether he be a judge, bailiff, court stenographer, lawyer, or journalist. And I have tried never to place one kind of person above another.

In my first days as a judge, reporters were as much a part of the landscape as were lawyers and defendants. The system was so overburdened and so insane that they hung around all the time just to observe the chaos. It seemed that every time I opened my office door, a reporter was in the hallway. "Judge, do you have a minute to talk about such-and-such?" "Sure," I'd say, and we would hold a quick, impromptu press conference right there.

Among the journalists I liked best was Edna Buchanan, the legendary reporter for the *Miami Herald*. Edna, who won the Pulitzer Prize for her police reporting, is a wide-eyed, hard-driving woman with a big heart and a great eye for detail. She was covering the courts when I took the bench, and, looking back on it, I suppose it was inevitable that we would become friends. We had a lot in common. We both had come a long way in professions traditionally dominated by men. Neither of us had much use for people who did awful things to innocent folk. And we both loved cats. At any given time, Edna and I may have had six or eight cats between us. We still do.

The remarkable thing was that my friendship with Edna did not interfere with the way she treated me professionally. If she had a story to write, she wrote it just as she saw it, friendship or no friendship. And let me tell you, being the subject of an Edna Buchanan investigation is like being examined by a proctologist with no other appointments. When Alex and I were having terrible fights at the courthouse, Edna reported every bit of what happened. I had no quarrel with that. Nobody wants her divorce covered in the press, but Edna didn't write a single word that wasn't true. Alex did indeed stand outside my office and bang his head against the wall. Edna had every right and obligation to report it.

The woman was everywhere. When John Rowe and I were preparing for our wedding ceremony in Miami, we didn't want anyone to know it if we could help it. Alex was still awfully upset, and we didn't want to antagonize him. So, one afternoon, John and I drove to Naples, clear across the state, to get a marriage license. (We had already been married in the East St. Louis funeral home, of course, but no one in Florida knew that.) We drove back to Miami the same day. When I walked through the door, the phone was ringing. It was Edna.

"Inasmuch as you're the only Ellen Morphonios I know," she said, "I thought you might be able to tell me why someone named Ellen Morphonios got a marriage license in Naples."

I damn near fainted. I later learned that there was no magic to what Edna had done—the *Herald*'s Naples reporter had found the license while doing his routine checks at the courthouse. But it came as no surprise to me that Edna was the first with the story. Naturally, she got an exclusive. I couldn't exactly deny I had gotten the license.

I try never to lie, especially when someone's taking notes. Lying is a bad idea for the simple reason that, after you've done it, you can never remember what you said. The next time someone asks the same question, you invariably come up with a different untrue answer. And then it's all over for you. I may not always tell the whole truth—that is, I may not always go into intimate and personal detail to answer a reporter's question. But I certainly don't try to deceive or mislead people. That's suicide, and I'm not a suicidal person.

Having good relationships with reporters doesn't mean they'll always write nice things about you. But it usually means they'll give you the benefit of the doubt and listen carefully to your side of the story. Edna Buchanan is the only reporter who has the number of my private telephone at home. When she calls, she is likely to hear Dale pick up and say, "City morgue—you stab 'em, we slab 'em." Edna has spent a lot of time around the morgue, so she can appreciate that line. Most of the other people who cover the courts have my other home phone number—the one I answer only when I don't mind being disturbed. The reporters can call anytime. I ask only that they don't let anyone know my address. As far as I know, no one ever has.

Most of the time reporters call me about things that don't even involve me, or that involve me only peripherally. I suppose they call partly because they know I like to shoot my mouth off. I mean, I'm not the kind of person who is going to say, "Sorry, no comment." Miami is a big town, full of very accomplished criminals. So I get a lot of calls about people I once sentenced who have now gotten loose and killed or robbed a few more people. By law, I can't comment on cases pending before me. So I always welcome the chance to spout off about cases pending before somebody else.

The case of Odell Hicks was just such an opportunity. Hicks was one of the worst offenders I had ever seen. He once stood in my courtroom and told me that he had raped more than one hundred women—had grabbed them off the sidewalks or out of their cars, thrown them into the bushes, beaten them up, and raped them. He didn't care if they were twelve years old or seventy—he liked to terrorize them all. I had sentenced Hicks to what I hoped would be a good long time behind bars, but of course the geniuses in the prison system had released him early.

Now a reporter was calling to tell me that Odell Hicks was dead. He had died, it turned out, in a particularly cruel and barbaric way. It seemed that a man named Prentice Rasheed had gotten fed up with having people break into his store at night. The perpetrators always gained entry the same way—through the ceiling. Finally Rasheed decided to put a stop to it. He rigged an elaborate trap that consisted of some metal grating, some electrical wire, and a switch. He placed the grate in the opening in the ceiling. The idea was that any would-be burglar would step down onto the grate and get the shock of his life.

That's just what happened to Odell Hicks. Rasheed found him dead the morning after the attempted break-in. He had been cooked like a Christmas turkey.

The reporter on the other end of the phone wanted to know if the state attorney's office should prosecute Rasheed.

"Prosecute him?" I said. "Hell, we should give him a medal. He has done this community a great service."

The remark was strictly on the record. When I talk to reporters, I usually let them use whatever I say. I don't mind being quoted as having said something outrageous, as long as it doesn't cause trouble for someone else—say, a fellow judge or a police officer. If I'm going to hurt someone by saying something stupid, it's going to be me. But from time to time, I have to go off the record with a reporter. For example, people have made threats on my life several times in my career. It comes with the territory. On a couple of occasions, reporters have learned of the threats and called me looking for a story. If I trust the reporter, I'll talk about it, but only off the record. I'm not going to antagonize one of those crackpots by calling them crackpots in print.

I am not normally the kind of person who holds grudges, but there are some news reporters who have treated me so badly I will no longer talk to them. Brian Ross is one I have mentioned already. The others were *Miami News* reporters who wrote a series of articles about the way bail bonds are handled in the courts. One story was especially full of cheap insinuations. It needlessly hurt a lot of people, including me. The reporters asked me for my side of the story, but they used precious little of it, for which I'll never forgive them. It was sad to see the *News*, which was a fine paper in Don Petit's time, stoop to innuendo to get a story. A good reporter understands that he has the power to make or break people, and knows that because of that power he always has to be fair. These *Miami News* reporters didn't understand that.

I didn't know how angry I was at them until the next time I saw a *News* staffer. One day not long after the stories appeared, I heard a knock at the private door to my office. My staff doesn't like it when I answer that door—it's a good way to get machine-gunned—but I do it anyway. A *News* reporter was standing there when I drew the door open.

"Hi, Judge," she said, holding her notebook and pen. "Can I talk to you about something?"

I surprised myself with my answer.

"No, you can't. I don't want to talk to anyone from the *News* ever again."

And then I shut the door.

If the law had allowed it, I would have sentenced Jimmie Lee Wilson to death by electric chair. But in the end, it didn't matter. Someone else sentenced him to death by sharpened spoon.

When you've met as many disgusting thugs as I have, it's hard to say which one was the worst. But Jimmie Lee Wilson has to be a contender. He was a dangerous lunatic, a menace to anyone unfortunate enough to cross his path. His list of convictions included six rapes, four robberies, two murders, and two attempted murders. His big-time criminal career began in 1964 with the rape of two Mexican sisters who worked in the fields of Dade County. The judge in that case properly gave him two death sentences. That should have been the end of him, but it wasn't. He spent eight years on Florida's Death Row before a federal judge overturned the sentences. The judge said the jury had been selected improperly. The sentence was reduced to fifteen years.

That was not the last injustice. Not by a long shot. Six months later, Wilson was back on the streets. His sentence had been cut in half because, the prison people said, he had behaved well during his eight years behind bars. I myself found it hard to believe that Wilson could have behaved like a decent person for more than eight minutes, but, then, nobody consulted me.

He quickly took advantage of this bright new opportunity to haunt the community. One August night, he abducted a twenty-one-year-old man and his twenty-five-year-old girlfriend from the Tally-Ho Lounge and forced them to drive to a rock pit. There, he raped the woman, then shot and robbed them both. Both survived. He repeated the crime six weeks later. This time, he abducted a couple from the Gateway Inn and forced them to drive to a tomato field, where he raped the woman. Then he robbed and murdered them both. The police solved the crimes when they found Wilson's fingerprints on the victims' car.

Bernard Yedlin, one of the lawyers who represented Wilson, called him "one of the most dangerous psychotics I ever represented in my life." This was from someone who defended him.

I sentenced Wilson for the tomato-field killings. I gave him two life sentences for the killings and 130 years for ghouling the bodies. I also recommended that he never be paroled. Another judge later tacked on some more life sentences for the other crimes.

At the sentencing in my courtroom, I asked Wilson if he had anything to say.

"It is obvious that I haven't been given a fair trial. There's been a grave denial of justice," he said. Killers are so quaint when they lie.

When he walked out of my courtroom, there was little chance he would ever draw another free breath. The inmates at Florida State Prison made sure of it. One Sunday morning, the guards on Ward V found Wilson dead on the floor of his cell. He had been stabbed repeatedly in the middle of the chest. The prison officials weren't sure what the assailant or assailants had used as a weapon. It was possible that someone had smuggled a knife into the cell block, but the prison people thought it more likely that the killer had taken a spoon out of the lunchroom and sharpened it into a crude stiletto.

No one knew who had done the killing. There were nearly one hundred other men on Ward V, but—surprise, surprise—they all said they hadn't seen a thing. The wardens didn't know if Wilson had been killed by one man, ten men, or one hundred men.

I don't know either. But I have a preference.

I got married for the third time in 1978. Some people never learn.

In every other case in this memoir, I have tried to use real names. Here, I am going to change a few names—not to protect myself, but to protect the other people involved. Despite what happened in my third (and, God knows, final) marriage, I still care deeply for all the people who were involved in the story. I would lay down my life for any of them. If I were to publish their real names, outsiders might take the opportunity to ridicule or embarrass them. I'm not going to let that happen if I can help it.

Louis was a police officer—a lieutenant attached to the Metro-Dade narcotics unit. I met him for the first time in the mid-seventies. He called the office and told me he wanted to meet to discuss a case. I wouldn't meet him without other people present because I didn't know him. So we made an appointment to meet in the hospital room of a police sergeant who had been injured in the line of duty.

What a first date. I should have taken it as a sign.

In the next couple of years, Louis and his squad came to my house regularly to have me sign search warrants. One judge in Miami is always assigned to this duty on evenings and weekends. In Florida, as in other states, the police must have a judge's signature on a warrant in order to search someone's home. The warrant explains why the police think a crime has been committed and gives a detailed description of the place to be searched. The judge who signs a cop's warrant never knows if he or she will ever see the cop again. Bursting through doors into the homes of criminals is dangerous work.

I signed a lot of warrants for Louis on weekends and in the middle of the night. Soon, he started to drop by once in a while just for a cup of coffee and a chat. Then he started to drop by a lot, and sometimes he stayed even after he finished the coffee. The kids were curious. "What is that cop doing here all the time?" Dale said. I think he must have had a hunch.

Finally, Louis got around to taking me out instead of the warrants.

He was a good-looking guy. He had brown hair, fashionably long sideburns, and a thick mustache. He stood just under six feet tall and was made of stone. A lot of other women, I'm sorry to say, couldn't resist him. Once, I gave a speech to a civic group at the Four Ambassadors Hotel in Miami. Louis and I were sitting together at the head table. When I got up to take the dais, a couple of young women came along and began to hit on my man. The table was set on a platform, so I could see only the women's heads. I didn't like it, so I decided to do something about it.

"Well, would you look at that," I said into the microphone, right in the middle of my speech. "I leave my seat for a second and already somebody's moving in on my husband." It sounded like a big joke, and everybody laughed. But the babes moved on, and that was what mattered.

Before becoming a cop, Louis had been a big hero in Vietnam, where he had served as part of a high-powered marine sniper outfit. He had taken several gunshots in the legs (the doctors told him he would never walk again, but he did) and had won dozens of medals and commendations, including a Bronze Star. Hubert Humphrey personally pinned one of the medals on him. He was a marine through and through—tough, stubborn, smart, fearless.

He also was sixteen years younger than I was. When we met, I was forty-six and he was thirty. That never bothered him as much as it did me. He seemed to enjoy getting to know an older woman, especially one in my position. But I had to put up with jokes about how I was robbing the cradle. I can take a joke, but after a while I started to wonder if I should look for someone my own size. Louis always talked me out of it. He might have been younger, but he was no less mature. Indeed, I often thought he was more mature.

One day in September 1978, I performed a double wedding ceremony in my courtroom. The two grooms, prosecutors in the state attorney's office, had met their brides in the courthouse, so they thought it was appropriate to get married there. It was a nice ceremony. A short time later, I performed another ceremony for a prosecutor. And as it happened, these newlywed couples weren't the only ones thinking about matrimony. Louis and I were also discussing getting married.

At the second reception, I took a long walk with my friend Harvey Shenberg. We discussed the pros and cons of my getting married, and there were a lot of both. On the pro side, I really cared for Louis and thought he would make a terrific husband. I also didn't like being alone. I liked having a man around—not just for sex, but also to handle the things I think a man should handle. The truth was, I liked having someone to take care of me, and I thought Louis would do a superb job of it.

On the con side, Louis was young enough, at least biologically, to be my son. When I got to be eighty, he wouldn't even be collecting Social Security. And if God granted us children, they would be younger than Dale's oldest child. That might be hard to explain on the playground. Besides, neither of us had done too well at the altar. Louis had been married twice before and so had I. As much as I cared for him, I didn't want to swing and miss again. You know the saying—three strikes and you're out.

Harvey and I didn't come to a conclusion that day. I made the decision on my own a few days later.

The decision: I was getting married again. I still had some

doubts in the back of my mind, but my excitement about being with Louis enabled me to ignore them. We decided to get married in Reno. I was scheduled to go out of town for a judge's conference anyway, so nobody would suspect we were going to get hitched. The decision to get married was a private one, and I wanted to keep it that way.

Before we left, I told my parents I was getting married again. They reacted as if I had said I was going to the store to pick up a gallon of milk. When someone announces her engagement as many times as I had, I guess the thrill starts to fade.

We got married in the chapel of the MGM Grand Hotel in Reno. It was a lovely ceremony. The chapel is beautiful, and music played in the background. We didn't mind that it was on tape. I wore a brown skirt and blouse that my niece Carole had given me, and a white shawl handmade by my aunt. Louis wore a business suit, the one he wore when he testified in court cases. He looked good for a guy his age. Afterward, we drove up to Lake Tahoe to look at the scenery. When I saw the mountains and the lakes, I was more certain than ever that there was a God. Nobody else could make something so beautiful.

When we got back to the hotel, I called Dale on the phone. He told me Joe Oglesby, a reporter for the *Miami Herald,* was looking for me.

"The secret is out, Mom," he said. "Joe said he wants to do a story."

So much for keeping it private. The wedding of another judge might have merited only a line in one of the gossip columns. But the wedding of a judge who got married after each Olympics was big news. (Surprisingly, the *Herald* did not have a reporter assigned full-time to cover my marriages.) I figured, what the hell. I liked Joe Oglesby and knew he would do a good story. So I called him and told him everything. The article appeared under the headline HANG-ING JUDGE, COP TIE KNOT.

We were married on Friday the thirteenth, under a full moon. What happened a few years later was enough to make a person superstitious.

Sometimes society is victimized worse by the justice system than it is by criminals. In my opinion, the story of cop killer Manuel Valle was just such a case. The story began on April 2, 1978, in Coral

Gables, a lovely and historic suburb of Miami. People who live in Coral Gables like to think they are insulated from the dangers of city life, but the events of that day proved they are not. Police officer Louis Pena was on duty that afternoon. At forty-one, he was an eleven-year veteran of the force, a good cop, and a good family man. With him that day was his German shepherd police dog, Abraham, who was by the officer's side every day. They were partners. It would be their last day together.

At 6:37 P.M., Pena saw a brown Chevrolet Camaro glide through a red light. He pulled the car over and asked the driver for his license. There was a passenger in the car too. The license said the driver's name was Manuel Alvarez. It wasn't. The driver was really Manuel Valle, a career felon. When Pena stopped him, he was wanted for a parole violation and for the attempted murder, three years earlier, of a Sweetwater, Florida, police officer. He was a man who was desperate to avoid capture for those reasons, and for a new reason as well: The scumbag had just stolen the Camaro. Valle was prepared to do anything to avoid arrest. He had a pistol in the front seat of the car.

Officer Pena went back to his car to run a computer check on the driver's name and the car registration. Valle and his buddy, a cheap hood named Felix Ruiz, knew they had been nailed. They talked for a moment. Then Ruiz walked away, saying he had to make a phone call. Valle leaned against the Camaro and lit a cigarette. The police officer was in the patrol car, talking on the radio. It didn't take long for Valle to decide what to do. He put out the cigarette and grabbed the gun off the seat.

Pena was shot three times—once in the neck and twice in the stomach. His dog barked frantically behind the cage in the backseat. By then, a backup police officer named Gary Spell was arriving at Almeria Avenue, the scene of the traffic stop. Spell, the son of a cop, had been on the force only a couple of years. When Valle saw him, he fired and hit the officer in the back. Normally, Spell did not wear a bulletproof vest on the job. But for some reason he wore one that day, and it saved his life. Valle scrambled back to the Camaro and sped away. Spell fired at the car, but unfortunately did not hit the driver. The police later found the car on Miracle Mile, the shopping center in Coral Gables.

Louis Pena's last words, gasped into the police radio, were, "I'm shot. I'm shot. I'm shot." The medical examiner later testified that he drowned in his own blood.

Valle would later say that he found Ruiz and hitched a ride with him back to Miami. The two men and their wives spent that night at the Ramona Motel on Flagler Street. Louis Pena's widow, Lana, spent the night alone. The killer and his sidekick were arrested the next day in Deerfield Beach, a few miles north of Fort Lauderdale. Hours later, Valle confessed to Metro-Dade police. They told him he could have a lawyer, but he said he didn't want one.

"I had violated probation. They were looking for me, and I didn't want to give myself up. I told Felix that they were checking on the car and they were going to find out it was stolen, that we were both going to be arrested. I just told him that I was going to have to blast the cop," Valle said in the confession.

He went on to say how he took Pena's life. "The first time I shot, I wanted to try to wound the officer so I could get away. I pointed the gun inside the car. Honestly, I couldn't see him because of the windshield. I knew where he would be sitting. At that time, I was nervous, you know. But I was almost positive I would hit him."

The confession was made public three weeks after the killing. People had been searching for justice from the start. Now they were calling my office and writing letters to the editor demanding that Valle be tried swiftly. I was happy to oblige them. This was a simple, straightforward case, and I was not going to let the defense lawyers drag it out, as they did in so many other cases. There was no reason they could not immediately take sworn statements from the witnesses. I set the trial date for May 8—twenty-four days after Valle was arraigned. Such a quick trial on a charge carrying the death penalty was unusual, I'll admit. But it was the right thing to do.

It was some trial. Police officers and reporters filled the courtroom every day to hear the awful details of the crime. Valle's lawyer, David Goodhart, did a fine job, but he did not have much to work with. In the confession, his client had supplied details of the crime that only the killer could have known. In a desperation move, Goodhart put Valle on the stand. The story Valle told was quite different from the one he had told the police. But he started by telling the truth.

"Is it true you shot Officer Pena?" the lawyer asked.

"Yes, it is," Valle said. He later said that he didn't consider himself "a model citizen," which I think no one in the courtroom would have disputed.

Valle admitted that he had picked up the handgun when he saw Pena calling in the car registration. He said he walked slowly to the patrol car, pointed the gun at Pena, and said, "Freeze." That was where his testimony departed from what he had told the police.

"My hand hit either the frame of the windshield or the mirror of the police car, and the gun went off," he said. "I don't know what it hit. I panicked. I didn't see the officer."

The defendant testified later that he had heard on the radio that Pena was dead. He pretended to be surprised about it. He also said that he had not given his confession voluntarily. "I was afraid," he said. "Afraid for my life."

Prosecutor Hank Adorno cross-examined Valle. "You'll break the law if it's to your benefit?"

"I have done so," Valle said.

"And you've lied when necessary to protect your own personal safety?"

"Sure."

"Would you lie to avoid death in the electric chair?"

From the bench, I could see Valle looking at his shoes. "I don't believe I deserve the electric chair, sir," he said.

The trial lasted three days. The jury deliberated only thirty minutes before finding Valle guilty. Testimony was then presented on whether Valle should go to prison for life or die in the electric chair. The jury took twenty minutes to recommend the chair. Naturally, I followed the recommendation. There was no alternative, as I saw it. If ever someone had committed a crime deserving of the death penalty, Valle had.

My son Dale, a conservative who was also outraged by Valle's crime, came to the sentencing. He took a seat in the gallery next to a young man he had never seen before. During the hearing, the young man raised his right hand as if it were a gun and pointed his finger at the defendant. Then he pulled the imaginary trigger again and again. Dale didn't learn until later that the young man was the dead officer's son.

Unfortunately, I had not heard the last of Manuel Valle. Nearly three years after the trial, the Florida Supreme Court ruled on his appeal. By a 6–1 vote, the court decided that Valle should not only not face the death penalty but also get a new trial. The next day's paper excerpted the court's ruling.

"We find that requiring Valle to go to trial within 24 days after arraignment resulted in a denial of effective assistance of counsel," the court said. The opinion went on to say that the court knew of no other case in recent history that had been tried so quickly. (Indeed, there was no other case. The speediest judge before me was the one who tried Giuseppe Zangara for the murder of Chicago Mayor Anton Cermak in Miami in 1933. Zangara was trying to kill Franklin Delano Roosevelt, but missed him and hit Cermak instead. The killer was tried, convicted, and put to death by electrocution within thirty-three days of the crime.) The Supreme Court said defense lawyer Goodhart had not had enough time to take sworn statements from some prosecution witnesses, and had no chance to have Valle examined by a psychiatrist. The case, the court said, would have to go back to square one.

Before I begin raving about the decision (I can hardly contain myself), let me tell you what happened next. In 1981, Manuel Valle was retried before Judge James Jorgenson. Valle's lawyers—he had two this time—asked the judge to keep the confession out of evidence. The judge refused, saying Valle knew what he was doing when he admitted to killing Pena. Gary Spell, the officer who was saved by his bulletproof vest, watched the trial from the back of the courtroom. It was Spell who adopted Pena's dog, Abraham, after the officer's death. The outcome of the second trial was the same as the first—the jury found Valle guilty. After the verdict, it again recommended death, and the judge followed the recommendation. Manuel Valle at last would go to the electric chair, right?

Wrong. The Florida Supreme Court, Valle's only friend in the world, upheld the conviction but overturned the sentence. Twice the people of Florida had thought justice had been done in the Valle case, and twice they had learned they were wrong. A police officer had been shot dead in cold blood as he radioed back to the station, and so far the state had not been able to effect justice in the case.

A few more years went by. In 1988, Valle's case came before Circuit Judge Norman Gerstein for resentencing. There was, for the third time, a full hearing of mitigating and aggravating factors. Again, the jury recommended the death penalty. It would be up to Judge Gerstein to decide Valle's fate. Now, I respect Judge Gerstein very much. But let me tell you, he is no conservative. My impression is that he would sooner walk barefoot over hot coals than sentence a man to death. He agonized for days over the Valle case. The decision was so difficult for him that it affected him physically—he lost weight and began to look haggard and worried. But in the end he followed the law and imposed the death penalty.

Unbelievable. It took the justice system ten years of nitpicking and fooling around to reach the same conclusion I had reached in twenty-four days. Some would say the delay was my fault. If I had given Goodhart more time to prepare a defense, the argument goes, the Supreme Court never would have overturned the sentence in the first place, and the taxpayers would have been saved the expense of all those extra proceedings. I know some people think that way, and that's fine. But I don't see it that way. To begin with, Manuel Valle was not crazy, and there was no sense in spending six months and thousands of dollars trying to find out if he was. Valle was an opportunist, plain and simple. The defense was looking into the insanity defense in desperation. It would have been an injustice to permit it.

I will admit that the defense did not have time to take statements from all five dozen witnesses on the state's list. But it didn't matter. There were only a few witnesses who were really important to the case, and the defense knew who they were and took their statements. The rest were on the witness list only because the state is required to name everyone who has had even a peripheral involvement in a case. The prosecutor didn't call anywhere near five dozen witnesses. It was a nonissue, but the Supreme Court had bought it.

I couldn't—and still can't—understand the court's thinking in that case. I can only surmise that it was scared by the speed with which I tried it. People in the justice system are accustomed to waiting months and even years for murder cases to come to trial. I upset that expectation. And when I did, the system was shocked. I see no reason why a simple case has to rot in a file while the witnesses lose their memories or grow old and die. But when I tried to do something about it, the Supreme Court stepped on my neck.

The system has more than observed the rights of Manuel Valle, in my opinion. I know the Supreme Court would disagree, but I think I respected his rights when I heard the case, and I'm sure Judge Jorgenson did too. Judge Norman Gerstein was painfully aware of Valle's rights. That's great. But what about the rights of Pena's widow, his son, and the rest of his friends and relatives? They do not have a right to grab Valle by the throat and throttle him, as they may well like to do. But they do have a right to see justice done—a right to see Louis Pena's killer tried quickly and fairly. For them, the pain of the officer's death has lingered for a decade. The system that Pena worked so hard for has failed them terribly.

And what about the rights of society? Those of us who obey the law have a right to live apart from the likes of Manuel Valle. One of the functions of civilized society is to identify and punish those who do wrong. In the Valle case, the system has failed to do that. The right of society to see justice done has been denied.

Valle has not yet exhausted his rights. He will have several more chances to appeal his conviction and sentence before he is strapped into the chair. It is not unusual for prisoners in Florida to wait on Death Row for ten years while the wheels of justice creak and groan. That's an outrage, and society shouldn't put up with it. I hope and pray that Norman Gerstein's sentence in the Valle case will be upheld and, more important, carried out. The death of Louis Pena has gone unavenged too long.

SIXTEEN

FORCED TO

SET A KILLER FREE

Manuel Valle was not the only defendant I brought to trial in a hurry. Except for the fact that he was a killer, I had nothing against him. At the time, I was working hard to try all my cases as quickly as I could. The unthinkable had happened in my court: I had built up a large backlog of cases.

It happened, ironically, because I was working harder. In late 1977, I became the administrative judge for the criminal courts. That meant lots of headaches and no more money. As administrative judge, I was responsible not only for my normal caseload but also for the day-to-day operation of the courts. When judges went on vacation, it was up to me to find other judges to handle their caseloads. When a judge recused himself from a case because of a conflict of interest, it was my job to find another judge to take over. And when a judge got way behind in his work, it was up to me to assign another judge to help out.

That was the ironic part. Because I was spending so much time on my duties as administrative judge, I wasn't getting my work done in the courtroom. Being an administrator meant I had to attend lots of long, boring meetings. And that meant I spent less time in the courtroom. Part of the swelling caseload was my fault. On many days when I attended meetings, I returned to my office late in the afternoon. Instead of climbing onto the bench and starting a new trial, I would pack my briefcase and go home, bushed. It was no way to run a railroad. I should have stayed longer and worked harder. When I didn't, it showed. In my years on the bench, I had prided myself on keeping my caseload as small, or almost as small, as any other judge's. Now, out of twelve judges, there were only three with caseloads larger than mine. Justice wasn't getting done quickly enough in my courtroom, and I couldn't stand for that. I knew the public wouldn't, either.

Under Florida law, I had 180 days after arrest to bring each case before a jury. On average, it took first-degree murder cases 149 days to get to trial. I thought 60 days would be more like it. There is no reason in the world why competent attorneys—and the Miami courts are full of fine lawyers—can't prepare a case for trial in that time. So I served notice on the lawyers who practiced before me that 60 days would be the standard. If the state wasn't ready, the case was going to trial anyway. If the defense wasn't prepared, I was going to shed no tears.

To reduce my caseload, I was going to have to work my tail off. Only long hours on the bench trying cases could get me out of the hole I had dug for myself. Where I once started court at nine A.M. sharp, I now backed it up to either eight-thirty or even eight, depending on how early the jurors could make it. (As for the lawyers, they had to be there when I told them to.) I also began to hear cases in bunches. It wasn't unusual for me to handle three at a time. One jury would be deliberating in the jury room, a second would be hearing evidence, and the lawyers would be picking a third in another courtroom.

I also served notice of my intentions by refusing to grant continuances. Unless a defense lawyer or witness was in the hospital with a verifiable illness, I didn't grant them, period. Everything set for trial went to trial.

The cases of Jimmy Lee Ashley and Elton Edwards were among those that were brought to trial lickety-split. They were accused of going on a deadly rampage through Claude Pepper Towers, a senior citizens' housing project. They were charged with killing two people. One was a sixty-one-year-old woman. The other was an eighty-two-year-old blind man who wrote poetry. Ashley was also charged with the rape and robbery, at gunpoint, of a seventy-year-old woman at the same housing project. The two defendants appeared in my courtroom on June 2. I told them to be ready for trial on June 19. I appointed Edward O'Donnell, a fine attorney, to represent Ashley, who could not afford to pay a lawyer.

"Your Honor," O'Donnell said, "I just met Jimmy Ashley a few minutes ago and I don't believe I can effectively prepare a defense in eighteen days."

"I think you can," I said.

The case touched off a war of editorials and letters to the editor.

The *Miami News* fired the first shot, tearing me apart in an editorial titled "Speedy Trial Tests Justice." The newspapers, always a little to the left, didn't like the tactics used by this conservative judge.

"Circuit Judge Ellen Morphonios, seeking to add to her reputation as a 'hanging judge,' is sorely testing the justice of the criminal justice system with her handling of a case involving two teenagers accused of murdering two elderly persons," it said. "It is one thing to be a tough judge and hand out stiff sentences within the law after a jury's finding of guilt. But it is quite another matter for a judge to take an action which could result in considerably less than a fair trial, yet that is the direction in which Morphonios' speedy trial action leans.

"While the crimes involved in this case are heinous, no one has been convicted. Trying to lessen in any fashion the chances of a fair trial is not only unfair to the accused, but it is an assault on the justice system which protects the innocent until they are proven guilty.

"A speedy trial is important to accused persons, but when it is too speedy it is unjust. And speed should not supersede the overriding need for a fair trial no matter what the crime. Judge Morphonios should stick to her role as judge, and stop trying to be prosecutor, defense attorney and jury."

Well, I thought the *Miami News* should stick to covering fires and printing department-store ads. But the *News* was not the only publication on my case. The *Miami Herald* weighed in a short time later, saying, "We're not entirely comfortable with the get-tough stance being taken by Dade Circuit Judge Ellen Morphonios. A few weeks of preparation . . . hardly seems enough time to prepare cases where the penalty could be life imprisonment or death." The paper went on to say that my tactics were "a predictable backlash" against the trend of letting cases drag on "at the expense of justice." The *Herald*, it seemed, wanted me to slow down and speed up. If I were in the habit of taking advice on how to do my job from editorial boards, and I was not, I wouldn't have known what to do.

Several gallant readers rushed to the aid of this poor damsel in distress. A member of one anticrime group sent a letter to the *News*. "I have observed the judge, and if our courts had more judges with her unswerving desire to protect the citizens, who are the victims of the criminals, crime would be reduced the only way possible: jailing

those who are guilty of crimes against the state. Judge Ellen Morphonios should be honored for her integrity and courage." I swear, I
didn't pay him to write it. Another writer called the *News* editorial
"a disgraceful injustice to a fine jurist. Judge Morphonios has a
proven track record of fairness, competence and courage." I didn't
commission that one, either.

I even got a vote of confidence from a defense lawyer, a member
of the group that was supposed to be so terribly aggrieved by my
speedy-trial policy. His name was Henry Prebish. "From my own experience, I have demanded and obtained from Judge Morphonios a
speedy trial for a public official accused of crime, with favorable results. Currently, I have demanded a speedy trial for a public official I
represent accused of crime." I appreciated the letter. But if Mr. Prebish was trying to butter me up, it didn't work.

I think substantial justice was done in all the cases I tried in
that hectic period. Certainly it was done in the cases of Jimmy Lee
Ashley and Elton Edwards. Ashley was convicted of raping the seventy-year-old woman. He pleaded guilty to killing the two others. At
sentencing, I salted him away. Edwards was going to face trial for his
part in the killing of the old blind poet, but at the last minute he
pleaded guilty. The prosecutor had already made his opening statement when Edwards's family persuaded him to confess to the crime
and accept his punishment. I sentenced him to life.

Trying those cases quickly meant that I could get my court back
on schedule—meant I could deliver better justice to society. Within
a few months after I stopped granting continuances, I had reduced
my caseload considerably. Where once there were only three judges
slower than I was, there were now only three judges who were faster.
And they didn't have to worry about a lot of meetings.

I always prided myself on maintaining a certain detachment on
the bench. I might have thought someone deserved to go to prison,
or worse, but I tried not to take anyone's crimes personally. The case
of Jimmy Lee Coney changed that—and temporarily drove me out of
the criminal courts.

Coney, a career criminal, committed his worst crime on March
24, 1976. The horrendous part of the case was that he was already in
prison when he committed the crime. Coney had been convicted of
rape in 1965, when he was eighteen, and had served ten years of a

twenty-year sentence. Now he was being held at the North Dade correctional facility, a small detention center for prisoners on their way back into society. Coney would be eligible for parole in a year. If he could behave just that long, he would be a free man.

It was too much to ask. The day of the crime, he was beginning his thirty-first day in a program that allowed him to leave the prison during the day to go to work. He had a job as a landscaper at a housing development in the southwest section of Miami. The prison officials dropped him off there early in the morning. By nine-thirty A.M. he was gone—he stole a car from a co-worker and disappeared.

This time, Coney's victim was not a woman but a twelve-year-old girl. She was home alone that day. Her mother was at work. The child was inside the house, playing, when Coney forced his way in. No one saw him enter. The little girl didn't know he was there until he was almost on top of her.

I do not know how to describe the violence with which he assaulted the girl. He seemed to go out of his way to traumatize her, to make sure she would never forget these few terrifying moments of her life as long as she lived, if she lived. The medical testimony about the rape of the child was almost more than I could bear to hear. But he didn't stop at rape. When he was done tearing her up, he grabbed a thick macrame cord, knotted it around her neck, and choked her with it. Then he loosened his grip and left her for dead. On his way out he stole a few things for good measure.

But the girl was not dead. When he left, she fell unconscious, struggling to breathe because of the trauma to her throat. Her mother found her that way when she arrived home a short time later.

The child, who eventually recovered from her physical injuries, was able to give a description of the attacker. Coney was arrested a short time later and his case was assigned to my courtroom. Based on the girl's testimony and medical evidence, he was convicted. I sentenced him to 420 years in prison—130 years each for rape, burglary, and robbery, and another 30 years for attempted murder.

It was a reasonable sentence under the circumstances, and I had to work hard to be reasonable. Never had I been so affected by a criminal. I hated Jimmy Lee Coney for what he did. I wanted to sentence him to death and administer the punishment myself, with my bare hands.

That was when I started thinking about leaving the criminal

division. It's healthy to feel outrage when someone commits a terrible crime. But a judge who can't maintain a sense of detachment will
go crazy in a week. I calmed down when the Coney case was over—
fortunately, you hear testimony that disgusting only once in a great
while—but I still wanted to pursue the idea of a stint in the civil
division.

It was something Daddy wanted me to do anyway. He lectured
me only a few times in my adult life, and one of the lectures was
about that.

"You've been working in the criminal courts your whole career,"
he told me. "It's time for a change. You weren't raised to stand in
one place your whole life. You're supposed to go places, or at least try
to. What is going to make you understand that?"

There was another reason to move to the civil division. Don
Petit was no longer my political guru, but I still harbored hopes of
becoming an appeals court judge, even if I never made it all the way
to the Florida Supreme Court. But there was no way I would get that
chance if I didn't hear some civil cases. Finally, the chief judge
granted my request. Maximum Morphonios, the hanging judge,
could no longer hang anyone.

What a mistake. Lord, what a disaster. To begin with, I never
came close to being named to the appeals court. Appeals court
judges were appointed, which meant that anyone who wanted to be
considered for an opening had to make application to a nominating
commission, which would then recommend a candidate to the governor. Well, I wasn't surprised to find that the folks there didn't put my
application at the top of the pile. The selection of appeals judges was
an intensely political process. It was fine if you were qualified, as I
felt I was. But it was more important that you be well connected,
and that you be the politically correct choice. I didn't fit the description. No politician would name me to the appeals court because,
frankly, I shot my mouth off too much. The governor wanted candidates who wore button-down suits and never got laid—or, if they
did, didn't enjoy it. No, I was the wrong woman for the job.

Being in the civil division was a nightmare all its own. Civil
judges preside over personal-injury cases, lawsuits between corporations, and so on. Let me tell you, it's dull. Nothing numbs my cra-
nium faster than a discussion of civil liability. Worse than the
boredom was the feeling that I wasn't doing a damned thing for the

community. The tweedy stiffs who practiced law in the civil division
were in no hurry to get anything done. They were making hundreds
of dollars an hour and saw no reason to turn off the money faucet.
Even when I managed to bring a case to trial, what good did I do? If
some company beat some other company out of millions of dollars,
how was the community served? It wasn't, so far as I could see.

I couldn't stand it. Within a year I was back on the criminal
bench, throwing thunderbolts. I had left criminal because I wanted
to strangle Jimmy Lee Coney. I had left civil because I wanted to
strangle the lawyers.

In 1982, the Florida Supreme Court made me set a killer free.

His name was Anibal Jaramillo. I think his first name should
have been Animal. He was charged with killing three people in
Dade County in a little over two weeks. In the first case, the police
said Jaramillo shot to death a twenty-four-year-old woman named
Graciella Gomez. She was driving a Corvette on a busy city street
when her assailant pulled up alongside her and began blasting away.
Somehow, the young woman escaped the attack. She skidded to a
stop, scrambled out of the Vette, ran through traffic, and jumped
into the rear seat of a car whose driver and passenger had offered
help. But the presence of other witnesses didn't stop the killer. He
walked up to the second car, took careful aim, and blasted Gomez as
she cowered in the backseat. I can only imagine the terror that
woman must have felt when she heard the killer's footsteps coming
toward her.

The second case was worse. Jaramillo was accused of executing
two men in a town house in southwest Miami. The killer got into
the house, tied up the two victims, gagged them, and sat them
down. Then he blew their brains out with a silencer-equipped machine gun. Gilberto Caicedo and Candelario Castellanos were given
no mercy.

Jaramillo first stood trial in my courtroom for the murder of Graciella Gomez. The state's theory was that Jaramillo was a hit man
hired to do away with people who had reneged on drug deals. It was
a believable theory. Gomez died during the most violent period in
Miami's history. The illegal-drug trade was growing quickly, and
dealers were killing each other with regularity. Miami's drug lords
were every bit as ruthless as Al Capone's mobsters were in the days of

the liquor rackets. I wouldn't say the state's evidence in the case was overwhelming, but I think it was sufficient. Jaramillo's fingerprints were found on a gun and a car abandoned near the scene of the slaying. But the prosecutor could not prove that the gun was the one used to kill Gomez.

The jurors found Jaramillo not guilty. At first, I could not imagine why. But then it dawned on me that perhaps the jurors were scared. During the trial, a photographer for *Time* magazine had come into my chambers and asked for permission to shoot in the courtroom. He said he was working on a story about juries and needed some good pictures of jurors hearing evidence. I gave him permission, of course. The courts in Florida are open to the public, and I did not have the authority to keep him from doing his job. A few times while he was shooting, I noticed the jurors glancing at him worriedly. I considered telling them who he was and why he was there, but I decided not to. Anything a judge says about the media's presence could prejudice a jury, and I didn't want to take that chance.

Maybe I should have. When the case was over, the first question the jurors asked me was, "Who was that man taking pictures of us?" I think they feared that they too might be hunted down and murdered in traffic if they found Jaramillo guilty.

I thought the evidence in the second case was stronger. When they searched the house of the two dead men, the police found Jaramillo's fingerprints on a butcher knife, a paper bag, and a piece of plastic in which some rope had been wrapped. The machine gun was never found. The prosecutor's theory was that Jaramillo had brought the rope into the house in the paper bag, and had then used the butcher knife to cut the rope so that he could tie up the victims. But again, he had no witnesses who could testify about the shootings themselves. The only potential witness, a nephew of one of the deceased, fled the house after the shootings and never returned.

The second trial sticks out in my mind because it was during that trial that John Hinckley, Jr., tried to kill President Ronald Reagan in front of a Washington hotel. I had been reluctant to tell the jury in the previous case about the photographer. But I didn't hesitate to tell this jury about the assassination attempt. The citizens have a right to know when their President has been shot. We took a recess, and when it was clear that the President would survive, we went back to work.

Jaramillo took the stand in his own defense. He said he had visited the two dead men a day before they died. He said he had used the butcher knife while helping them to unpack boxes in their garage. The police fingerprint technicians could not clearly disprove the story because they could not say exactly when the prints had been left on the knife. But that didn't matter to me. I, for one, found Jaramillo's testimony incredible. He was a man trying desperately to save his own skin.

The jurors saw it the same way. They convicted Jaramillo on both counts of first-degree murder and recommended that he go to prison for life. That wasn't good enough for me. I saw Jaramillo as the worst kind of murderer—the kind who kills not because of passion but for pay. I sentenced him to death in the electric chair on both counts. I also ordered that the sentences run consecutive to one another. That way, if an appeals court reduced the sentence to life in prison, Jaramillo would still serve at least fifty years without parole.

But, oh my, the appeals court went further than that. In Florida, all death sentences are appealed directly to the state Supreme Court. In their wisdom, the justices not only overturned the death penalty but also ordered Jaramillo set free. A dozen reasonable, conscientious jurors had decided unanimously that the state had proved its case against the defendant. But the court came along, stepped right over the jurors, and ruled that the state had not presented sufficient evidence to convict.

"This proof is not inconsistent with Jaramillo's reasonable explanation as to how his fingerprints came to be on these items in the victim's home," the court said. Hell, Jaramillo's explanation may have been reasonable, but anyone sitting in the courtroom could see that it wasn't true. The jurors certainly saw it. The court went on, "The state failed to establish that Jaramillo's fingerprints could only have been placed on the items at the time the murder was committed." I was ordered to call Jaramillo to my courtroom and release him. It was the first time the state Supreme Court had ever freed a man sentenced to death by a judge.

Letting him go was among the most unpleasant duties I have ever had to carry out. I felt pure fury and frustration. The smirking killer, fresh from Death Row, appeared in my courtroom on a Tuesday morning. His lawyer, Louis Casuso, stood next to him. I am not one who likes to give speeches from the bench, but this time my emotion got the best of me.

"Frankly, this is the most incredible thing I can think of. I think he's guilty of murder. The jury thought he was guilty of murder. The minute he gets on the street he'll probably kill again. I think he's a contract murderer. He's everywhere. He's like Spiderman. He's everywhere." I was getting too worked up, so I thought it best to get it over with. "But in accordance with the mandate from the Florida Supreme Court, he's discharged."

Jaramillo's lawyer said, "Thank you, Your Honor."

"Don't thank me," I snapped. "He'll be back."

I haven't seen the return of Mr. Jaramillo. Yet.

Don't say anything bad about the Miami Dolphins. I love 'em. I have ever since the team was founded. When I was married to John Rowe, I never missed a game. If the team was out of town, I watched on TV. If it was in town, I went to the Orange Bowl and cheered in person. Even when I couldn't get a ticket and the game wasn't televised in Miami, I managed to follow the team. John and I would drive four hours to Naples, rent a motel room, and watch from there. In 1972, the Miami Dolphins were literally the perfect team. They went 17-0 and won the Super Bowl. Eugene Morris, the star running back known as Mercury, was at the heart of that perfect team.

So you can imagine my disappointment when, in the summer of 1982, Mercury Morris showed up in my courtroom, charged with trafficking in cocaine.

Injuries had forced him out of football in 1976, but he had continued to live in Miami, continued to make himself visible. In the early seventies, I saw him give a speech on motivation at a banquet I attended. He was electrifying. Using his great charm and poise, he grabbed the audience's attention and never let go. Every word seemed full of deep meaning. I was so enthralled with the speech that my male companion, someone more than a friend, was sure I was getting the hots for the retired running back. I wasn't. But I thoroughly enjoyed his speech.

Unfortunately, he had a reputation for doing things less admirable than public speaking. After football, he was arrested for writing bad checks and was put on probation. Pretty soon, word started to spread that he might be involved in drugs. As the wife of a narcotics officer, I was aware of the talk. But arresting people was Louis's business, not mine. So I didn't ask any questions.

By the summer of 1982, Morris was in bad shape. He was hooked on cocaine, he owed money to a couple of drug dealers, he couldn't pay his mortgage, and he was in hot water for writing more bad checks. That was when his gardener offered to help. Freddy Donaldson, a guy with a long police record, told Merc he could make some quick money by doing a drug deal. The gardener offered to set up the deal. The plan was that Merc would sell a couple of kilograms of cocaine to a guy Donaldson knew. What Merc didn't know was that Donaldson then went to agents of the Florida Department of Law Enforcement and told them what the football star was planning.

A couple of days before the deal was to go down, Donaldson called Morris on the phone to discuss it. Donaldson told Merc that the buyer—an undercover state agent—had the money. When the gardener mentioned money, Merc said, "Don't talk this way over the fucking phone." Near the end of the call, Morris said, "Hey, man, you better make sure this is no fucking setup, boy. Did you hear me? Did you hear what I said?"

The state law-enforcement agents heard him. They were taping everything.

Morris later met the buyer—an agent named Joe Brinson—at a mall. The agent was wearing a body microphone. If Morris had been a more skillful drug dealer, he would have checked the guy for a wire, but he didn't. So everything he said wound up on tape. The agent said he was nervous. Could he trust Morris?

"You ever heard of Mercury Morris?" Merc said. "What I'm telling you is I've got kids. I've got as much to lose as you."

The deal was set. On August 18, the agent went to Morris's house in South Miami. He carried shoe boxes and paper bags with $120,000 in $100 bills. Morris's beer-drinking buddy, a pipe fitter named Edgar Kulins, was at the house with Merc. The agent showed Morris the money, and Morris gave him a sample of the cocaine he planned to sell him. Then he and Kulins freebased some cocaine and watched a dirty movie while they waited for their coke supplier to arrive. On the tapes the agents made, you could hear people screwing and moaning.

The supplier, Vincent Cord, showed up with the coke. Morris gave it to the agent. Brinson was counting out the cash to pay for the cocaine when his fellow agents moved in.

Morris's last words as a free man were, "It's a goddamn bust."

When he heard the agents coming, Merc grabbed the bag of cocaine. He was thirty-five years old, but still pretty quick. Then he tried to throw the stuff over a fence and into the canal behind his house. Merc was a much better runner than he was a passer. The stuff—456 grams of white dust—landed at the feet of George Ray Havens, the state attorney's chief investigator. It wasn't Mercury Morris's day.

The story made headlines from the first day. Merc's coach, Don Shula, and his former teammates were quoted as saying they felt terrible about what had happened. People in Miami felt shocked and betrayed. The Dolphins, the only big-time professional sports team in Miami at the time, were the pride of Miami. Morris might not have been the most popular player on the team, but he was close. His arrest was an insult to the team's fans. And in Miami, that meant everyone.

"I don't believe this," a high school football player said in the newspaper story the day after the arrest. "This is a shock to me."

The case was randomly assigned to my courtroom. I felt from the start that Merc had no chance of getting acquitted at trial. The evidence was too strong. Merc didn't feel that way. Within a couple of weeks after the arrest, prosecutor George Yoss told him he would recommend a lighter sentence if Morris would plead guilty and lead the investigators to other dealers. But Merc wouldn't have any part of it. He was hell-bent on having a trial. He seemed to think that a jury would go easy on him because his gardener had initiated the deal, and because he used to be a great running back. It was pure hubris, in my opinion.

Things got even worse for Merc when the supplier, Vincent Cord, copped a plea. In exchange for lenient treatment, he agreed to testify against Morris. With his testimony, Morris would have a hard time persuading the jury that he was a poor, unwitting soul duped into a drug deal by his gardener.

On the witness stand, Morris never denied that he made the drug deal, or that he used cocaine. But he said the gardener "kinda persuaded [him]" to do things he wouldn't otherwise have done. If Donaldson hadn't pushed him, and if the agent had not been so insistent on making the deal, it never would have happened, he said. "I am not a drug dealer," he said. "I have never been a drug dealer."

The next day, Morris's buddy Kulins also pleaded guilty. Now Merc was all alone. The jury was left with only him to judge, and he apparently no longer liked his chances. All the testimony had been heard and the lawyers were ready to give their final arguments when Yoss, defense lawyer Ronald Strauss, Merc, and I gathered outside earshot of the jury to discuss the state's plea offer. Morris, looking confident as always, let his lawyer do the talking.

"We're prepared to plead guilty to possession in exchange for a recommendation of one year in the stockade," Strauss said.

One year? Under a tough new law, people convicted of trafficking in cocaine would have to spend a minimum of fifteen years in prison. That means fifteen years without parole. In any case, Morris wasn't asking for a light sentence here. He was asking for a birthday present.

"No way," Yoss said.

"Ludicrous," I said. "I won't do it."

"He can plead right now to conspiracy and trafficking, and we'll waive the fifteen-year mandatory. It's the best I can do," Yoss said.

"Not good enough," Strauss said.

That was the end of the discussion. Morris had come this far. Now he was going to take his chances with the jury. I finished reading the instructions to the jury about four P.M. Then the jurors left to begin their deliberations. In the hall, reporters for newspapers and TV stations across the country sat and passed the time. I waited in my office, wondering what it was like to be Mercury Morris just then. Wasn't he terrified at what was about to happen? Or could he still believe the jury was going to excuse him because he used to be someone?

The jury took three hours to convict him of four of the six charges against him, including trafficking in cocaine and conspiracy to sell cocaine. I always watch the defendant's face when a verdict is being read. Usually, the defendant's expression is full of hope. When the guilty verdict is read, the look of hope changes to an expression of disappointment or despair, but hardly ever surprise. Most people convicted of crimes don't seem surprised. Mercury Morris didn't. He just sat there, rigid as a steel beam. Behind him, his wife broke into tears. Even the prosecutor looked grim. Like everyone else, George Yoss, a big Dolphins fan, had admired Merc.

When the clerk finished reading the verdicts, I said, "Sorry, Merc." I had no quarrel with the verdict. But I really was sorry.

The sentencing was in January 1983. Morris came to court in jeans and a sweater. "As I sit here this day, I'm perplexed how I was convicted," he told me. I believe he was perplexed. He had been perplexed from the start, though I can't imagine why. Then his lawyer said, "Putting Eugene Morris in jail is a judgment of destruction." He asked me to ignore the law requiring me to give Merc fifteen years without parole for trafficking.

I couldn't do it. I had to follow the law. Fifteen years without parole was more time than I was required to give first-time offenders who commit second-degree murder. It didn't seem entirely fair, but I had to give it to him anyway. Then I tacked on another five years, for a total of twenty years in the state prison. I gave him the extra five not so much to punish him but to give him incentive to behave. Someone who is sentenced to a mandatory fifteen years has little reason to be good—he'll get out in fifteen years whether he behaves or not. The prisoner sentenced to a mandatory fifteen plus five has to watch his step. If he's good, the prison people will let him out after fifteen. If not, they'll keep him five more years.

I could have sentenced him to thirty years, but I didn't want to. As I've said, I liked him and felt sorry for him.

Most prisoners go straight to the state prison after sentencing, but I let Merc stay in the county jail while he and his lawyer worked on his appeal. The other prisoners didn't seem to like him. Every day, the jail officials sent me a new series of complaints about Merc. One said he had rubbed the thigh of a woman visitor. Another said a visitor had flashed her breasts at him. Some of the other guys on the cell block didn't like Morris because he was writing a book and because the media paid a lot of attention to him. They were piddly little complaints, nothing worth paying attention to. So I sent word to Morris to behave himself and left it at that.

Later, I got a report that Merc had roughed up a younger inmate. Morris had taken a role as a leader in the jail. A few times a week he met with younger inmates to lecture them on the evils of drug abuse and crime. During one of these rap sessions, a juvenile offender apparently laughed at something Merc said. The kid said Merc grabbed him and slammed him against a desk. Then, the complaint said, Merc told the kid he was going to put him in a coma. Morris said the young man merely fell out of his chair.

When I got that report, I was tempted to send a message back saying, "Nice job, Merc! Do it some more!" I thought throttling the kid was an outstanding idea. I'm sure it got his attention. Morris probably did more for the rehabilitation of that kid than the system could have done in a lifetime. And the jailers wanted me to discipline him for it? Come on.

Morris didn't let himself waste away in prison. He kept in good shape, and tried to help other prisoners to go straight. I appreciated it. Several times I let him out so that he could speak to various civic groups. Prisoner No. 088586 got to see more of the outside world than most other prisoners, but still it was no picnic. He was in handcuffs the whole time, even when the jailers brought him to fast-food restaurants for dinner. He was a living example of what can happen to an essentially decent person who gets in with the wrong crowd, gets hooked on drugs, and makes a bad decision. And he admitted as much in his speeches.

But in the courts, he always stressed that he was entrapped. During the trial I had been faced with a difficult decision. The defense wanted to call a witness who said he had spoken to Freddy Donaldson, the gardener, about Morris. This witness was going to testify that Donaldson told him, "I'm setting up Mercury Morris for a bust." Naturally, his testimony would have bolstered Morris's case immensely. If the gardener had conjured up the whole thing to entrap Morris, the jury might have been willing to forgive Merc for going along with it. But I didn't let the witness testify. Under the law, as I read it, what he said the gardener said was hearsay and was not admissible.

Morris's appeals were based on that decision. His lawyers argued that I had made a mistake in not allowing the witness to testify. They said Merc was entitled to a new trial. The appeals court in Miami upheld the decision twice. But then, in 1986, the Florida Supreme Court reversed it. The testimony, the court said, "should have been before the jury for consideration as to whether, as an agent of the police, Donaldson impermissibly induced Morris . . . to commit the crimes for which he was convicted." Merc must be given a new trial, the justices said.

The decision didn't shock or upset me. I had ruled on a very complicated area of law, and had done my best to be fair to both sides. The local appeals court had agreed with my decision. I took no offense at the reversal. I have attended numerous legal seminars since the decision came down. Every seminar discussing hearsay evidence has used that case as an instructive example. No, there was no shame in that reversal.

For Morris, there was pure joy. The state saw no point in trying him on the same charges again. Justice could be done without trying to send him away for fifteen years. Morris agreed to plead no contest to a cocaine conspiracy charge. Even if I gave him the maximum sentence under the state guidelines of four and a half years—which I eventually did—he would get out of prison immediately because he had already served more than three years and had behaved well.

We all had a great time at the sentencing. It was one of the rare hearings that ends with the defendant walking out of court a happy man, completely free.

First I read the part of plea colloquy that tells the defendant he can be deported to his native country if he is convicted of a crime. "Where is that for you?" I asked. "Pittsburgh?"

"You got it," he said.

"You understand a plea of nolo contendere is tantamount to a guilty plea?" I said.

"Yes, ma'am," Merc said.

"Has anyone forced you, threatened you, or coerced you into entering this plea?"

Morris, a tough, solid man, didn't say anything. He just smiled. Can't blame him. It was a silly question.

SEVENTEEN

THE PRISONER
COMPLIMENTED ME
ON HIS SENTENCE

Most of the people I send to prison don't seem to like me. I guess that's understandable. But Juan Esteban de los Santos liked me. He complimented me on the way I sentenced him.

The defendant was in my courtroom for a violation of probation hearing. Already on probation, he was now accused of committing another relatively minor crime. The prosecutor had offered to recommend a two-year sentence in exchange for a guilty plea, a sweet deal indeed. But De los Santos didn't seem to understand how much trouble he was in. He just kept complaining that he wasn't happy with his court-appointed lawyer, Arturo Hernandez. I took it upon myself to make him understand the situation.

THE COURT: You will be getting seven years in the state prison, hear me well, if you are shown to have violated probation. Mark my words, I do not speak lightly. Now, what you do is entirely up to you, but I am telling you what is going to happen. You have a constitutional right to defend yourself and be your own lawyer, if that is what you want to do. It would be an idiotic thing to do, but you have a right to do it. Your choice is this: You are going forward on the violation of probation hearing with your lawyer, or you are going forward representing yourself. Is that clear?

THE DEFENDANT: Okay. I'll take the two years. Look, Your Honor is doing an excellent job, and—

THE COURT: I know that.

THE DEFENDANT: Your Honor, all the judges should be like you.

THE COURT: Huh?

THE DEFENDANT: All the judges should be like you, Your Honor. You are doing an excellent job.

THE COURT: Thank you very much, sir.

MR. HERNANDEZ: Judge, I think that merits about a six-month reduction in the sentence, wouldn't you say?

THE COURT: Won't work.

Juan Hernandez's mother was a bitch. I knew it the first time I saw her. The trouble was, I couldn't be sure if she was bitch enough to frame her ex-husband for the rape of a child.

The alleged rape of six-year-old Juan Hernandez (because of the nature of the case, I have changed his name and the names of his parents) was among the most troubling cases I have ever heard. It broke new ground in the law, inspired several long, probing articles, and left me wondering if I had sent an innocent man to prison for life.

The defendant's name was Luis Hernandez. He was an electrician who had been a political prisoner in Cuba in the 1970s. In 1980, he and his wife, Olga, came to the United States and took an apartment in Miami Beach. In court later, several people would testify that Olga was emotionally unstable. The marriage was a difficult one. In 1984, Olga kicked Luis out of the house and took up with another man. When the two were divorced, Luis's only concern was that he be allowed to visit his six-year-old son, Juan.

Late that summer, Olga began making plans to move to California with her new boyfriend. She couldn't take little Juan with her, so she left him with Luis and his sister, Alicia, in Hialeah Gardens. There, the father and the son shared a bed. One morning, Luis went to work and Alicia helped her nephew get ready for school. Just before Juan was supposed to leave, he called to her from the bathroom. "Look," he said, pointing into the toilet. There was blood mingled in his feces.

Luis's sister took Juan to several doctors in the next few weeks, but none could say for sure what was wrong. When Juan's mother heard something had happened, she postponed her move to California and took the boy to yet another doctor. This doctor examined him and found a bleeding sore in his large intestine. Another examination eight days later showed the same sore. The doctor, fearing sexual abuse, asked Olga some questions about whom the child spent time with. It was enough to make Olga very, very suspicious.

The person she suspected was her ex-husband, Luis. What she

did to confirm her suspicions made my skin crawl. She was working in a Laundromat owned by her boyfriend. In back, there was a small utility room. She took the child there and turned on a tape recorder. Then she proceeded to terrorize the child, in Spanish, into admitting that his father had abused him. The child denied it again and again—more than twenty times in all—but she just kept pushing him. The translation of that interview has haunted me since the first time I heard it.

"Your father has never touched you in your little behind?"

"Never," the boy said.

"For sure? Swear it to me, son."

"I swear it to you."

Later, she said, "It seems to me that what you are saying to me is a lie."

"No, it isn't."

"Because it shows in your eyes. Tell me the truth. If you tell me the whole truth, you are going to go on seeing your father and you are going to see your aunt. You are going to see your cousins. You are going to be able to go to Hialeah. If you don't tell me the truth, you are not going to go to Hialeah anymore nor are you going to see your father again. So tell me the whole truth about what happened to you."

"The truth, uh . . . I am not sure."

He insisted for several more minutes that his father had not done anything to him. Then he began to cry. After several minutes, he broke down and said Luis had touched him in the anus. But he denied seven times that his father had touched him with his penis. Mommy still didn't quit.

"Tell me, my son. Nothing is going to happen to you. Remember well and tell me what happened to you. You must remember: You are six years old. You are already a little man. Tell me what happened to you. Don't cry and tell me what happened to you. Tell me, come on, don't cry. What did your father put into you there, my son? What did your father put into you? Huh? Tell me."

His tail, the boy finally said, using a slang word for penis.

That did it. Olga took the tape recording to a detective. In an interview with the cop, the boy repeated that his father had put his finger and his penis inside him. Juan said the same thing to the next doctor who examined him. Luis Hernandez was eventually charged with sexual battery on a child under age eleven. At the least, his reputation was ruined forever. At most, he would spend the rest of his life in prison. The case was assigned to my court.

It wasn't going to be like other trials. In Florida, the defense is allowed to take sworn statements from prosecution witnesses before trial. The defense lawyer may question the same witnesses again in the presence of the jury. But under a new law designed to protect victims of child sexual abuse, little Juan would have to testify only once, on videotape. The videotape would then be played during the trial. At least that was the way it was supposed to work.

Florida's lawmakers had written this spiffy new law, but they hadn't said how the court was supposed to put it into effect. A person charged with a crime has a right under the U.S. Constitution to confront his accusers. To me, that means that the defendant has a right to look his accuser in the eye while he is testifying. The Florida law wouldn't allow Luis to be in the room while Juan gave his videotaped statement. So the lawyers and I had to figure out a way to put him in the room without really putting him in the room.

We came up with a pretty good plan, or so I thought. First, I appointed a special master—sort of a surrogate judge—to sit in the room with the lawyers while Juan gave his statement. The master was Melvin Black, a fine lawyer. Then we hooked up a system of TV monitors that would allow Juan and Luis to look at each other without actually being in the same room. While Juan testified, he would see his father's image on a TV screen, but he wouldn't feel physically threatened by him. I stayed in the room with Luis Hernandez.

It didn't work. The kid wouldn't say a damned thing. Those lawyers questioned him for an hour and a half, and not once did he say his daddy had buggered him.

Prosecutor Don Horn said, "Did anyone stick anything into your butt?"

"I don't remember," the boy said.

Well, most people would have remembered it. That's essentially what defense lawyer Akhtar Hussain said when he asked me to dismiss the case. The prosecution had brought in its main witness, and he had refused to implicate Luis Hernandez. How, he asked, could I let the case go on?

Easy. I had to. Just because the kid didn't say anything in front of a court reporter, two lawyers, a special master, and the televised image of his father didn't mean something hadn't happened to him. Judges can't apply the same standards to cases involving children that they do to cases involving adults. If an adult rape victim won't implicate anyone, that is his or her choice. If a child won't do it, the reasons may be complicated. I ruled that the case would go to trial, and that the child could testify via closed-circuit television again.

Lord, it was a frustrating trial. I don't know how the jurors stayed awake in some parts. Before the trial, the child had been interviewed in a psychologist's office. The doctor had given him some toy trucks to play with while he talked. Except that he didn't talk. He played with the trucks. This came as no surprise to me as a mother. If you give a child a choice between playing with some great trucks or talking about the time his daddy stuck his finger up his anus, he's going to play with the trucks. In the background, the doctor could be heard asking, "Now can you tell me about what happened to you?" And the kid just said, "Vroom, vroom." It was pathetic.

The boy's live testimony went a little better. I set him up in my chambers with the lawyers, Melvin Black, and a TV monitor. At first, he didn't want to say anything. But after some pleading by Don Horn, Juan picked up a couple of anatomically correct dolls and acted out what had happened in his father's bed. He said his father had inserted both his penis and his middle finger into his rear end. It was spine-tingling stuff. You would have had to be made of wrought iron not to feel sorry for the kid.

Until Akhtar Hussain started to ask questions, that is. When the defense lawyer questioned him, Juan said he made the accusations only because he thought his mother would beat him if he didn't.

The jurors heard the tape of Olga's interview with her son. They found out for themselves what a lousy investigator she had made, and what a terrible shrew she had been.

The prosecution and the defense went back and forth for the rest of the trial. The state's doctors said the bleeding intestine could have been caused by Luis's fingernail. The defense's doctors said that there was no evidence of sexual abuse, and that it was all a mistake. The jurors' heads must have been spinning. I know mine was.

I was hoping that Luis's testimony would help me to make up my mind, but it didn't. He said his ex-wife was trying to destroy his life, which I thought was entirely possible. On the other hand, every child abuser says someone is out to destroy him. If we simply believed everyone who said he wasn't guilty, no one would ever go to prison.

I was still unsure of the case when I sent the jury out to deliberate. People have asked me why I didn't just dismiss the case if I had doubts. Well, that is not my job. The state clearly had presented enough evidence to support the charges. Once it had done that, it was up to the jury to decide whether the evidence could overcome a reasonable doubt in their minds. I can't impose my will on the process. Luis's guilt or innocence was a question of fact for the tryers of the fact—the jurors.

They found him guilty in forty-five minutes.

I couldn't believe it. I thought there was a fair chance that the jurors would find reasonable doubt and let Luis go. When they deliberated for less than an hour, I thought I was losing my mind. It had been a long time since I was so surprised at the outcome of a case.

At sentencing, I had no choice but to sentence Luis to life in prison, which meant he would serve at least twenty-five years without possibility of parole.

I usually try to forget about my cases when they're over, but I couldn't forget about that one. Olga Hernandez had picked on that little boy mercilessly. By the time she was through with him, he would have admitted that he had been abducted by Martians and buried neck-deep in Jell-O. Yes, there was evidence that something had happened to the child, but there was also evidence that nothing had happened to him. One day long after the trial was over, Don Horn stopped by my office. I asked him if he still believed Luis was guilty.

"Absolutely," he said. "I really feel he is."

In 1989, the Supreme Court took a load off my mind by ruling that Luis deserved a new trial. The court said defense lawyer Akhtar Hussain should have done one thing he didn't do: He should have questioned the boy's very ability to tell the truth. The mistake, the court said, meant his client didn't get adequate representation and deserved a new trial.

The case was never retried. The state attorney's people dropped the charges and Luis was released from prison. The prosecutors wouldn't say why they did it, but I think they realized there was a strong possibility that Luis's mother had indeed set up her husband. But they had no way of finding out. Olga vanished and has not been seen since. I guess that's how much she cared about her boy.

I learned one other astonishing thing about that case. When Luis was released from prison, he went back to live with his sister and his son, Juan. He and his son, I was told, soon began to share the same bed again. Luis was not afraid to admit it. That was when I figured he was not guilty. Nobody who was guilty could be a big enough jackass to get out of prison and do something like that.

I have a little toy in my chambers. It is a tiny model of an electric chair. It stands six inches high and has real electrical cables attached to it. Contrary to what some people think, I do not strap it to the arms of recalcitrant lawyers and zap them with house current. I use it only as a symbol—a symbol of the ultimate form of justice and retribution.

It is an ironic symbol for me. In my tenure on the bench, I have sentenced eight men to die in the electric chair, but the sentence has never once been carried out. In six cases, the Supreme Court reduced the sentence to life. In the case of cop killer Manuel Valle, the court ordered a new trial. And in the case of Anibal Jaramillo, once convicted of murder, the court simply let the bastard go. No one sitting on Florida's Death Row can blame his predicament on me, I'm sorry to say.

I did not sentence these men to death lightly. I believed in each case that the death penalty was appropriate under the law. Take the case of Adelbert Rivers. One day, Rivers and two of his buddies decided to stick up a Chinese restaurant. I guess there was nothing good on television that day, so they decided to terrorize a couple of dozen diners, waiters, and waitresses. They barged into the place with their guns drawn and demanded money. One of the waitresses panicked and ran for the kitchen. Rivers leveled his shotgun and shot her in the back. She had made absolutely no threat to him— what could she do, poke him with her pen?—and now she was dead. He fired a couple more shots as he left, but, by some miracle, he didn't kill anyone else.

Johnny Perry got the death penalty too. Perry stabbed a woman to death with a foot-long kitchen knife. He had done yard work for Kathryn Miller, who lived in a lovely section of Miami called Pine

Acres. It is not far from where I live. Perry stopped at the house that day only to rob it, but Miller apparently panicked when he tried to force his way in. So he killed her—beat, strangled, and stabbed her. It was a savage killing, almost the worst death imaginable.

But in both cases, the Supreme Court reduced the sentence to life. The juries in both cases had recommended sentences of life in prison. Under Florida law, I could override the recommendations and sentence the defendants to death if I could list compelling reasons for doing so. I appreciated the careful thought that the jurors had put into their recommendations, but I couldn't go along with them. Adelbert Rivers shot an innocent woman in the back so that he could enrich himself. Johnny Perry killed Kathryn Miller because he wanted to get rid of the only witness to the robbery. If those weren't compelling reasons for ordering the death penalty, I don't know what would be.

I think the Supreme Court was just plain wrong in those cases. If the state's legislators didn't intend for judges to override the jury in some cases, why did they write the law the way they did? By reducing those two sentences, the court thwarted the intent of the legislature—and denied substantial justice to the people of Dade County. It's just unfair.

I think the Supreme Court sometimes loses touch with reality. The justices sit in great big offices in Tallahassee, the friendly, countrified state capital, watching the flowers blossom and enjoying the cool air. Some of them don't have any idea what it is like to live in a community where rape and murder are as common as summer rain. I'm sure politics is part of the problem. In Florida, Supreme Court justices are appointed by the governor. After that, they face only a retention vote to keep their jobs. It is mighty rare for anyone to lose his job on a retention vote. If the justices lived in Miami and had to face a vote to keep their jobs, as I do, I'm sure they would find out that people don't like having the likes of Anibal Jaramillo put back on the streets.

In a way, I don't care what the Supreme Court does. It has always been my practice as a judge to do what I think is right. I thought, and still think, that Adelbert Rivers and Johnny Perry—and all the rest—deserved the death penalty. If the justices want to reverse my rulings, fine. Let them go ahead.

I don't know how they sleep at night, but let them go ahead.

*   *   *

Louis and I had a tremendous marriage. I pray I'll never have to live through anything like it again.

For the first month of our marriage, we lived in my house in Miami. Dale, his wife, Jean, and their son, Rondle, also lived with us. A month after Louis and I were married, Jean gave birth a second time, this time to a girl, Reagan. The house got pretty crowded at that point, so Louis and I decided to move to his house in the country.

Louis, who had always loved being outdoors, raised and sold quarter horses in his spare time. His ranch, called Misty Farms, was in the southwest section of Dade County, almost an hour from the courthouse. The house was a big wooden building with nineteen rooms, many of which had been added on long after the house was first built. Alongside the house were the stables and the rings where Louis worked with the horses. I liked to look at the animals, but I never rode them. As a rule, I don't ride anything with such a large body and such a small brain.

As much as Louis enjoyed working with the horses, he eventually had to sell the ranch. His job with the narcotics unit often kept him out late nights, which made it hard for him to get up early and work with the horses. And a couple of years into our marriage, he decided to attend law school at night, which cut into his time even more. So, when Dale and Jean found a place of their own, Louis and I left the rustic horse farm and moved back to my house in Miami.

We had a stupendous marriage. We were great friends and great companions, and we got along famously on every score. It was just a wonderful friendship with sex privileges. We both liked to travel, so we left Miami as often as we could and visited other parts of the country. Our first love was Montana. We also enjoyed talking about our work. His job was exciting, glamorous, and dangerous, and I liked to think mine was too.

With Louis, I was as faithful as a St. Bernard dog. Not once during that marriage did I fool around with another man, and I certainly had my chances. Hell's bells, at the Metro-Justice Building you have opportunities going down the escalator. I'm not sure Louis could say truthfully that he was true to me. Many times, Louis would say he would be home from work at one A.M., but he wouldn't show up until four. It would tick me off, but I wouldn't show it. I would assume he had been screwing around, but I never really knew. I was realistic about it. I know that the world turns on a whole lot of screwing around. I never expected any of my husbands always to be true blue and never touch another chick. I had good reason to believe that John Rowe and Louis each did a little diddling on the side, but so what? It isn't going to fall off just because it winds up in the wrong trough one day.

I think people screw around because what's old is familiar and what's new is exciting. It's really that simple. But pretty soon, what's new gets old and a man goes back to his wife. I took the position that it didn't matter what Louis did when he wasn't with me. I insisted only that he wake up in my bed, have breakfast at my table, and pay his part of the living expenses. Sure, it would have hurt if someone had called me and told me he was at a certain motel with a certain woman. Sure, I would have been angry. But if someone had done that, I wouldn't have gone looking for him. Because if I had found him in bed with someone else, I would have had to do something about it. And I didn't want to. I loved him and wanted to keep him.

If, in the end, he had run off with just another woman, it would have been all right. But it wasn't. The other woman was my daughter-in-law, Jean. It was Dale's wife.

I sometimes think nothing ever would have happened if not for me. Without thinking, I did things that brought them together. And when they started growing closer and closer, I didn't do anything to stop it. It began with an automobile trip. One week, Louis decided to go to North Carolina to do some hunting. He had been a hunter since he was a kid and had never lost his love for it. About that time, Jean was planning to go to South Carolina to visit her folks. So, just trying to be helpful, I suggested that Louis drive Jean up there. Louis wasn't too crazy about the idea. He was in a hurry to go hunting and wasn't interested in stopping on the way. Besides, he had never really liked Jean. He never put his finger on it, but there was just something about her that turned him off. But in the end he agreed to take her along, I think, because I wanted him to.

On the way north, Louis and Jean had a nice chat. When they stopped at a motel for the night, Jean was rather bored. There wasn't much to do and she was restless. Louis called me on the phone that night and told me nothing much was happening. Then I got one of my great ideas. "Dale never takes Jean dancing," I told Louis. "You love to dance. Why don't you take her out, buy her a drink, and have a good time?" Dale, who was much smarter than I was, couldn't believe what I was saying. When I got off the phone, he wanted to kill me for throwing the two of them together that way. It never entered my mind that anything could happen, but it entered Dale's, and he let me know it.

When Louis got home from the hunting trip, he couldn't say a complete sentence without mentioning Jean's name in it. One day that week I came home from work and he said, "I asked Jean to come over to help me wash the bugs off the truck." By now I could see that he was infatuated with her. I assumed it was a passing fancy. But it wasn't. A short time later, I went to San Francisco on a business trip. When I got back, Dale and Jean's neighbors commented on how nice it was that Louis had visited every night I was gone.

"Yes," I said. "Nice. Very nice."

There was a tide rising, and I was trying to hold it back with rationalizations and self-deception. The water was up to my neck and I was about to drown. But I didn't do anything about it. I didn't even stand on my tiptoes. Pretty soon the tide would wash over my head, and then it would be too late. But I couldn't, or wouldn't, see it happening.

A trip to Yellowstone was going to be our time together. It was going to make everything all right. Our plan was to go out there, just Louis and me, and enjoy the mountains the way we had on our honeymoon. We drove out there a week after I returned from San Francisco and had a wonderful time. The scenery was breathtaking, and we enjoyed each other thoroughly. The only hitch was that I had a minor bladder infection and I had left my medicine at home. But it didn't bother me much. I could have lasted to the end of the trip without it.

One afternoon, Louis and I were eating lunch in a restaurant in Gardiner, Montana.

"Wouldn't it be nice," he said, "if your grandson were here? He would love this."

"He sure would," I said.

"I'll tell you what. Let's call him up and tell him to catch the next plane. Dale and Jean could join us, and we could all have a good time together. And they could bring your medicine with them."

I knew what he really wanted. I was no fool. Maybe I should have told him that I wanted only to be with him, that I wanted to relive our honeymoon. But my marriage wasn't the first thing I thought of when he made the suggestion. My family was. Louis may have been asking me for permission to see Jean. But he was also offering me a chance to be with my son and my grandchild. And that is an opportunity no grandmother can ever resist. My children and grandchildren meant, and still mean, the world to me. What could it possibly matter what Louis was doing if Dale and Rondle were with me?

Dale, Jean, and Rondle flew out and met us the next evening. Reagan stayed in South Carolina with Jean's folks. We had a great time building snowmen, having snowball fights, and enjoying the scenery of the West. At first, Louis and Jean didn't seem to pay much attention to each other. I was watching closely, and they seemed to be restraining themselves. I learned later that Dale didn't think so. He and Jean were fighting every night because he felt Jean was neglecting him. Again, he probably was right.

Things started to get out of hand the day we rented snowmobiles. We got three of them and rode them all day. At first, Dale and Rondle rode one, Jean and I rode another, and Louis rode the third by himself. But then there was some subtle switching of seats. Pretty soon Dale was riding with Rondle, I was riding alone, and Louis and Jean were riding together. It tore me apart to see my daughter-in-law ride up a hill clutching the waist of my husband. It was clear she wasn't just clutching him to keep from falling off. She was grabbing him away from me. It was then that I began to realize she might never let go.

The night before we were to leave, I heard Louis tell his mother on the phone that I wasn't feeling well, and that I would have to fly home instead of driving. My illness was news to me. The bladder infection wasn't bothering me much at all by then. When he got off the phone, Louis announced that he, Jean, and Rondle were going to drive back in the car, and that Dale and I would fly home. All right, fine, I said. As long as Rondle was with them, everything would be all right. But at the last minute, Louis decided Rondle couldn't ride in the car because it was too cold in the backseat. It was a pathetic excuse, but at that point Dale and I couldn't seem to do anything to put an end to what was happening. The next day, they drove off.

Dale, Rondle, and I stopped in Chicago on the way home to see the sights. Then we flew back to Miami to wait for Louis and Jean. Their plan was to drive through South Carolina, pick up Reagan, then come straight home. I was expecting them to arrive early on Christmas Eve. But the hours passed and they didn't come. Dale and I sat up most of the night, tapping our feet and keeping each other company. It was Christmas Eve, the most important family night of the year, and the family wasn't together. I went to bed way past midnight, partly disgusted but mostly just sad. How could this be happening?

Louis and Jean strolled in at eight-thirty Christmas morning. We did not shout "Merry Christmas" when they crossed the threshold.

After that, Jean and Dale couldn't keep their marriage together anymore. They had had a good marriage, but this stress was too much. Two months after Christmas, Jean took the kids and went back to South Carolina to live with her parents. It was a sad day for Dale and me, the saddest in our lives.

Louis and I hung on for seven months after that. He was in love with someone else, but somehow our relationship lingered. I felt terribly out of control. My ability to guide events, to get things the way I wanted them, abandoned me completely. At times I felt that the attraction between Louis and Jean was fading, that the romance would peter out. Other times I thought it would be only a matter of days before I would again be alone.

My birthday that September was the worst I ever had. To surprise me, Louis flew to South Carolina—he was a licensed pilot—and picked up Jean, Rondle, and Reagan. I was delighted to see the grandchildren, and, yes, pleased to see Jean. For all my misgivings about what had happened, she had meant a lot to me and my son for a long time and nothing would make me forget it. I cared for her and still do. We all had a nice day together. That night, Louis, Jean, and I went to a retirement party for a police officer I knew. I was the master of ceremonies, so I spent most of the evening at the microphone, calling out dances and introducing people. Late in the evening, I looked out on the floor and saw Louis and Jean dancing. They were so close, so in love.

That's it, I thought. It's all over now but the shouting.

I got so drunk. I don't like to drink, so it doesn't take much to get me drunk. But this night I was really looped. Jean was too. When the night was over, one of the sergeants who worked with Louis helped me out to my van and loaded me into the back like a crate of oranges. He helped Jean in too. When Louis got in to drive us home, I began saying all kinds of crazy things about the situation. I think I even suggested, facetiously, that Jean and I alternate weekends as his wife. It may have been a drunken discussion, but it was also an open discussion about the problem, and about possible solutions. The next day, Louis said it was quite an experience to hear Jean and me in the backseat dividing him up.

That day, Louis flew Jean and the kids back to South Carolina, then turned right around and flew home. When we went to bed that night, I heard his voice in the dark.

"Maybe we better think about getting a divorce."

There was a moment's silence. "I suppose so," I said.

There was no more conversation. I went to the office in the morning and drafted the divorce papers myself. Louis came to the office and my friend Harvey Shenberg led us through a quick divorce proceeding. My third marriage was over by lunchtime.

That afternoon, Louis and I drove around Miami looking for a new place for Louis and his future bride, my daughter-in-law, to live. People have asked me how I could have helped him, but I couldn't have imagined not helping him. My family had fallen apart. If I hadn't gone with Louis that day, he might have decided to find another place to live, and then I would have lost the grandchildren too. I wanted them to live close to me. If that had meant finding the apartment and paying the rent myself, I would have done it. I truly wished them the best.

Louis and Jean were married a short time later. I sent flowers to the wedding.

At the courthouse, the ending of that marriage was the subject of many hot rumors and cruel jokes. It was like something out of the *National Enquirer*, and people couldn't help gabbing about it. But for me, it was just a tragedy. I spent much of the next year crying. I tried to concentrate on my work, but for the first time seeking justice wasn't the most important thing to me. Merely staying well was. I wanted only to keep my balance, to find some way to feel better about my life.

The experience changed me. I didn't think it was possible for something to change me, but I learned otherwise. Louis was the first person who ever burned me. A lot of people said, "Now you know how it feels." They were right. When I got burned, I lost all my confidence. Once I rushed into romance like a sixteen-year-old kid driving too fast on a crowded street. Like a kid, I thought I was immortal. Losing Louis the way I did showed me I wasn't. After that, I no longer trusted my judgment when it came to love. I still don't. I still don't.

EIGHTEEN

LIFE SENTENCES

One day in 1989, I was trying to decide whether to send a guy to prison or give him a break and put him on probation. It doesn't matter what the charge was, or what the guy's name was. It was just another case in the endless series of cases, another name I would forget as soon as I turned the page on the calendar. The folks in the courtroom thought I should give the guy a break. I looked at his record, which wasn't bad, and took into account that he had a family and a steady job. Then I thought it over for a few seconds—that's all the time I had, all the time I ever have. Before I made the decision, I took a long look at the guy. Then I put him on probation. He was free to go home to his family.

After court, the probation officer approached me.

"I knew we were getting somewhere when I saw you looking at him," she said. "I knew then that you were going to treat him like a human being."

Some might have taken what she said as an insult, but I didn't. She didn't mean any harm. She was merely pointing out that I sometimes don't even look at the people whose lives I hold in my hands. I thought long and hard about that. The more I did, the more I silently thanked the probation officer for saying something. I made it a point after that to try not to treat people like numbers. I tried to do better.

It is never easy. Any judge will tell you that. In today's world, a judge can easily become insensitive. The sheer volume of crime is part of the reason. On the bench, I am little more than a spectator at a parade of misery. Trying to remember the faces and names of people going to prison in Florida is like trying to recall the face of a single drummer in an entire parade of drummers. The faces blend together. I sometimes can't remember if it was Hernandez or Horton or Blake or McCormick that I just sent away for most of his life. Unless the defendant does something to make me remember him (such as, say, urinate on the floor in front of me), I am likely to forget him before the bailiff escorts him out.

We judges also become insensitive because of the constant escalation in the types of crime we see. When I took the bench, I could get into a real lather over a single burglary. But the world was different then. People's values were different. Today, if someone is only a burglar or a shoplifter, I'm sometimes tempted to give him the key to the city. Armed robbery used to be big news in Miami. To get on the front page now, a criminal has to kill a guy, cut off his head, and throw it at a police officer. (This is something that really happened in Miami.) The world is going crazy. Who can get upset about burglaries?

People at the courthouse say I have mellowed quite a bit. When Ellen Morphonios first became a judge, Her Honor could be a raging bitch. I didn't get nicknames like "The Hanging Judge," "Maximum Morphonios," and "The Time Machine" for nothing. Once, I sentenced a guy to life for the murder of a Florida Highway Patrol trooper. At the hearing I made headlines by saying, "I hope it isn't considered that I'm bloodthirsty, and I hope I'm not, but nothing would give me greater pleasure than to impose the death penalty." I used to get people so riled up that they would faint right in the aisles. When the paramedics came to revive them, they would get to the courthouse and say, "Fourth floor, huh? I guess Morphonios is beating them again."

I generally go easier on people nowadays. (Not that there aren't a few people I'd send to the chair with a smile.) I have mellowed as a judge because I have mellowed as a person. Advancing age has succeeded in doing what all the lectures from friends failed to do. I have calmed down like an old fixed cat. I have a boyfriend whom I see a couple of times a year, and once in a while I slip away to the Caribbean with a friend. But those times are rare. Mostly I spend time in Miami with Dale and our close family friend Martica Monsalve. When I can, I go to Tallahassee to visit Dean and his family. My life has been quiet for several years now. It appears that it will stay that way, but if I were you I wouldn't bet cash money on it.

When I think of the way I spent my younger days, I am often amazed that I lived to see this age. But the fact is that I have outlived many of the people who were most important to me. Don Petit, my best friend forever, died in 1983 of lung cancer. (It was the same year I lost Louis—the worst year I ever had.) Jack Headley had a heart attack in 1989 and remained in a coma for several months before he died. In the last days, his ex-wife Donnel and I stood by his bedside and held each other. Some might have thought it strange for us to console each other, considering she had been his wife and I had been his girlfriend. But we had something in common—we both loved Jack.

The loss of my father was the hardest by far. Daddy quit driving the cab in the early seventies. Mama, who was so much like me, and who therefore butted heads with me so often, died July 14, 1980. Daddy spent the last years of his life as a sort of unpaid member of my staff. He came to the office early each morning and made coffee for everyone. The folks on my staff called him Pop, and they loved him almost as much as I did. My friend and secretary Shirley Lewis still keeps her desk drawers full of pictures of him. He died one night in 1987. I was scheduled to fill in on a talk-radio show that night. Daddy had been getting sicker and sicker, and we all knew that it was almost time. I damn near backed out of the radio show. But then I realized that Daddy would never stand for that. Once you made a commitment, you kept it, no matter what. So I did the program with my friend Harvey Shenberg at my side. When I got home Daddy was waiting for me. He died an hour later. I held him while the rest of the family stood by the bed. He was ninety years old.

I will never, ever be the same.

It has always been my plan to work until age sixty-five, then collect a full pension and retire to the farm in North Carolina. But some of my friends say I should retire early. The extra money isn't that important, they say. (Easy for them to say: They don't have half a dozen cats to feed.) They tell me it's time to relax. They have a point. I have high blood pressure, and trying to slog through one hundred cases a week is no way to bring it down. Maybe nineteen years on the bench is enough. I know killers who have done less time than that. It might be fun to take it easy for a while, or maybe start a new career. I have always wanted to work in radio full-time. I have even had some offers to work in television. Who knows what might happen?

No, I might not stay on the bench until I keel over dead. But

I'll stay there for now, and I'll like it. Working in the justice system is a frustrating business, sure. But even so, I like to think I'm accomplishing something. Each sociopath I send to prison is one less for you and your family to worry about. It's a small contribution, I know. There is always a new killer or robber to take the place of the one I just sentenced. But dispensing tough justice is the only contribution I can make. It's the only one that makes any sense. When I step off that bench for the last time, whenever that may be, don't say I was the best judge ever to don a robe, or the best lawyer ever to crack a book. It wouldn't be true. Just say what I said to Harry Reasoner of *60 Minutes* when he interviewed me on my patio, next to my pool.

Say, "She was a stand-up broad." It's the nicest compliment I can imagine.

ACKNOWLEDGMENTS

I wish to thank Daddy, Mama, and Don Petit, who created me, and Fuller Warren, B. K. Roberts, and Richard E. Gerstein, who respected Don enough to take a chance on me. Without them there would be no me.

More in the present, I wish to thank Mike and Carol Wilson, who met me as a stranger and now know more about me than my own children do. And without Anne Cates, Al Sepe, Harvey Shenberg, Shirley Lewis, Mona Gesse, Susan Tepper, Tyrone Cobb, Cathey Mincey, and Donnie Wright, none of us ever would have been able to put all this together.

As always, my kids worked on this project right along with me, but they had to put up with some things Mike did not. Some of these memories hurt, and the kids had to put up with some sadness around the house that we could have lived without. When the decision was made to do this book, I went into it as I do everything else—openly and honestly. If I was going to tell the story, it would have to have all the warts as well as the flowers. And pulling the shades from around shadows can be traumatizing to the soul.

I would also like to thank Carl Hiaasen, Richard Ovelmen, Sam Terilli, Gene Miller, Polk Laffoon, Rick Reilly, Nora Paul, and the staff of the *Miami Herald* library. Attorneys Ira Loewy, Anthony Musto, and Arthur Berger were of great help in researching one story in the manuscript. I would especially like to thank attorney Bill Hussey of Fort Lauderdale, who helped us to retrieve two chapters from our computer disks after we deleted them by accident. His gracious assistance saved us several weeks' work.

It was not my idea to write this book. Mike Wilson wrote a profile of me for the *Miami Herald* in 1988. He did a very thorough job and spent a long time working with me. I was impressed—by him, his thoroughness, his writing, and, above all, his fairness.

A few months later he wandered in and suggested he write a book about me—a book by me as told to him. I can't write diddly-squat, so all writing would be done by Mike. I couldn't think of a really valid reason why not to do it, so I agreed. There had been a rash of other such offers, none of which I seriously considered. Someone pointed out that no one needed my permission to write a book about me, and suggested that it might be a good idea to beat them to the punch and try to get it right. If you think it's easy to go back over sixty years and remember everything—the good things you did and the bad things you did—then go off in a corner and try it. It's not as easy as it looks.

We were just getting serious about the project when the 60 Minutes segment on me aired in December 1988. One of the first phone calls I got was from a fellow named Bill Adler of Bill Adler Books, Inc., in New York. I have spent the greater part of my life making decisions based only on my instinct about a person and the way the hair on the back of my neck reacts. When I talked to Bill Adler on the phone, I liked him. The next thing I knew, he was my literary agent—and Mike's—and through him we signed a book contract with William Morrow & Company, Inc.

I didn't have the opportunity to actually meet Mr. Adler and his lovely wife until many moons later, when my friend and judicial assistant Shirley Lewis and I were in New York. The hair on the back of my neck had once more served me well. He's a great guy, and I'm proud to have worked with him.

We're also lucky to have worked with Lisa Drew and Bob Shuman of William Morrow & Company, Inc. Their help in our first venture into publishing was invaluable.

I don't know if you have enjoyed this book, but I hope you have. I don't know if, after reading it, you like me. Probably not, but I hope you do. I make no excuses for anything. I came up the hard way. I made it myself with the help of a lot of wonderful people and I have very few regrets. The ones I do have relate only to the hurt I caused some people in my personal life. Other than that, if I had it all to do over again, I'd just throw that sucker into instant replay and let 'er rip.

—Ellen J. Morphonios
Miami, Florida

INDEX